The 21st Century Ladz

EMERALD ADVANCES IN MASCULINITIES

Series Editors: Steven Roberts, Tess Bartlett, and Rosemary Ricciardelli

Emerald Advances in Masculinities brings together diverse discussions of masculinities to develop alternative voices and perspectives that push the boundaries in discussions of masculinities.

Books in the series explore some of the major current concepts that traverse a range of methodologies, theoretical perspectives, and conceptualisations related to the critical studies of men and masculinities.

Previous titles:
Debating Childhood Masculinities: Rethinking the Interplay of Age, Gender and Social Change edited by Utsa Mukherjee

Hegemonic Masculinity, Caste, and the Body: Intersections in Local and Transnational Spaces by Navjotpal Kaur

EDITORIAL ADVISORY BOARD

The 21st Century Ladz: Continuity and Changes among Marginalised Young Men from the South Wales Valleys

BY

RICHARD GATER

Cardiff University, UK

emerald
PUBLISHING

United Kingdom – North America – Japan – India – Malaysia – China

Emerald Publishing Limited
Emerald Publishing, Floor 5, Northspring, 21-23 Wellington Street, Leeds LS1 4DL.

First edition 2025

Copyright © 2025 Richard Gater.
Published by Emerald Publishing Limited.

Reprints and permissions service
Contact: www.copyright.com

British Library Cataloguing in Publication Data
A catalogue record for this book is available from the British Library

ISBN: 978-1-83797-634-8 (Print)
ISBN: 978-1-83797-631-7 (Online)
ISBN: 978-1-83797-633-1 (Epub)

INVESTOR IN PEOPLE

In Loving Memory of Loki Gater

April 19th 2015 – December 30th 2021

Contents

About the Author

Richard Gater is a Research Assistant at the Centre for Adult Social Care Research (CARE) at Cardiff University. His research interests lie in masculinities, education, employment, and health and well-being.

Foreword

It's not something that the academy likes to admit or even necessarily comprehend, but the scholarly treatment of working-class boys and men – and the working class more generally – remains replete with deficit-laden accounts. Implicitly, and sometimes explicitly, working-class boys and men are situated as being the big part of contemporary social ills. Against the grain of this reading, Richard Gater contributes to a budding research literature with an important, compelling and thought-provoking first book. Preconceptions of a lack of ambition, a lack of achievement, a lack of adaptability, and even a *lack of humanity* are absent here in part because the author's own working-class roots provide a lens for understanding that stereotypes of working-class masculinities should be troubled. Instead, this book features an unwavering commitment to uncovering the richness, complexity, and contradictions inherent in the lived experiences of the young men it so carefully studies.

Drawing from immersive ethnographic research in the South Wales Valleys, Gater's nuanced portrait of working-class youth illustrates that there is much to learn *from*, not just about, working-class boys and men. This feels to me especially important given the research site is part of the former industrial heartlands, the kind of place that has often been considered to surface static, unchanged forms of masculinity and a people seemingly stuck in time. However, Gater's vivid opening account – a bewildering moment of observing a group of young men engaged in an unconventional act of camaraderie – captures the essence of this book: a journey into understanding behaviours that both align with and disrupt traditional notions of masculinity. These young men, that Gater describes as the 'Ladz', defy easy categorisation. They embody toughness and risk-taking but also display sensitivity, physical tactility, and gender-egalitarian views. Such a portrayal demands that we rethink what it means to grow up working-class young man in contemporary Britain.

One of the most striking aspects of this book is its refusal to settle for one-dimensional explanations. The 'Ladz' navigate conflicting social expectations, with their interactions with education and employment revealing an ongoing negotiation between inherited cultural practices and the demands of a post-industrial economy. The concept of 'amalgamated masculinities' – introduced here as a fusion of protest masculine traits and softer, more inclusive characteristics – provides a powerful framework for understanding these young men's identities. It is a testament to the book's analytical strength that it captures not only continuity with past generations but also the emergent forms of masculinity shaped by changing social and economic contexts, and that it does so in a way that avoids a reductive turn to framing social change as only camouflage for persistent (and very real) unequal gendered power relations.

Moreover, this work speaks to broader questions about the future of work and social mobility. The young men's pragmatic attitudes towards education, their partial rejection of traditional manual employment, and their engagement with evolving forms of masculinity all suggest that working-class identities are more adaptable and forward-looking than often assumed. In an era where automation and economic shifts threaten to marginalise low-skilled labour, understanding these adaptations is more important than ever. And, of course, this is not only a story of adaptation but of contemporary working-class struggles and broader class power relations.

What makes this book truly stand out is its personal tone. Gater's reflections on his own working-class upbringing add depth and authenticity. The struggle to reconcile past and present identities mirrors the journeys of the 'Ladz' themselves, making this more than an academic study – it is a story of growth, confusion, and understanding. I am excited for the readers of this book. The voices and the analysis presented in this book will entertain you, will challenge you, and if approached in good faith, will teach you.

Professor Steven Roberts
Head, School of Education, Culture & Society
Professor of Education & Social Justice
Faculty of Education, Monash University, Australia

Acknowledgements

I want to acknowledge many people's contributions in helping me complete this book. First and foremost, I would like to thank the research participants and the host organisation for making this book possible. I hope I have done justice to your stories and captured the complexity of your lives.

Work on drafting this book began whilst I was employed as a post-doctoral research fellow at the Wales Institute for Social and Economic Research and Data (WISERD). My post was supported by WISERD's Civil Society research programme, funded by the Economic and Social Research Council (ES/S012435/1). The support of the ESRC is gratefully acknowledged.

I am also immensely grateful to everyone who has contributed to the academic journey that led to this publication. While this list is not exhaustive, I would like to give special thanks to Kerry Merchant, Stephen Williams, Howard Williamson, Stuart Jones, Robert Jones, Andrew Thompson, Paul Chambers, Dawn Mannay, Phillip Brown, and, in particular, Valerie Walkerdine. More recently, I would also like to thank Steven Roberts, Jonathan Scourfield, and Paul Willis. These individuals, along with others, have supported me and helped me gain the confidence, skills, knowledge, and passion necessary to produce this book.

Lastly, I would like to express my sincere and heartfelt gratitude to my family and friends for their continuous encouragement, for listening to my ideas and helping me make sense of them, and for supporting me on my academic journey.

Introduction

A Bewildered Researcher

It was 2020 on a mild December night in the Aber Valley, a deprived former coal mining community deep in the heart of the South Wales Valleys. I had spent almost three months at a youth centre in this community, which was the base for my ethnographic research and the foundation for this monograph. I had established a good rapport with the staff and many of the young people at this organisation. On this particular night, the youth centre was a hive of activity, and many of the young people were in a boisterous mood. I had positioned myself at the centre's main entrance, where many of the young people often gathered, as it offered them quick and easy access to the outside and the ability to smoke, an activity that many of the young people engaged in. Whilst standing at the entrance, I heard an outpouring of laughter and noise coming from outside. I decided to investigate and find the source of what sounded like enjoyment. However, I was about to witness one of the most bewildering scenes of my time at the youth centre.

As I walked through the entrance door and approached the main road outside, I was greeted by a group of young men chasing each other around a car. The sound of retching filled the air as the young men drew phlegm from the back of their throats and nasal passages and then proceeded to spit it in each other's faces, all the while laughing as they did it. Observing these working-class young men engage in this act and watching nasal mucus drip from their faces as they laughed dumfounded me because, as I document in Chapter One, I was a research insider (Merton, 1972) both concerning the area where the research was situated, which is my place of residency, and I was once a laddish masculine working-class young man (Jackson, 2006; Willis, 1977). Within the culture I grew up in, spitting in another man's face was considered a cowardly and dishonourable deed; it was an act that transgressed the 'man code' (King et al., 2021) and ideas of masculine toughness (McDowell, 2003), courage and respectability.

In line with the centre's operational rules, we had a staff meeting later that night to discuss and debrief the night's events. I was still stunned and puzzled by the spitting episode and decided to discuss it with the staff. I explained to

The 21st Century Ladz: Continuity and Changes among Marginalised
Young Men from the South Wales Valleys, 1–5
Copyright © 2025 by Richard Gater. Published by Emerald Publishing Limited.
This work is published under the Creative Commons Attribution (CC BY 4.0) licence. Anyone may reproduce, distribute, translate and create derivative works of this work (for both commercial and non-commercial purposes), subject to full attribution to the original publication and authors. The full terms of this licence may be seen at http://creativecommons.org/licences/by/4.0/legalcode
doi:10.1108/978-1-83797-631-720251001

Dafydd – the centre manager – my confusion surrounding the young men's behaviour and how it conflicted with the working-class laddish code I adhered to growing up. He responded: *'That category of young men [laddish] doesn't exist anymore. These young men have been changing for the last ten years'*. This statement puzzled me because, as Chapters Four and Five will show, the participants of this research do demonstrate laddish (Jackson, 2006) qualities, which include 'having a laugh', sexism, being cool, hard, risk-taking and interest in activities constructed as masculine (Francis, 1999). However, as Chapter Six illustrates, Dafydd's statement would eventually become partially justified, and this would not be the first or last time that this group of working-class young men who became the focus of my study and whom I would come to term the 'Ladz' would bewilder me and make me question my identity – who I once was and who I had become.

Several concepts in this book originate from my engagement with relevant literature and my undertaking of 120 hours of ethnographic observations at the youth centre. These observations were influenced and are interpreted through reflections on my youthful laddish biography and my confusion from witnessing the Ladz express views and engage in behaviours I once practised, including a disaffected relationship with education and manual employment aspirations, criminal activity, violence, and drug/alcohol use, all of which have become synonymous with working-class and/or protest masculinity and laddish behaviour (Connell, 1995; Jackson, 2006). While also observing the young men demonstrate somewhat contradictory, though not exclusively (see Chapter Three), softer masculine displays, such as physical tactility, sensitivity, gender-egalitarian views and rejection of homophobia (McCormack, 2014; Roberts, 2013).

Based on the Ladz contrasting displays of behaviour that conform and conflict with the historical understanding of marginalised working-class young men, and in conjunction with an exploration of their school-to-work transition that involved semi-structured interviews and the use of visual methods, this book attempts to decipher these behaviours and answer key questions that guided my research. These questions included: to what extent is the young men's masculine identity representative of common laddish understanding, and how is this identity formulated? How do the young men make sense of education, and how is this understanding constructed and influenced? How do the young men understand employment in the context of their biography and changing social and economic circumstances? And what do the young men's masculinities, employment and education findings tell us concerning discussions about the future of work?

When making sense of the young men's behaviours and in response to the research questions, I argue that the continuities and changes in gendered expressions collectively shape the young men's identity and attitudes towards education and employment, and produce what is conceptualised as 'amalgamated masculinities', a fusion of locally constructed protest masculine characteristics and softer masculine attributes adopted through external cultural influence (Gater, 2024). The following sections provide a contextual overview of the literature concerning this publication and outlines the book's structure.

Background

Post-World War II education and employment-related literature often identify the significance of social relations and the inheritance of a masculine identity (Tolson, 1977; Willis, 1977) associated with stoicism, risk-taking, toughness and resistance to authority (Connell, 1995; Kimmel et al., 2005). The inheritance of this identity led some working-class young men to reject education and a manual work orientation that supported the expression of this identity (Ashton & Field, 1976; Carter, 1966; Veness, 1962; Willis, 1977) yet also led to monotonous, unrewarding jobs (Beynon, 1973; Goldthorpe et al., 1969a).

However, the "Thatcherite Revolution" (Nayak, 2003a, p. 149) and the UK's subsequent rapid deindustrialisation from the 1970s onwards led to a decline in such work and an increase in service sector employment. Much of the latter consists of low-skilled, poorly-paid jobs, especially for those from working-class backgrounds (Lindsay & McQuaid, 2004; McDowell, 2003; Roberts, 2020). Much service sector employment also requires historically associated 'feminine' attributes, such as customer service, interpersonal communication, and the presentation of self (McDowell, 2003; Warhurst & Nickson, 2020).

Despite all this, post-industrial research continues to recognise the significance of masculinity in the UK, especially among sections of working-class youth in former industrial locales once reliant on coal, steel, and manufacturing. The research often identifies issues around education and employment (see, for example, McDowell, 2003; Nayak, 2003a; Nixon, 2009; Walkerdine & Jiménez, 2012; Ward, 2015) that often derive from the intergenerational transmission of previously essential ways of being, including community-related attachment and working-class masculinity characteristics (Ivinson, 2014a; Walkerdine & Jiménez, 2012; Ward, 2015). These features oppose the neoliberalist ideal of individualism (Beck, 1992; Gidders, 1991) and service sector employment requirements of emotional labour (Hochschild, 1983), and deference and docility, features claimed to be at odds with working-class and/or protest masculinity (Connell, 1995; McDowell, 2003).

Adjacent to these studies, research has documented the changing nature of manhood and male displays of softer expressions of masculinity in the form of hybrid masculinity (Bridges & Pascoe, 2014) and inclusive masculinity (Anderson, 2009). It is within the scope of inclusive masculinity that Roberts (2018) offers an additional perspective on working-class young men and employment and suggests that his 'missing middle' participants (working-class young men who have not disengaged from school/employment, yet neither achieved degree-level education or a professional occupation), no longer fully subscribe to traditional norms of masculinity and are instead demonstrating a more inclusive form of masculinity that is more in tune with the emotional labour (Hochschild, 1983) requirements of service sector work.

Roberts (2018) and, more recently, Brozsely and Nixon (2022) make important contributions to working-class studies through the focus on the missing middle or ordinary kids (Brown, 1987). However, this book provides a contemporary accompaniment to place-based comparable studies of class and social change in post-industrial locales (McDowell, 2003; Nayak, 2003a; Walkerdine & Jiménez, 2012; Ward, 2015) and returns the focus to marginalised working-class young men. This focus is needed because, firstly, 'masculinities are configurations of practice that are constructed, unfold, and change through time' (Connell & Messerschmidt, 2005, p. 852). Secondly, because of surrounding claims regarding changes in social class distinctions (Beck, 1992; Giddens, 1991; Savage et al., 2015) and working-class identity (Ainsley, 2018). Thirdly, research on future employment changes suggests that young men with low educational attainment and manual forms of employment will be negatively affected (Frey & Osborne, 2013; Hawksworth et al., 2018; McKinsey Global Institute, 2017). Furthermore, the UK government policy response to future employment changes – increased automation and new technologies – often include upskilling and lifelong learning (Bell et al., 2017; Brown et al., 2020; HM Government, 2021; Leopold et al., 2018; Schlogl et al., 2021; Wheelahan et al., 2022). Subsequently, based on the current understanding of marginalised working-class young men and the associated negative and complex relationship with education and employment, the success of this policy response is questionable.

This book offers a valuable contribution to working-class studies by reversing the recent school-to-work participant shift (Brozsely & Nixon, 2022; Roberts, 2018), refocusing on a group of marginalised working-class young men in the context of the 1977 research on the lads conducted by Paul Willis (1977), whilst also considering relevant contemporary studies. I argue that the young men from this study share some similarities with the lads from Willis (1977) study and with other research concerning marginalised working-class young men, education and employment, including the intergenerational transmission of previously essential ways of being, a complex relationship with education and manual employment orientation (Ashton & Field, 1976; Carter, 1966; Mac an Ghaill, 1994; McDowell, 2003; Nayak, 2003a; Nixon, 2009; Veness, 1962; Walkerdine & Jiménez, 2012; Ward, 2015; Willis, 1977). However, there is also evidence of inconsistencies and a change and departure from traditionally associated values of working-class and/ or protest masculinity (Connell, 1995). This includes the young men's struggles with learning disabilities and/or mental health, which contributes to a pragmatic approach to education as opposed to anti-learning (Jackson, 2006; 2010; Willis, 1977), softer displays of masculinity (Anderson, 2009) and some deviation from manual employment orientation that was often the consequence of specific social circumstances. Within the latter, I refer to a rupturing process that destabilised modes of being associated with heavy industry (Ivinson, 2014b; Walkerdine & Jiménez, 2012; Ward, 2015). The differences in the young men's attitudes and behaviour are significant, especially in the context of future employment changes and the notion that manual employment, low-skilled and poorly educated young men will be negatively affected by increased automation and new technologies. The changes in attitude and behaviour allow us to think about how we could harness and develop them through targeted intervention and a locally-based initiative delivered by trusted community members and organisations to increase educational engagement and consider employment futures other than low-skilled manual employment and increase the life chances of marginalised working-class young men.

Structure of the Book

This book covers several aspects, including social class and masculinities, future employment changes, and current knowledge concerning working-class young men, education, and employment. This collection of components and their complexity requires a discussion of several works of literature. For this reason, the literature review consists of two chapters. The chapter structure includes:

Chapter One introduces the Ladz, offering some personal insight into the young men and demonstrating their laddish association. It also discusses myself, the Valley Boy, and my researcher positionality.

Chapter Two reviews significant literature and the trajectory of ideas concerning working-class young men, education, and employment and identifies commonalities and disparities along with a research knowledge gap. The chapter also discusses future of work changes and social class.

Chapter Three critically assesses the literature and theories on masculinities, highlighting shortcomings in these ideas regarding related aspects of this book and identifying missing issues.

Chapter Four empirically explores the young men's educational experiences, demonstrating similarities and dissimilarities between the lads from Willis's study and contemporary studies on marginalised working-class young men.

Chapter Five empirically explores the young men's employment orientation and reasoning, identifying commonalities with the lads through some attraction to manual work and highlighting a deviation from this career aspiration.

Chapter Six presents and discusses empirical findings relating to the young men's social relations and masculinities, demonstrating views and behaviours that contradict working-class and/or protest masculinity-associated characteristics.

Chapter Seven discusses the main findings from this book, incorporating theoretical and empirical literature from previous research whilst also suggesting policy approaches. The chapter concludes with some final thoughts.

Chapter One

The Ladz and the Valley Boy

Introduction

The first section of this chapter introduces the Ladz and offers some personal insight into the young men while discussing their laddish association (Jackson, 2006). The following three sections then explore my researcher positionality. Given the collaborative and qualitative nature of the study and the crucial intimate role that a researcher plays in collecting, selecting, and interpreting data (Finlay, 2002), it is important that I document and consider my own positionality on the research (Unluer, 2012) which included an insider status (Kanuha, 2000), outsider status (Bridges, 2001), and overt full membership (Bryman, 2016). As the chapter demonstrates, these positions were both advantageous and disadvantageous and evoked a personal emotional response. However, collectively, these three forms of researcher positionality have arguably helped contribute to a rich 'thick description' (Geertz, 1973, p. 7) while also influencing my ethnographic lens.

Introducing the Ladz

The Ladz were a group of marginalised working-class young men aged 12–21 that my research predominantly focused on alongside interviews with three youth workers and a schoolteacher. These young men became the focus of my study through 120 hours of ethnographic data collection and subsequent interaction that enabled me to build a good rapport and trusting relationship with them. Based on trust and rapport, I adopted a purposeful sampling technique (Patton, 2002) and recruited participants that would 'yield the most relevant and plentiful data, given [the] topic of study' (Yin, 2015, p. 93). Owing to the impact and curtailing effect of COVID-19, the research predominantly became a case study (Yin, 2012) of nine young men, which I gave individual pseudo names: Stan (age 13), Tommy (age 14), Dan (age 16), Craig (age 12), Lewis (age 18), Billy (age 15),

The 21st Century Ladz: Continuity and Changes among Marginalised
Young Men from the South Wales Valleys, 7–18
Copyright © 2025 by Richard Gater. Published by Emerald Publishing Limited.
doi:10.1108/978-1-83797-631-720251002

Ian (age 17), Cole (age 20) and Wesley (age 17). This group of young men were relatively representative of young men who frequented the youth centre at the time of the research. All of the Ladz gave verbal and written consent to their involvement in the research, with those under sixteen also supplying parental or guardian consent, and the Cardiff University ethics committee provided ethical approval for the study.

Stan

Stan typified laddish culture (Jackson, 2006), displaying hostility towards author-ity, volatility, and often engaged in racist, misogynistic, and homophobic dis-course (McRobbie, 1991; Skeggs, 1992; Walker, 1985). Despite his youthful age, Stan had already gained notoriety in the community and was banned from two local organisations for vandalism and destruction. Furthermore, community shop owners often had to call the police on him due to his intimidating, anti-social behaviour. Stan's run-ins with the law meant that almost all local police officers could personally identify him. He seemed to take great delight in this police notoriety. For example, on one of the many occasions that the police vis-ited the youth centre – often merely on liaison visits – Stan confronted a police officer and said: '*Do you know me?*'. The police officer replied: '*No, should I?*'. Stan responded: '*I'm Stan Jones. You're obviously new*'. Stan clearly thrived on the infamous status and seemed disappointed that the police officer failed to rec-ognise him and acknowledge his reputation.

Tommy

Tommy was the first participant with whom I established a rapport. Tommy and Stan were relatively close friends, and both displayed similar protest and/ or hegemonic masculine values, including courage, toughness, stoicism and risk-taking (Cheng, 1999; McDowell, 2003). Although Tommy demonstrated hyper-masculine behaviour (Mac an Ghaill, 1994), it seemed milder compared to Stan's. He presented a 'cheeky chappie' persona with a confident, masculine swagger and bounce in his step. Akin to Stan, Tommy had a negative reputation in the com-munity and had been involved in criminal activity. However, unlike Stan, when questioned and speaking about his misdemeanours, Tommy often presented the idea of victimhood as opposed to Stan's boastfulness. He often claimed that the problems he got into were usually not entirely his fault and were either accidental or the result of peer pressure.

Dan

Dan was not a regular user of the youth centre and only appeared on sporadic occasions. However, my relationship with Dan extended beyond the centre; I knew him through our involvement in the local rugby club as I had trained the youth team. Therefore, there was already an established relationship between Dan and me, and I decided to capitalise on this connection as I felt it would be helpful during an interview. This decision would later be justified through the richness of Dan's data. At 16 years of age, Dan was an exceptionally large young man. Standing at roughly six feet and five inches tall, with broad shoulders and weighing around 18 stone, Dan was a formidable figure who towered over me and all the youths at the centre. Despite Dan's powerful presence, he had a relatively laid-back character. However, this persona was occasionally offset with hyper-masculine, aggressive displays of violence (Maguire, 2020). On one of the occasions that Dan attended the centre, he got into a violent altercation with another young man. I did not witness this fight myself, but I was told Dan had inflicted considerable damage on the other young man because he had apparently bad-mouthed one of Dan's family members.

Craig

At 12 years old, Craig was the youngest of the nine participants. Due to Craig's age, I deliberated about including him in the research. However, despite his age, he was a relatively confident young man, and my ethnographic observations and interviews revealed that he had clear ideas about his future employment trajectory. Unlike the three previously mentioned participants, Craig's outward bodily display of laddish qualities was less forceful and assertive. He was a relatively small young man with a happy-go-lucky demeanour. Craig's disposition appeared to help generate a confident conversational ability, leading him to express his thoughts and views freely. Subsequently, Craig was an easy young man to engage with verbally, further supporting his inclusion in the research. Despite Craig's less distinct physical displays of masculinity, his discourse had significant masculine and laddish qualities. He frequently used misogynistic and homophobic discourse (Willis, 1977) and talked with boastful enthusiasm about his violent physical encounters and the injuries he had inflicted on opponents whilst playing rugby.

Lewis

Lewis was one of the oldest participants at 18 years old and was a suave, stylish young man, often dressed in designer clothes. He also seemed to have a penchant for women and dedicated significant parts of his interview to discussing his various relationships with girls. Despite his confident, macho masculine front (Ward, 2015), Lewis was a very complex young man who suffered from various mental health issues and had previously had a marijuana addiction. During his interview, he spoke candidly about his mental health and behavioural problems (explored more thoroughly in Chapter Six), including issues with anger management. As he commented in an interview: '*I got anger issues. That's why I smoke so much. I smoke a fag, and it calms me down. Then an hour later, I'm angry again*'. Lewis's problems with anger had led to his involvement in more than twenty brawls.

Billy

Akin to Dan, Billy was another relatively sizeable young man, yet less muscular in his appearance. In some ways, Billy's persona was similar to Craig's. Billy displayed a cheerful and laid-back demeanour and was articulately spoken. His laid-back demeanour was often intensified due to his use of marijuana. Like several youths at the centre, he engaged in cannabis use, often leaving the centre, using the nearby lane to partake in drug use, and then returning to the centre. Like the following three participants, Billy's outward displays of laddish behaviour at the centre were limited, and he may seem like an outlier peripherally. However, his laddish qualities and those of the following three participants become more pronounced and distinguishable in their interview data.

Ian

Ian was an energetic, inquisitive young man. Unlike some of the other Ladz, Ian did not demonstrate any outright physical laddish qualities, and as the following interview excerpt shows, he was entirely against some historically associated laddish activities like smoking (Willis, 1977). '*I tried smoking once. I hated it! Never again! Why waste my money on that? I wouldn't do it again. I don't understand why people waste their money on that*'. However, verbally, Ian did demonstrate his commitment to this classification. For instance, in the following ethnographic excerpt, Ian discusses his involvement in rugby, which highlights his masculine laddish characteristics (McDowell, 2003), such as toughness and competitiveness: '*I'm fast as fuck, faster than Kyle. I'm not scared to tackle anyone, don't give a fuck how big they are. I will tackle them!*'.

Cole

Cole was another young man who only sporadically attended the youth centre – he was 20 years of age and had possibly started to outgrow the place. Cole was not initially a person I considered for the research because of his irregular attendance at the centre and the subsequent lack of ethnographic data. However, Cole was almost the 'poster boy' of the youth centre and had spent time there on work placement. Therefore, the centre staff encouraged me to include Cole in my research. Cole described himself as a 'nightmare' teenager and displayed laddish qualities, including a desire for manual work (Connell, 2005; Willis, 1977). However, it would be disingenuous to slot Cole into the laddish category neatly because, as some of the later sections show, unlike the rest of the Ladz, laddish culture and some of its adverse outcomes are almost imposed on Cole due to his childhood experiences, which included being a victim of both physical and verbal abuse inflicted by his father.

Wesley

Wesley was another centre 'poster boy' and was heavily involved in many of the centres' activities, including the youth committee. Therefore, like Cole, I was encouraged to incorporate Wesley into the research. However, I would have included Wesley myself in reflection because he offers contrasting characteristics and an element of comparative analysis. In some ways, but not all, Wesley was the outlier of the Ladz group. He was a shy, timid young man. This temperament was coupled with a tall, slender frame and a muffled form of speech that some-times made him difficult to understand. Wesley was a frequent user of the centre, and although he was friendly with many of the other youths, he often spent his time sitting in the corner of rooms or with his headphones on, listening to music. Physically and verbally, Wesley's data reveals a limited direct association with the laddish category. However, as later chapters demonstrate, Wesley's education and potential employment outcomes resemble laddish consequences.

Alongside the group of nine young men, four adults were also interviewed and involved in the research. These included Dafydd, the youth centre manager and Martin, the lead youth worker. Both of these men were university-educated and included because of their senior roles in the youth centre, their 20 years or more of longstanding service to the organisation, and considerable youth work experience and knowledge of young people in the community associated with the study. The third youth centre staff member involved in the research and interviewed was Amy, a relatively young female youth worker in her mid-twenties. The fourth adult included in the research and interviewed was Tony. Tony was the manager of the local secondary school pupil referral unit[1] that some of the young men attended.

The Valley Boy Insider

As mentioned previously, the research setting was the Aber Valley, my place of residency and a deprived former coal mining community deep in the heart of the South Wales Valleys. The Aber Valley is situated in the borough of Caerphilly in South East Wales and comprises of two villages, Abertridwr and Senghenydd. This community previously had two coal mines, the Universal Colliery and Wind-sor Collieries. The sinking and construction of these two coal mines in the 1890s helped transform the Aber Valley from a rural farming area with a population of 86 to a thriving industrial community of 11,000 inhabitants. At their peak, the two coal mines collectively employed almost 5,000 people (Llywelyn, 2013; Phillips, 1991). The Universal Colliery closed in 1928, and the Windsor Colliery closed in 1986. Due to the Aber Valley's geographic location and the relatively isolated nature of the area, it has failed to effectively replace the employment lost with the demise of the two coal mines. Subsequently, the Aber Valley is now classified as a deindustrialised area and suffers from elevated levels of deprivation across several social and economic indices (Welsh Government, 2019b). Unemployment rates, especially for men, are, for example, significantly above the national average: male unemployment in Aber Valley is currently 9.4 per cent compared with the UK average of 5 per cent, although female unemployment, which stands at 4.8 per cent, is only slightly above the UK average of 4.5 per cent (ONS, 2021a,

---

[1]Pupil referral units are a particular type of educational setting for young people of compulsory school age who, for different reasons (i.e. challenging behaviour and/or temporary and permanent school exclusion), have been removed from mainstream and special schools (Meo & Parker, 2004, p. 103).

2021b). Nearly 35 per cent of Aber Valley residents have no academic qualifications (ONS, 2021a). This community contains my family, friends and everything dear to me. Not having an emotional attachment to this place would be almost unthinkable to a working-class man like myself who cherishes the ideal notion of community and togetherness (Walkerdine & Jiménez, 2012). Subsequently, the strength of my insider status is inescapable and extensive (Merton, 1972). In some ways, I may be described as what Adler and Adler (1987) refer to as a complete member, a researcher who possesses a lived understanding and shared experiences similar to the research subject.

The similarities between the participants of this study and me extend beyond living in the same community. Many of the young men from this study partially display a form of working-class and/or protest masculine laddish resistance to education (Connell, 1995; Jackson, 2006). My school years were also spent as a laddish young man, and unlike 'most of the male sociologists who have … chronicled the rebellion and resistance of the hooligans to schooling … worked hard at school, did their homework, passed exams, took the advice of teachers' (Delamont, 2000, p. 99), I rejected education. I placed minimal importance on academic qualifications in my youthful years and left secondary school with not a single GCSE. A sociological examination of oneself is often a complicated process (Bourdieu, 2001). However, on reflection, I believe there are a few possible reasons why I rejected education.

As a young boy, I had poor coordination skills that I now know stem from my recently diagnosed severe dyslexia and dyspraxia. Subsequently, my childhood ability to successfully engage in sports was hindered, and although my dyslexia and dyspraxia were undiagnosed during my school years, I now assume that they must have caused me difficulties. Therefore, I guess my resistance to the school was an attempt to carve out an identity for myself and demonstrate my teenage masculinity through an avenue other than sporting prowess (Frosh et al., 2002) or academic achievement (Mac an Ghaill, 1994).

My resistance to education and what quickly escalated into early teenage smoking, drinking alcohol, drug-taking and 'petty' crime, were intensified by my youthful admiration and what later became a friendship with a group of young men from my village termed the 'Square Boys'. This group of working-class young men shared an association with the coal mining forefathers of the area, demonstrating toughness and stoicism (Ward, 2015) and epitomised (Haywood & Mac an Ghaill, 2003), epitomised what has become known as working-class and/or protest masculinity (Connell, 1995). Using a play on the words of Richard Burton (Dick Cavett Show, 1980), for me, and young men from the area like myself, our ambition was to become a 'Square Boy' who stood on the street corner because, for us, they were the kings of the contemporary underworld. Neighbouring groups of young men revered them and knew that entry into the 'Square Boys'' territory would potentially be met with violence. The 'Square Boys'' rough and ready displays drew the attention of local girls who seemed attracted to the young men's strong, lively masculine characteristics (Frosh et al., 2002). This popularity intensified the 'Square Boys' attraction to myself and others like me.

The connection between myself and the laddish category goes beyond a rejection of academic qualifications. My father was a carpenter, and relatively early in my teenage years, I committed to manual employment and becoming a carpenter like my father, because it seemed like the obvious employment route (Veness, 1962). This commitment led me to enrol on a local college carpentry course that, at the time, had a no qualification entry requirement. Although I completed this two-year course, other than a couple of brief spells on building sites as a carpenters' labourer, I could not get any substantial experience in building-site carpentry because apprenticeships were in minimal supply. I also lacked the know-how and confidence to successfully transition from a college-qualified carpenter to one that was building-site proficient. Without building-site experience and being unable to find a building firm or someone to support me further in my carpentry development, the two years I spent at college were worthless. Subsequently, with no GCSEs, my employment trajectory cascaded into a series of what are often referred to as 'dead-end jobs' (MacDonald & Marsh, 2005). Although I do not entirely subscribe to the notion of dead-end jobs, because I am not convinced that everyone seeks career progression and social mobility (Reay, 2013; Walkerdine et al., 2001), the jobs I have been employed in, fall into the definition of this term: low paid, with minimal room for progression (Lindsay & McQuaid, 2004) with some being precarious.

You name it, I have done it! I have: made washing lines in a factory; worked as a local park attendant; sold sports nutrition supplements in a health shop; worked in a factory producing concrete products, including garden ornaments; laboured on building sites, and I have worked at a supermarket picking products for home delivery. However, at age 32, I had what Thomson et al. (2002, p. 339) refer to as a 'critical moment': an event depicted in narrative 'considered to be important or to have had important consequences'. I have chosen to leave this event undocumented. However, this experience brought about an early midlife crisis and made me realise my life was going nowhere. My lack of educational attainment had significantly reduced my employment opportunities, and my life lacked meaning. Consequently, based on a 'nothing to lose' attitude and expected failure, I returned to education and enrolled on a youth, community and social work access to education course. I chose youth, community and social work because I wanted to become a youth worker and help younger marginalised versions of myself and prevent a life trajectory similar to mine. Additionally, my park attendant job led me to believe that I could gain young people's trust. However, a spell of youth work employment experience dissuaded me from this career path, and I fell in love with sociological theory through the work of Ferdinand Tönnies, Karl Marx and Émile Durkheim and made my way through education to PhD level.

Although my forthright biographical documentation adds integrity to the claims in this book, my association with the laddish category and research sample type, coupled with my emotional and physical attachment to the place of study, partially create researcher insider positionality, which potentially raises questions regarding my ability to be objective (Breen, 2007). In contrast, it is suggested that an outsider researcher may have increased value due to their objectivity and the ability to emotionally distance themselves from the study group (Kerstetter,

2012). However, there are very few cases where someone can be categorised as a real outsider or insider (Breen, 2007; Mercer, 2007; Merton, 1972), and it is equally necessary to recognise the benefits of my insider status. Firstly, my insider status increased my understanding of the study topic (Bonner & Tolhurst, 2002). Secondly, it made me aware of social codes and colloquialisms that enhanced my interaction with some participants (Bonner & Tolhurst, 2002). Thirdly, my shared understanding with the participant encouraged an open and honest discussion (Bonner & Tolhurst, 2002) while potentially providing me access to individuals who might have been closed to outsiders (Dwyer & Buckle, 2009). Fourthly, as Bourdieu (2001) argues, I believe my insider status and personal experience potentially sensitised me to things an outsider researcher would not have noticed.

Despite the benefits of shared experience, similarities have also presented me with difficulties. The young men's behaviour and mannerisms often generated a dual psychological and emotional response within me. These included fond youthful recollections, contrasted with a sense of sadness for opportunities lost, consideration for what might have been had I averted laddish culture (Willis, 1977) and engaged academically, and the thought that I might have been a well-established academic at this point in my life, instead of having to return to education at the age of 32 after years of doing numerous low paid precarious jobs.

These affective responses produced an undeniable affinity between some of the participants and me, but this link was also beneficial. Unlike criticisms that suggest insider researchers may have an affinity with the research participants and thus only partially report empirical findings to portray the study group more favourably (Saidin, 2017), I understand and have personally experienced the negative implications of laddish culture and its ability to reduce life chances (Weber, 1948). This understanding increased my researcher reflexivity (Attia & Edge, 2017). It raised my awareness of the potential pitfalls of insider positionality and understanding of 'the role of the self in the creation of knowledge' (Berger, 2015, p. 220).

An additional aspect worthy of documentation includes my demeanour. I do not feel that I fit into the stereotypical academic image. My sense of place identity (Proshansky et al., 1983) has generated a strong South Wales Valleys working-class associated accent. My right arm exhibits a virtually full-sleeve Japanese tattoo. I have a bald head littered with scars collected through my participation in rugby, with my deformed ear being particularly noticeable. The reality of my non-traditional academic image was once made clear to me by an established senior Russell Group University lecturer, who, upon initially meeting me, presented me with the following response: '*What is someone like 'you' doing at Cardiff University? We don't normally see people like you here*'. My demeanour and commitment to a traditional working-class identity often make me feel like a 'fish out of water' (Bourdieu & Wacquant, 1992, p. 127) in academia. However, as the following example demonstrates, this personal attribute is often advantageous within specific fieldwork settings.

My initial experience at the youth centre began with an early encounter with Tommy. As stated previously, Tommy was 13 years old and slightly built, yet his confidence and swagger gave him an undeniable noticeable presence that offset his slender frame. On my first day at the centre, I was standing at the entrance, and Tommy approached me with an air of self-assurance that belied his young age; he looked me up and down and said: '*You are new here. Are you a rugby player? I can tell because of your ear. I like you. I think you're going to be OK*'. Tommy's early positive assessment of me seemed intuitive based on my image. Furthermore, the response illustrates favourable recognition of my demeanour instead of the adverse reaction received from the senior Russell Group University lecturer, thus possibly highlighting the benefits of an 'unconventional' academic image in specific fieldwork settings.

However, the intuitive connection between myself and Tommy may partly resonate with the criticism that insider researchers may seek out participants similar to themselves and fail to explore a full range of participants that may otherwise offer varied sources of information (Stephenson & Greer, 1981). However, a researcher's identity is often relative and altered due to time, space, and research participants (Dwyer & Buckle, 2009). Therefore, there are very few cases where someone can be categorised as a real outsider or insider. Dwyer and Buckle (2009, p. 60) refer to this relational research position as 'the space between', a notion that challenges the simplistic dichotomy of insider versus outsider status and suggests that researchers are likely to fill different spaces at various times. 'The space between' offers an additional researcher role perspective. However, together with this section, as the following discussions demonstrate, my researcher positionality included multiple roles incorporating (Kanuha, 2000), outsider (Bridges, 2001), participant-observer (Gold, 1958) and overt full member (Bryman, 2016).

The Outsider

Although there were many shared similarities between myself and Ladz, apart from the three youth centre staff and Tony, all of the young men who participated in the study were 21 years or more my junior and significantly younger than me, to the extent that I am a similar age to many of their parents. Thus, although there were many shared similarities between myself and the Ladz, my generational position arguably also makes me an outsider.

The birth years of the young men I observed ranged from 2002 through to 2009. The case study sample situates itself within the demographic cohort of Generation Z (Gen Z) (Grow & Yang, 2018; Seemiller & Grace, 2018). Though it may be counterintuitive to generalise based on epoch (Mannheim, 1970), Lub et al. (2015, p. 655) argue that 'people born in different generational cohorts have experienced different events and circumstances in a formative phase of their lives, and have developed different mental schemas about the world they live and work in'. Subsequently, generational consideration can help make sense of differences between age groups and locate individuals within a specific period (Pilcher, 1994). Within the context of my research and status as a researcher, the notion of generational disparity was significant.

Unlike myself and my generation, Gen Z has generally grown up with mobile phones and has never known a world without the internet (Twenge, 2017). The participants' use of phones initially alerted me to the extent of my outsider status.

I was aware of young people's extensive phone use, but my early observations revealed an intensity that I was neither accustomed to nor conscious of. Further-more, although the participants used many colloquial terms that I was familiar with, they also adopted unfamiliar terminology. For example, the phrase: '*Alright fam*' was communally used by young men as a friendly way of greeting each other. 'Fam' is a slang word short for family but does not mean biological relations; instead, it relates to people they feel close to. The term 'fam' is closely associated with American hip-hop and features in grime lyrics by Lethal Bizzle and Stormzy. Stormzy's music was favoured by many of the participants of this study and was often accessed using the internet and YouTube.

In contrast to the term 'fam', my favoured choice of greeting is the Welsh col-loquial term 'butt' ('Alright butt'). This word is commonly used across the South Wales Valleys by many men of my generation and links back to an era of indus-trial work, 'where the term "butty" was synonymous with coal miners working together underground' (Ward, 2015, p. 49). The comparison between these two greetings arguably demonstrates a generational difference, my outsider status and the possible influential strength of the technology and contemporary popular culture. The significance of music was further cemented when one of the partici-pants (Dan) was sat in the computer room listening to the Eminem song entitled Stan. Stan was released in the year 2000, and the lyrics from this song evoked happy, youthful memories for me. Subsequently, I said to Dan: '*Like this song, do you, butt?*' Dan replied: '*Yeah, it's a good song, but it is a bit old*'. At this point, I recognised that Dan also potentially viewed me as old, a reality that highlighted my outsider status due to the age difference between myself and the participants.

The 'Makeshift Youth Worker'

My initial fieldwork began with me having a relatively free role, and I was allowed to move around the youth centre with considerable ease, choosing which rooms to situate myself in and whom to observe. However, as the weeks progressed, this free role became restricted. Due to underfunding and staff illness, I was required to undertake an integrated position within the organisation and become a 'make-shift youth worker'. Subsequently, akin to the staff themselves, I was compelled to adopt the room rotation system, meaning each team member spends an hour in a specific room supervising youth activity and then swaps places at hourly intervals. This transition changed the dynamics of my researcher role. I was no longer a participating observer (Gold, 1958). I became an overt full member (Bryman, 2016) of the organisation with newly acquired roles and responsibilities that pre-sented me with challenges.

For example, one evening, when I was assigned to the pool room, two of the younger members were happily playing pool. During their game, Stan entered the room and asked one of the young men if he could take a shot for them. At Stan's request, the young man despondently gave Stan the pool cue. Despite being relatively small, Stan was a formidable figure and leader among some of his peers. After taking the requested shot, Stan continued to hit several other balls in a sporadic frenzied manner. The young man initially playing pool appeared dismayed by Stan's behaviour but seemed unwilling and afraid to challenge him. Stan was reluctant to stop, and his actions recklessly intensified, with him hitting balls forcibly off the pool table and around the room. Subsequently, I said to Stan: '*That's enough, Stan. You have taken the shot you wanted. Now give the pool cue back, please. You can play next*'. Stan replied: '*Fuck you, Rich*'. To which I replied: '*Don't speak to me like that, please, Stan. I asked you nicely and showed you respect. Now, give the cue back, or I will be forced to give you a warning. I don't want to do that, so just give the cue back, please*'. Again, Stan replied: '*Fuck you, Rich, I am playing*'. At this point, I was getting agitated.

I had worked hard to build up a good relationship with Stan. He was recognised as a 'difficult' character by all the staff, but I had invested much time into him, as I thought he would be particularly relevant to my research due to his laddish (Jackson, 2006) characteristics. However, Stan's behaviour had become dangerous. He had the potential to hurt others and damage equipment. My role as a 'makeshift youth worker' had put me in an awkward position. I could not let Stan's behaviour continue, but by intervening further, I was potentially going to jeopardise the relationship I had worked hard to build. I was angered that I had been put in this position, but I had no choice but to halt Stan's actions. Therefore, I said: '*Stan, I have given you fair warning. You have given me no choice now. This is your first warning. Please don't make me give you another. It is cold outside, and I don't want to give you another warning and kick you out. Just give the cue back, please*'. The centre operates on a 'two-strike rule'. You give an initial warning for wrongful behaviour, and upon receiving a second warning, the person is asked to leave. At this point, I was dejected. Stan was crucial to my research, and I had purposely emphasised the use of the word 'please' because I knew that he disliked authority, and I wanted to demonstrate respect.

However, in response to the warning, Stan once again said: '*Fuck you, Rich, you can't kick me out. That would be tight [bad], and you are sound [good]*'. Stan continued his reckless behaviour and forcibly hit what little balls were left on the pool table. I sat for what felt like an eternity, despondently knowing that as a 'makeshift youth worker', I had a duty of care to the other members, and I now had to eject Stan from the centre and potentially alienate him from my research. Downheartedly and full of internal anger towards the position I had been put in, I said to Stan: '*Stan, you've given me no choice. This is your second warning. You've got to leave, butt, sorry*'. Stan looked at me angrily, slammed the cue on the table and left the room.

Stan did not directly leave the building and lingered until the senior youth worker asked him to go and threatened a lengthy ban if he did not respond. I left the centre that night despondent, dejected and full of emotional turmoil, which led me to reflect on my researcher positionality (Attia & Edge, 2017). I was a 'Valley boy'; I was an insider; I was one of them! Why didn't Stan listen to me? Had I code shifted (Ward, 2015), lost my working-class 'Valleys' identity, and gained the middle-class academic status that I had desperately tried to avoid on my academic journey? Furthermore, I felt aggrieved that I had been put in a position where I had to penalise Stan's behaviour and jeopardise a relationship I had worked hard to build. However, I equally recognised that the youth centre was underfunded and understaffed and desperately required my help. I was conscious that as researchers, we continually 'take' in the pursuit of our research goal, yet sometimes fail to give our hosts anything directly in return, a thoughtless process that did not and does not sit comfortably with me. Thankfully, on his return to the centre, Stan bore no grudge against me and even apologised for his behaviour. Furthermore, reflecting on my data, I recognised that the role transformation to 'makeshift youth worker' had also been advantageous. Being fixed in a specific room for a set period heightened my focus and led to more detailed documentation than in the initial 'freelance' role.

Conclusion

This chapter has introduced the young men who became the focus of my research, or the Ladz as I refer to them, and highlighted their laddish association (Jackson, 2006), which later sections reconfirm and contradict. It has also introduced myself, the Valley Boy, and discussed the multidimensional nature of my researcher positionality during the study. This included an insider status (Kanuha, 2000), which was offset by an outsider status (Bridges, 2001) and the acquired 'makeshift youth worker' role and subsequent overt full membership (Bryman, 2016), all of which influenced the outcome of my research and this book. The following chapter reviews literature and the trajectory of ideas concerning working-class young men, education, and employment while also discussing predicted future employment changes and social class.

Chapter Two

Working-Class Young Men, Education, and Employment

Introduction

This chapter has two subsections: firstly, it explores prominent literature concerning working-class young men, education, and employment. The second part discusses future employment changes and social class, which are not directly addressed in the body of the book but have some significance concerning the labour market prospects of marginalised young men like the Ladz.

A chronological approach is used to identify key themes in the literature: working-class young men's views towards education and employment: how and why these aspects are constructed, and the effects on employability. The chapter identifies some consistencies concerning the Post-World War II Studies and post-industrial research; however, the chapter also demonstrates that these studies and their findings may be somewhat dated. It highlights, in contrast, a recent study by Roberts (2018) that presents a departure from prior research findings. The chapter argues, however, that Roberts's research findings need to be considered in the context of place-based specificity and working-class subgroup studies.

Post-World War II Studies

In the introduction to *Learning to Labour,* Willis (1977, p. 1) opens by offering a research statement that includes: 'the difficult thing to explain about how working class kids get working class jobs is why they let themselves'. This statement was partly the basis for Willis's qualitative ethnographic study, which documents the transition from school to work of a group of working-class young men. Although the study includes data from various participants, the research primarily focuses on two groups of young men, including the ear'oles and the lads, with the lads having a more central focus in the book. The lads consisted of a group of

The 21st Century Ladz: Continuity and Changes among Marginalised
Young Men from the South Wales Valleys, 19–34
doi:10.1108/978-1-83797-531-720251003

12 non-academic working-class young men attending a boys-only secondary modern school that was situated in a small industrial town in the West Midlands in the heart of a 'working class inter-war council estate' (Willis, 1977, p. 4), and the school intake consisted mainly of working-class pupils.

Willis's findings demonstrate the lads' immersion in a counter-school culture and rejection of school, which derived from a working-class, shop floor culture (Roberts, 1995) and a form of masculinity that has become known as working-class and/or protest masculinity (Connell, 1995; Haywood & Mac an Ghaill, 2003). This form of working-class masculinity was often inherited through social connections, including family and mainly male figures, including the father (Tolson, 1977) and honed within the peer group (Willis, 1977). These social connections and subsequent identity construction generated manual employment aspirations and a rejection of academic credentials based on the belief that these qualifications would not enhance future employment prospects, thus discarding the notion of meritocracy. Instead, the lads' school experience centred around 'dossing, blagging, wagging' (Willis, 1977, p. 26) and resistance to authority, behaviour influenced by their inherited and honed masculine form of working-class identity, which generated a desire and commitment to manual work and a rejection of mental labour and 'pen-pushing' (Willis, 1977, p. 149) based on the belief that these were effeminate and 'cissy'. Conversely, the ear'oles conformed to school norms and had more middle-class aspirations.

Essentially, Willis argues that the lads were not passively channelled into jobs; instead, 'they were actively choosing their own future in unskilled work' (Roberts, 1995, p. 88) and complicit in their own social reproduction (Griffin, 2005; Skeggs, 1992). The lads' cultural upbringing and the masculine environment in which they were raised instilled qualities that facilitated a simple transition to manual work due to the masculine nature of the employment and the ability to express aspects of their previously honed cultural identity, such as resistance to authority, banter and distrust of theoretical work. However, the employment experiences in unskilled and semi-skilled manual work eventually became monotonous and unrewarding (Willis, 1977).

Although *Learning to Labour* has been an influential study in school-to-work transition research and other research fields, this study is not without criticism. For example, Brown (1987, p. 24) argues that Willis creates a bi-polar depiction of working-class young men's educational experiences, including a pro and anti-school response that does not explain why 'large numbers of working-class pupils do not reject school'. Additional criticisms centre around Willis's focus on young men (Griffin, 1985; McRobbie, 1991), a lack of objectivity due to over-rapport with the lads and a 'celebration of their lifestyle' (Hammersley & Atkinson, 2007, p. 88) and a lack of focus and attention on the ear'oles (Griffin, 2005). Despite these critiques, Willis's bi-polar model offers 'an explanation of why pupils develop the responses they do' (Brown, 1990, p. 61) and shows how class is socially reproduced (France & Roberts, 2017).

Learning to Labour and Willis's study offers a cultural (Brown, 1987; France & Roberts, 2017) explanation of working-class young men's educational experiences and employment aspirations. However, additional school-to-work Post-World

War II studies (Ashton & Field, 1976; Carter, 1966; Veness, 1962) offer a structural explanation (France & Roberts, 2017). Despite the differing positions, there are recognisable commonalities between the studies. Akin to the identified significance and influence of family and peers in Willis's study, Veness (1962), Carter (1966), and Ashton and Field (1976) also demonstrate the significance of social class and socialisation through family and community traditions which determined young people's ambitions, school experience and employment aspirations.

Carter (1966), for example, focused on differing working-class family types and distinguished three groups, including 'home-centred and aspiring', 'solid working-class' and what he calls 'the rough'. 'These three types of background exert distinctive influences upon children[s] ... job aspirations and general attitudes towards work [and] knowledge about work' (Carter, 1966, p. 41). For example, home-centred families are categorised as having middle-class aspirations with husbands in skilled employment and positions of responsibility. Therefore, children are encouraged to study and do well in school and careers, whilst factory work and shop work are rejected because of the associated low standing. Solid working-class family types are defined by male fathers in semi- and unskilled manual employment and children who aspire to the same jobs as their fathers and neighbours and thus only partially engage in schoolwork. The rough family type is defined by deprivation, and their children bear a significant resemblance to the lads from Willis's (1977) study with males in semi and unskilled work and children that do not care about school and have no appreciation for the joys of learning and are ready-made for 'dead-end' jobs.

Like Carter, Ashton and Field (1976) define three family types with equally distinct influences and outcomes. including careerless, short-term, and extended careers. The careerless correspond with Willis's (1977) lads and Carter's (1966) roughs and are defined by large working-class families living in impoverished conditions with parents in careerless, low-income jobs with little formal education. Children often develop a negative attitude towards education, reject meritocracy, and enter jobs like their parents, with extrinsic reward and financial gain being the primary motivator. Conversely, extended careers include mainly middle-class families with few local ties and whereby children experience minimal school difficulties. Academic achievement is deemed necessary for career orientation, and manual occupations are seen as demeaning and beneath them. Veness (1962) also offers a three-model typology regarding school leavers' employment aspirations and expectations, including tradition-direction, which 'refers to the situation in which the choice [of] employment is predetermined by family or neighbourhood traditions because no other choice would be thinkable to the young person' (Veness, 1962, p. 69). Inner-direction, whereby the choice of employment is made with reference mainly to a person's interests and talents, often overlapping with tradition-direction (Carter, 1966). And other-directed, where a young person's career orientation is influenced by external sources of information and stimulated by 'talks, conversations, pamphlets, broadcasts and so on' (Veness, 1962, p. 73).

In summary of the Post-World War II Studies, although there are variations in the point of focus and differing terminology used, there are commonalities among these studies. These include varying forms of working-class responses to education and employment aspirations that derive from cultural and structural influences and socialisation or intergenerational transmissions of ways of being that generate a range of outcomes, including young men that conform to school norms with middle-class aspirations together with those that reject education and manual work orientation. Despite these variations, during the Post-World War II period, the labour market was defined by a segmented structure with a clear division between unskilled, skilled, and professional forms of work and relatively full employment rates (Tomlinson, 2013). Therefore, various educational outcomes and employment aspirations were accommodated, thus generating a relatively smooth, fluid school-to-work transition (Tomlinson, 2013) and enabling working-class young men who left school with no qualifications to find manual employment with satisfactory rates of pay and some prospect of security with reasonable ease (McDowell, 2003; Roberts, 2020; Willis, 1977). However, as the following section shows, these labour market conditions have altered significantly.

The Shift from Manual to Service Sector Work

The late 1970s 'Thatcherite Revolution' (Nayak, 2003a, p. 149) and Conservative Government policy contributed to a move away from industrial work, a decline in manual jobs and a shift towards service-sector employment. This employment shift lessened the need for male manual workers who once dominated employment in the heavy industries, while the growth in the service sector employment stimulated demand for female workers. Service sector employment consists of a range of work, from well-paid, high-tech, and professional occupations to low-status, insecure jobs (Ward, 2015). Therefore, unlike in the Post-World War II era, working-class young men who leave education with no qualifications are now likely to have limited job opportunities in minimum wage employment such as 'hospitality (hotels, bars, cafes, restaurants) and in retail shops' (Roberts, 2020, p. 35) and job roles requiring traditionally associated 'feminine' attributes and skills including emotional labour interpersonal communication and presentation of self (Hochschild, 1983; Leidner, 1993; McDowell, 2003). However, the deference and docility features of emotional labour have historically been claimed to be at odds with working-class and/or protest masculinity (Connell, 1995; Nixon, 2018) and 'the right to "stick up for yourself"' (McDowell, 2003, p. 176). Although this section demonstrates significant structural changes in the UK labour market and economy, the following post-industrial studies related section highlights some continuations and consistencies concerning Post-World War II school-to-work transition research while identifying a significant disparity.

Post-Industrial Studies

Some post-industrial studies demonstrate a degree of continuity with Post-World War II research. For example, Williamson and Williamson (1981, p. 45) ethnographic study, conducted in 'Milltown' (a rough suburb of a Welsh city), documents five 13–18-year-old working-class young men who rejected school and 'didn't see much point in doing exams [because they] could not see any equation between educational attainment and financial reward'. The young men, characterised by strong machismo, aggressive sexism, and homophobia, aspired to masculine jobs that involved 'hard graft', including outdoor manual work (Williamson & Williamson, 1981, p. 52).

Mac an Ghaill (1994) ethnographic study at a UK West Midlands secondary school explored how boys learn to become men. In doing so, akin to Post-World War II research, Mac an Ghaill identified groups of working-class young men with differing approaches to school and employment aspirations determined by their 'relations with their families, their experiences of school and the local labour market' (Hopkins, 2013, p. 185). These groups of working-class young men included 'The Academic Achievers' who came from a skilled employment working-class family background, had 'a positive orientation to the academic curriculum' (Mac an Ghaill, 1994, p. 59), and saw academic credentials as a route to upward social mobility. 'The New Enterprisers' gravitated towards vocational curriculum subjects and saw these as a means of social mobility. The last group of working-class young men includes 'The Macho Lads'. Similarly, to 'the lads', 'roughs', and 'careerless' (Ashton & Field, 1976; Carter, 1966; Willis, 1977), these young men rejected 'formal school knowledge and the potential exchange value it has in the labour market' (Mac an Ghaill, 1994, p. 65). Instead, 'The Macho Lads' school experience centred around three Fs – fighting, fucking, and football and a 'valorisation of "masculine" manual labour that informed the group's social practices' (Mac an Ghaill, 1994, p. 71).

Similarly, Nayak's (2003a, 2003b, 2006) research in the North East of England identified a group of working-class young men with a 'prominent masculine legacy of manual labour [which] ran through their familial biographies' (Nayak, 2003b, p. 150) and a negative attitude towards education that derived from the belief that school was of little importance to their future. Instead, the young men expressed elements of an industrial heritage embodied in an appreciation of skilled physical labour and a commitment to the traditional working-class masculine ideal of 'hard graft'. Also situated in the North East of England, MacDonald and Marsh's (2005) youth transition qualitative study of 88 young people aged between 15 and 25 documents several participants' dismissal of formal education. This attitude towards education is attributed to local labour market conditions, the paucity of decent working-class jobs and the employment opportunities available, including serving in cake shops or stacking supermarket shelves, and the belief that these forms of employment did not require educational engagement.

McDowell's (2003) research on young men and their school-to-work transition yet again identifies a legacy of manual labour and attraction to typically masculine jobs, including semi or unskilled manual work, and who generally expressed a '"don't much care" [attitude] to school and its regulatory environment' (McDowell, 2003, p. 118). Furthermore, despite the identified significant labour market shift, although some of the young men did have some involvement in service sector work, McDowell (2003, p. 134) 'found little evidence … that the young men [were] … looking for work in the retail sector, in leisure or tourism or the hospitality industry'. Correspondingly, Nixon (2006, 2009) demonstrates low-skilled, poorly educated working-class men's rejection of anything other than male-dominated manual occupations, with socialisation and educational background being influential factors (Andersson & Beckman, 2018). Service sector work was generally only considered where customer interaction and emotional labour (Hochschild, 1983) were minimal, including a narrow range of 'masculine' service sector jobs, including distribution, transportation, and warehousing.

Similarly to the Post-World War II studies, although the post-industrial studies demonstrate some degree of plurality in working-class ways of being and educational experiences and employment orientation, despite the shift from manual to service sector work, there is a continued identification of a macho laddish subgroup of working-class young men that adopt a negative attitude towards education and manual employment aspirations (O'Donnell & Sharpe, 2000) that largely derives from socialisation or intergenerational transmission of working-class masculine ways of being and structural factors. However, these post-industrial studies are nearly two decades or more old, and the recent research of Roberts (2018) somewhat challenges these notions and offers an alternative understanding.

Roberts,' (2018, p. 2) research draws on findings from a 'longitudinal qualitative study covering a seven-year period with young men of working-class origins from Kent, in the South-East of England' and a historically industrial area with an employment source that included shipbuilding, milling, and coal mining. However, despite deindustrialisation and the dearth of industrial jobs, the research area ranked among the least deprived third of the UK (Roberts, 2011) and has witnessed significant regeneration and profound growth in retail, hotels, restaurants, and wholesale.

Drawing on a study sample that included 24 white, heterosexual working-class young men aged 18–24, Roberts (2018, p. 4) explores the educational and employment experiences and formulation of masculinity of a group of working-class young men that 'are not the most marginalised, most spectacular or most dispossessed members of the working class, as is the focus for many scholars'. Instead, he focuses on the 'missing middle' – 'those working-class men who, by virtue of being neither disengaged from school/work nor on a route to a "typically successful" adulthood characterised by a degree and a professional occupation'.

Roberts (2018, p. 126) states that his missing middle study sample 'had not merely inherited older generations of men's dispositions towards and understanding of appropriately masculine work'. Therefore, unlike Nixon's (2006, 2009) participants, Roberts argues that his working-class young men were not tied to traditional predispositions but have developed a form of inclusive masculinity more in tune with the emotional demands of retail work. Roberts claims that the differentiation in his findings can be explained through the contemporary nature of his research and participants' detachment from previous ways of being due to the decline in heavy industry and the coinciding rise in service sector work.

Although Roberts' findings demonstrate the discontinuity of intergenerational transmission of working-class masculine modes of being, Roberts seems to distinguish his research from previous studies based on geographic location. For example, Roberts (2018, p. 78) states that his study, based in Kent in the South East of England, was 'a contrasting setting to much academic work on young men and changing economies conducted in industrial "powerhouse" regions (e.g. Furlong & Cartmel, 2004; Jimenez & Walkerdine, 2011; McDowell, 2003)'. Roberts somewhat implicitly raises the signal of the importance of cultural and geographical specificity (Ivinson, 2014a; Walkerdine & Jiménez, 2012) in understanding young men's responses to education and work and seems to acknowledge that 'the industrial and social history of a place affects [the] identity of its inhabitants' (McDowell, 2003, p. 96). Within the 'industrial 'powerhouse' regions' distinction, Roberts includes the work of Jimenez and Walkerdine (2011), which was conducted in the South Wales Valleys, the same research location as the research upon which this book is based. Therefore, the following section explores the research in this locality regarding working-class young men and their experiences and relationships with education and employment.

South Wales Valleys

Jimenez and Walkerdine (2011) research was based in South Wales Valleys, UK, and a community referred to as 'Steeltown' due to the area's strong association with steel production owing to a steelwork, which was a major employer in the area up until its closure in 2002. The study demonstrates the 'intergenerational transmission of gendered codes of masculinity' (Jimenez & Walkerdine, 2011, p. 194) and the subsequent reluctance of young men to engage in low-status forms of service sector employment due to family and friends ridiculing, rejecting and shaming the young men about their engagement in jobs and wearing a work-related uniform that was communally viewed as 'feminine'. Furthermore, in the main publication resulting from the 'Steeltown' study, Walkerdine and Jiménez (2012, p. 119) discuss issues around education in the research locality, stating that young men in the area were 'a bit like Paul Willis's (1977) lads several decades earlier, [and] were longing to be men and had followed the path of many generations of men before them who left school with no qualification'.

As mentioned, a significant criticism of Willis's (1977) study concerns the bipolar depiction of working-class young men's educational experiences (Brown, 1990) and narrow focus on disaffected youths (Brown, 1987). In response to this, Brown's (1987) South Wales based 'Middleport Study' of young men's school-to-work transition, which was based on data collected from three comprehensive schools and using both qualitative and quantitative data collection, largely focuses on what Brown (1987, p. 31) terms Ordinary kids, working-class young men that 'neither simply accept nor reject school, but comply with it', which Brown argues is an attitude towards school adopted by the majority of working-class pupils. The 'ordinary' working-class young men's response to school was characterised by "getting on within the working class' (Brown, 1990, p. 68), which led them to make an effort in school based on the belief that a modest level of attainment and academic credentials would enhance their chances of employment. However, similarly to Post-World War II school-to-work transition studies (Ashton & Field, 1976; Carter, 1966; Willis, 1977), Brown equally identifies two other subgroups of working-class young men, including the Swots who adopted a 'getting out' approach to school and 'who were identified as spending all their time working and never having a laugh or getting into trouble with teachers' (Brown, 1990, p. 67), and 'Rems' who akin to Willis's (1977) lads, rejected school based on the belief that it was boring and irrelevant, and was mainly a venue for 'hav[ing] a laugh' (Brown, 1987, p. 72). Similar to the Post-World War II school-to-work transition studies, although Brown does not explicitly explore gender, his findings have been interpreted through the lens of masculinity and claimed to demonstrate that 'working-class boys construct a variety of masculine identities of which being macho is only one' (O'Donnell & Sharpe, 2000, p. 45).

Masculinity is a central aspect in the research of Ward (2015). Ward's research is a longitudinal study based in a former mining community in the South Wales Valleys. Using Goffman's notion of performance of self, Ward demonstrates how young men perform masculinity in different settings and concerning education, leisure and employment and engage in 'a degree of chameleonising ... where individuals can adjust and alter performances with different audiences' (Ward, 2015, p. 150). These subgroups of working-class young men include 'The Geeks', who were academic achievers and mainly demonstrated a form of masculinity based on educational success, which is often perceived to oppose laddish (Willis, 1977) working-class masculinity. However, outside the confines of school, 'The Geeks' visited strip clubs and engaged in sexist laddish associated behaviour.

The second subgroup of working-class young men included 'The Valley Boiz', whom Ward argues resembled Willis's (1977) lads and had a similar attitude towards education and employment and engaged in fighting and drinking large amounts of alcohol. However, these young men stayed on in education post-16, which was influenced by the limited employment options in the locale. Furthermore, some of 'The Valley Boiz' undertook part-time service sector work in pubs and fast-food outlets. However, although this involvement may be regarded as somewhat contradictory considering the young men's association with working-class/or protest masculinity, which is often deemed antithetical to the service sector requirements (Connell, 1995; McDowell, 2003), Ward surprisingly overlooks this disparity and does not explore the young men's experience of service sector work. Nevertheless, similarly to 'The Geeks', 'The Valley Boiz' also engaged in dual displays of masculinity by 'perform[ing] a "softer" side through intimate stories with close friends' (Ward, 2015, p.152).

The third and final subgroup in Ward's study is 'The Emos'. These young men adopted a similar approach to education as Brown's (1987) 'ordinary kids' and 'did enough to "get on" in school' (Ward, 2015, p. 98) whilst also displaying an alternative version of masculinity through a distinctive style including long hair and tight skinny jeans together with traditional displays of working-class masculinity. Essentially, Ward's (2015) study argues that despite social transformations, the influence of heavy industry continues to prevail and make working-class masculinity a "default reference point" for young men (Ward, 2015, p. 96).

This South Wales Valleys portion of this review reveals findings somewhat dissimilar from those of Roberts (2018), contradicting the notion that working-class young men are not tied to traditional predispositions. The literature demonstrates the persistence of working-class masculinity (Connell, 1995; Willis, 1977), a negative or complex relationship with education and the "intergenerational transmission of gendered codes of masculinity" (Jimenez & Walkerdine, 2011, p. 194). However, these studies predate Roberts and may be regarded as somewhat dated concerning social and economic change, especially considering that the findings from the most recent study are nearly a decade (Ward, 2013) or older. The following section considers the significance of future employment changes to the above debates.

Future Employment Changes

This section explores the literature concerning future work changes, new technologies, increased automation and the predicted impact on job types and individuals. The future of work debate is complex. However, this section confines itself to a broad outline that simply locates various positions to further situate the research in the future kind of work that awaits young men like the participants. There are consistencies between these positions principally centred around the notion that manual forms of employment and low-skilled, poorly educated young men will bear the hardest impact from future employment changes.

Therefore, rather than merely reconciling working-class young men's future to the hands of fate, this chapter errs on the side of caution and considers predicted future employment changes as a realistic outcome and thus identifies possible shortcomings concerning government policy response and current understanding of marginalised working-class young men, education and employment.

Future of Work Studies

Driven by capitalism, humanity is set to achieve even greater technological and scientific advances that may potentially deliver unprecedented social change, particularly concerning employment (Autor, 2015; Grace et al., 2018; Rifkin, 1995). The notion of a job apocalypse and a surplus population of human workers has stoked public fears surrounding a future of inequality, whereby employment will be limited to an elite few (Aggarwal & Nash, 2018; Beaudry et al., 2016). Contemporary media discourse has often been at the forefront of this portrayal, regularly emphasising the notion that automation is set to create thousands of job losses in forthcoming years. Examples of this media depiction include headlines such as: *'Robots are coming for your job: and faster than you think'* (Chan, 2016). *'Robots 'could take 4m UK private sector jobs within 10 years'* (Booth, 2017), and *'The Year the Robots Came for Our Jobs'* (Malesic, 2017).

Despite media portrayal, there is little research-based consensus about the future scale of labour substitution resulting from automation. However, it is widely believed that new technologies will primarily impact 'routine' jobs that are easier to automate. For example, Frey and Osborne (2013; 2017) estimate that around 47 per cent of total US employment is at considerable risk from automation in the next two decades or by the year 2030. Overall, the findings indicate that the jobs most at risk of computerisation are those that are predictable or physical forms of employment, including transportation, construction and extraction, manufacturing, office administration, and sales and services. The jobs least at risk from computerisation require complex perception, manipulation skills, creativity and social intelligence, such as skilled management, engineering and science, computers, education, healthcare, legal services and the arts and media, subsequently leading to anticipated increased demand for competencies including soft skills and social skills (Brynjolfsson & McAfee, 2012; Davenport & Kirby, 2016; Deloitte, 2016; Goodhart, 2020). Others who support this view include McKinsey Global Institute (2017), Grace et al. (2018), as well as non-American studies: Pajarinen and Rouvinen (2014), Deloitte (2016), and Frey et al., (2014).

The findings of Frey and Osborne are cited in several articles that relate to the future of work and automation, yet despite this popularity, their research has obvious shortcomings. Firstly, they fail to account for the possibility that automation will create new jobs, a notion that is particularly evident in several pieces of research, including that of Hawksworth et al. (2018), IFR (2018), and Leopold et al. (2018). Furthermore, much of this research contradicts the findings of Frey and Osborne by suggesting that rather than damaging human employment, automation is labour-augmenting and has the potential to increase employment levels due to the creation of new jobs (Arntz et al., 2016).

Secondly, whilst Frey and Osborne's findings and claims offer a very deterministic view of automation and employment, they fail to account for the economic aspects of automation (Brown et al., 2018), such as the cost of replacing humans with machines. Moreover, substituting workers with machines may not be economically viable or even worthwhile for all forms of business (Hawksworth et al., 2018). Arntz et al. (2016) also suggest that Frey and Osborne's research is methodologically flawed and thus overestimates the number of jobs that can be fully automated. The basis of Arntz et al. (2016) critique is centred on the notion that jobs are often made up of multiple tasks (Autor & Handel, 2013) and that not all tasks within an occupation are easily automatable, thus making the analysis of a job as a whole, and the occupational-based approach, flawed.

To substantiate their claims and critique of Frey and Osbourne and the occupational-based approach, Arntz et al. (2016) employ a task-based approach to the analysis of automation and its effects on employment. Rather than assuming jobs as a whole are displaced by automation, the task-based approach assesses employment tasks that machines can displace (Arntz et al., 2016). Employing this method, Arntz et al. (2016) analysed the percentage of jobs at risk from automation for 21 OECD countries, including America. This analysis involved using the "PIACC database (Programme for the International Assessment of Adult Competencies) that surveys task structures across OECD countries" (Arntz et al., 2016, p. 8). Using this data, Arntz et al. were able to take into account the way tasks varied by roles within the same occupation.

The findings of Arntz et al. (2016) estimate that for the 21 OECD countries included in their research, on average, 9 per cent of jobs are automatable. American jobs at risk from automation fall into this average category of 9 per cent, with the UK being slightly higher at 10 per cent. In comparison, Frey and Osborne (2013, 2017) estimated that 47 per cent of American jobs are at risk from automation, a contrast that equates to a 38 per cent discrepancy. Furthermore,

Arntz et al. (2016) also suggest that their own estimate of job risk and automation may be exaggerated due to social, legal and economic obstacles. Moreover, even if businesses were to employ new forms of technology, human workers may be able to adapt their skills and switch tasks and thus secure employment.

Leopold et al. (2018) offer a somewhat optimistic view of automation and employment. The estimates of these scholars suggest that by the year 2022, automation will actually increase jobs in emerging professions, which will subsequently offset any decline that may occur in other forms of employment. Leopold et al. (2018) predict that automation will lead to an 11 per cent increase in employment, an estimate slightly greater than their predicted job decline of 10 per cent, yet it still equates to a net employment gain overall.

The notion that automation will increase employment levels overall is also predicted by the data-driven research of Hawksworth et al. (2018). In relation to education, males face the most significant risk from automation. Men with low educational attainment are often over-represented as craft and related trade workers and machine operators. In contrast, low-educated women often have a high representation in service and sales work and elementary occupations such as cleaners and helpers, all areas estimated to be less affected by automation than the jobs undertaken by men with similar educational attainment.

Despite differing views on the impact of technologies and automation on jobs, all the estimates indicate that there is a clear distinction between the jobs most likely to be affected by automation and those least likely to be affected, with this difference being distinguished through the categorisation of routine jobs and non-routine jobs. Overall, the future of work research suggests that the employment forms most likely affected by automation are routine jobs, occupations relating to using fingers and hands, or exchanging information and selling (Brown et al., 2018). Many of these forms of employment are often performed by individuals with minimal educational attainment (Frey and Osborne, 2013). Routine forms of employment are identified as high risk because they are often repetitive and mainly consist of job tasks based on well-defined procedures that machines can easily replicate and perform (Reidy, 2014). Furthermore, not only can machines replicate these jobs and their tasks, but in many cases: 'if a machine can do job tasks currently done by humans, a machine will often do the task with greater precision, speed and at a lower cost' (Muro et al., 2019, p. 14).

Policy Response

The UK and Welsh governments have recognised the potential threat of automation and job loss: UK Government National AI Strategy (HM Government, 2021); the Welsh Government Employability Plan (Welsh Government, 2018); The Welsh Government Wales 4.0 Delivering Economic Transformation for a Better Future of Work (Welsh Government, 2019a). Generally, the policy narrative echoes the literature and studies surrounding the future of work (Arntz et al., 2016; Brynjolfsson & McAfee, 2012; Leopold et al., 2018) and has become entwined with education, reskilling, upskilling (Allas et al., 2020; Kapetaniou, 2019; WEF 2020, 2021), and the notion that 'If workers can up-skill through better education and training, they will be better placed to complement the intelligent machines of the future' (Spencer & Slater, 2020, p. 121).

A Future for Working-Class Young Men

This future of work discussion reveals little consensus, but it is widely assumed that employment changes will negatively impact low-skilled, poorly educated young people. In response to this impact, government policy largely focuses on the notion of lifelong learning and upskilling individuals to counteract the impact of new technologies. However, concerning the current understanding of marginalised working-class young men and the identified negative association with education, the benefit and success of this educational focus are currently questionable. Therefore, without addressing this potential policy shortcoming and considering methods to engage marginalised working-class young men in education, future employment changes may increase inequality due to the negative impact on marginalised societal groups and increase youth unemployment. Furthermore, automation and new technologies are predicted to affect manual jobs severely. These forms of employment have been traditionally associated with a working-class status due to the relationship to the modes of production and subsequent level of income, economic security, chances of economic advancement and position of authority and control (Goldthorpe, 1980, 2016). However, the UK labour market structure has altered significantly since these employment-related social class definitions. Therefore, the following section explores social class and the discussions surrounding this topic, demonstrating the trajectory of ideas and the shift in understanding this concept whilst also defining this book's use and interpretation of social class. Understanding social class is important to youth transition research, as it often shapes a person's understanding of the world and their decisions and choices (France & Roberts, 2017).

Social Class

The term 'class' is commonly used in various forums ranging from academic journals to tabloid newspapers, yet, despite this, it is frequently argued that there is no universal measure of class and thus no single correct definition (Crompton, 2008). The traditional definition of this term refers to groups of individuals that jointly share similar occupational statuses and incomes (Manstead, 2018). This classical objective notion of class is attributed to the emergence of 18th-century technological/scientific innovation and the subsequent birth of industrial capitalism (Crompton, 2010). These distinct social and economic changes created a social class distinction based on occupational relationships while also intensifying the importance of paid employment, thus making occupational status a key indicator of social advantage or disadvantage (Crompton, 2008). Thus social divisions under this model are based on differences between those that control and own material means of production, often referred to as the bourgeoisie or middle-class, a new class, distinct from inherited aristocratic wealth, and those possessing only their labour-power which they were forced to sell to the bourgeoisie to survive, these being the proletariat or working-class (Dorling, 2014; Marx & Engels, 1987).

The correlation between occupation and class status has guided significant, influential post-World War II (WWII) sociological studies. Lockwood's (1989) *The Blackcoated Worker* is the most notable, but others, such as The Affluent Worker Study (Goldthorpe et al., 1968a, 1968b, 1969), also exerted a profound influence (Savage, 2010). Goldthorpe et al.'s case study of three major manufacturing companies (Vauxhall, Skefkco, and Laporte), all based in Luton, UK, aimed to explore workers' class identity. One of the fundamental objectives of the research was to explore the theory of 'embourgeoisement', or in other words, whether certain more highly paid workers were incorporating middle-class norms and values (Goldthorpe et al., 1967). The findings from both studies inspired Goldthorpe to pursue further research, including *The Oxford Mobility Study* (Goldthorpe, 1980). From this, he developed a model, often referred to as the Goldthorpe or Nuffield Class Schema (Goldthorpe & Hope, 1974), which created a scheme of occupational grading used to measure class structure. This schema has had a lasting legacy, being central in the creation of the National Statistics Socio-economic Classification (NS-SEC) (Rose & Pevalin, 2003) and contemporary class-based analysis in Britain. To this end, the Goldthorpe schema was adopted as the foundation for the NS-SEC because the schema is seen as internationally accepted and believed to be theoretically balanced (ONS, 2010). It is also generally considered a good measure and predictor of education and health outcomes. Despite these assertions, Goldthorpe's schema has received significant criticism. Crompton (2010, p. 51) argues that there is 'a number of difficulties in using occupation (or job) as a measure of "class"'. Firstly, these complications include the difficulty of categorising individuals without a job. Secondly, Goldthorpe's schema was moulded to the contours of men's employment (Crompton, 2008) and thus placed little emphasis on gender, and thirdly, occupational rank does not indicate a person's capital or wealth holdings (Crompton, 2010). Devine (1998) also criticises Goldthorpe for being economically deterministic and failing to recognise the cultural aspects that also form class identity.

The Golden Age of Social Mobility

The critiques of Goldthorpe's work are particularly pertinent to this book, especially the gender-related issue, as this criticism emphasises the trajectory of socio-economic transformation that has occurred in Britain and the subsequent impact on particular societal groups, mainly the working class.

Goldthorpe's schema was created during the early 1970s, a period that was yet to experience the full impact of the 'gender role revolution' (Esping-Andersen, 2009) and was thus categorised by a sexual division of labour (Benería, 1979) and a male breadwinning ideology (Williams, 2008). These configurations were influenced by employment opportunities and the relatively high rates of male working-class dominated forms of manual employment, including manufacturing, shipbuilding, steel production and coal mining (Qayyum et al., 2020). Many of these jobs provided secure forms of employment, comparatively high rates of pay and generous employee benefits (Beck & Lau, 2005). Furthermore, traditional forms of manual employment were often a significant source of working-class identity (Willis, 1977). These jobs were often physical, dirty and dangerous, yet these employment characteristics and the ability to cope with them meant that working-class workers commanded social respect (Bottero, 2004). Moreover, traditional forms of working-class employment were often also categorised by high levels of trade union representation, providing members with a sense of strength, solidarity and power (Jones, 2012). These employment conditions, coupled with relatively balanced standards of living and elevated levels of social ascent, led this era to be associated with the 'Golden Age of social mobility' (Bukodi & Goldthorpe, 2018).

The trend towards declining inequalities in income and wealth in the Post-WWII period was not long-lasting. As previously stated, the introduction of a Conservative Government and the 'Thatcherite Revolution' (Nayak, 2003a, p. 149) led to deindustrialisation and the closure and demise of heavy industry and manufacturing. Certain jobs once a source of employment for many working-class men, were significantly offshored to other countries. The fracturing of these industries, coupled with a dramatic increase in service sector employment (Allen & Hollingworth, 2013), has entirely altered the prospects of the UK's working-class, with many men and women now forced to undertake precarious, low-paid jobs that offer little prospect of career progression (Ainsley, 2018). Furthermore, contemporary employment changes have also witnessed a significant increase in professional and managerial occupations (Goos & Manning, 2007). This employment shift has contributed to a modern British society that now suffers from distinct levels of income and class inequality (Rowlingson, 2011). Inequality has many detrimental implications on a person's life chances (Weber, 1948), especially for those deemed to be working-class (Wilkinson & Pickett, 2010).

Cultural Approaches to Class

Despite the identified significance of class, some scholars consider social class to be an obsolete notion (Tittenbrun, 2014). This idea is a strong theme among theorists and neo-liberalist advocates (Beck, 1992; Beck & Beck-Gernsheim, 2001; Giddens, 1991). Claims surrounding the 'death of social class' base themselves on contemporary transformations in employment, production and related institutions, including the expansions of female employment, a decline in manufacturing and trade union associations, the rise in service-sector employment, precarious work and zero-hour contracts, rising unemployment and more extended periods in education (Crompton, 1996). These changes are claimed to have detached individuals from older collective ways of life and shared identities; thus, people have become responsible for their own life biographies. Subsequently, this individualised societal shift has led Beck and Beck-Gernsheim (2001) to refer to social class as a 'zombie category', meaning the idea of this category still lives on in society, yet the reality that it relates to is dead. It should be noted, however, that these notions are theoretically grounded assertions and lack empirical substantiation (Atkinson, 2007).

The 'death of social class' assertion has coincided with what has been termed the 'cultural turn' (Bottero, 2004). The cultural turn is a genre of social class analysis that has dominated contemporary discussions around class. Unlike the employment-related approach to social class, where the class position is primarily derived from occupation (Goldthorpe & McKnight, 2006), the cultural turn addresses how social inequality can be produced and reproduced through cultural practices and 'focuses on people's identities, emotions and their subjective experiences of living in a particular class position' (Watson, 2017, p. 186).

Influential in this new approach has been Bourdieu's notion of class analysis which deviates from the idea of economic determinism and argues that social class arises from three kinds of capital; cultural capital, which refers to a person's interests, tastes and cultural knowledge (Bourdieu, 1989); social capital, which includes social networks, friendship and association; and, economic capital made up of income, property and material resources (Bourdieu, 1986). The primary but contested critique of Bourdieu's work stems from a failure to recognise agency within the notion of habitus and thus reducing people to mindless individuals who are merely influenced by their socialisation process (Ingram, 2018). Despite these critiques, Bourdieu enables us to think about class as a cultural phenomenon and 'explore the implicit ways that class is lived and reproduced' (Hebson, 2009, p. 28). As such, Bourdieu's work continues to influence contemporary class-based analysis, particularly the work of Savage et al. (2013) and the associated Great British Class Survey (GBCS).

The work of Savage et al. (2013) offers a fresh take on class analysis in the 21st century (Ainsley, 2018). Inspired by the writing of Bourdieu, the theoretical position used by Savage et al. (2013) assumes that occupations are not the leading indicators of social stratification. Instead, the adopted approach aimed to move beyond economic determinism and provide an analysis of class that represented its multi-faceted nature (Savage et al., 2015). Utilising a web-based Great British Class Survey, Savage et al. (2013) argued that the established model of class had altered and fragmented to such a degree that social stratification in contemporary Britain consists of seven categories ranging from the elite at the top, the precariat at the bottom and five categories in between (established middle class, technical middle class, new affluent workers, emergent service workers, traditional working-class) with the boundaries between these five categories being blurred.

Class and This Book

Despite Savage et al.'s (2013) claims, as stated previously, the associated cultural turn has received criticism due to its decreased focus on the economic aspect of class (Atkinson, 2015; Fraser, 2000) coupled with the scant attention paid to questions around work and employment (Vogt, 2018), criticisms that are particularly pertinent to this book. As the previous section demonstrated, predicted future employment changes and the influence of automation and Artificial Intelligence are potentially set to significantly affect un-skilled and semi-skilled forms of employment (Frey & Osborne, 2017) and jobs that have been traditionally associated with the working class (Goldthorpe, 2016). Subsequently, this possible occurrence and its discriminatory effect re-establishes the significance of occupation as a class indicator due to the possible detrimental effect of wholesale job loss and the prospect of reduced life chances (Weber, 1948) for a large section of working-class individuals across Britain. Thus, concerning this book and in consideration of possible future employment changes, social class is considered through a dual-lens that assigns equal importance to both the economic and cultural dimensions.

Conclusion

This chapter has described the trajectory of studies and ideas around working-class young men, education and employment. Although the literature demonstrates the plurality of working-class identity, it also largely identifies a subgroup of working-class young men with a negative or complex relationship with education and attraction to manual employment that derives from socialisation or intergenerational transmission and structural factors. However, Roberts' recent finding shows some deviation from these associations and demonstrates working-class young men's engagement with education and attraction to employment other than manual labour. However, the context of Roberts' study is significant because Roberts' study was conducted in an area that has seen significant societal development, a changing labour market structure, was not an industrial heartland and included a missing-middle or ordinary kids study sample, as opposed to 'the lads', 'careerless', 'roughs', 'The Macho Lads, 'Rems', 'Valley Boiz' and young men that have been continually associated with a negative or complex relationship with education and attraction to manual employment. Therefore, although Roberts' work offers a valuable contribution to working-class studies, this book returns the focus towards more marginalised working-class young men because existing knowledge may be considered somewhat dated, especially considering prior related study findings are almost a decade or more old, which generates queries around the contemporary identity construction of this subgroup of working-class young men in deindustrialised locations. Furthermore, this chapter has also discussed future employment changes and highlighted the potential negative impact on low-skilled, poorly educated young men and forms of manual employment often associated with a working-class status while also discussing social class, the competing perspectives and arguing for the importance of assessing social class through a dual-lens that assigns equal importance to both the economic and cultural dimensions.

The following chapter assesses the literature and different theories relating to masculinities, highlighting shortcomings in these ideas concerning related aspects of this book and identifying missing issues.

Chapter Three

Critically Exploring Masculinities

Introduction

This chapter includes an assessment of masculinities theory and analyses how and why differing masculinity explanations exist and the criticisms in order to establish the current understanding of masculinity. The chapter concludes by arguing that masculinities theories need to consider the significance of place-based specificity together with the effect of broader contemporary societal change and the dual impact of these aspects on shaping current working-class young men's masculine identities for the purpose of understanding continuity and changes in masculinity-related views and behaviours.

Contextual Information

Masculinity as a core concept has been subject to continuous debates and evaluation regarding its nature, origins, and existence (Carrigan et al., 1985). This conceptualising of masculinity and gender has included the notion that men behave differently from women because they are biologically programmed to do so (McCormack, 2012). This notion of sexual variation is based on the idea that hormonal, psychological, and genital differences determine disparities in behaviour, temperament, and emotions (de Boise, 2015). A prominent contemporary proponent of the biological notion of masculinity is the Canadian psychologist and YouTube personality Jordan Peterson. Peterson has attracted an extensive following of young men due to his critique of feminism and his 'traditionalist' ideas of masculinity grounded in the notion of gender identity based on biological sex (Stern, 2019). However, as the following sections demonstrate, this biological notion of masculinity has been challenged by opposing ideas, often presenting a social constructionist perspective of masculinity and gender.

The 21st Century Ladz: Continuity and Changes among Marginalised
Young Men from the South Wales Valleys, 35–44
doi:10.1108/978-1-83797-631-720251004

Sex-role Theory

Despite enduring biological notions of masculinity, many sociologists have tended to focus on the structural and social formulation of gender identity and masculinity. One of the first sociologists to engage in the structural and social approach to gender identity was Talcott Parsons (1954), who argued that biological differences were incapable of explaining social patterns of sex roles – a notion that is centrally based on the idea that 'men learn to be men' (Roberts, 2018, p. 44), and thus gender identity and masculinity are socially constructed through families, schools, peer groups, and societal institutions (Parsons, 1964). Parsons argued that sex roles – which included men as breadwinners and women as primary caregivers – were crucial features of a well-ordered society. Furthermore, any deviation from these roles would generate 'role strain' and ultimately undermine society's stable fabric.

Robert Brannon (1976) further developed the sex-role theory and identified four specific components males needed to uphold to achieve their sex role status. The first of these was 'No Sissy Stuff', the idea that masculinity and a male identity require a dissociation from femininity. The second aspect was 'Be a Big Wheel', masculinity was measured by success, power, wealth, and status. Thirdly, 'Be a Sturdy Oak' denotes stoicism, emotionlessness and strength over weakness, and finally, 'Give 'em Hell', the notion that masculine men engage in risk-taking, aggressive and courageous behaviour. The sex-role theory maintained a respected position in theoretical thinking and still holds some utility today (McCormack, 2012). However, the growth of the 1970s women's movement and the increased emergence of feminist theorists began to challenge sex role theory (Ward, 2015).

Hegemonic Masculinity

One of the most prominent and influential challenges to the sex role theory came from Carrigan et al. (1985), who critiqued the sex role theory based on its failure to recognise power relations and men's dominance over women. Carrigan et al. (1985) presented a new model of gender identity and masculinity that aimed to understand how some groups of men asserted social power over women and some men. This theoretical model moved beyond a singular notion of masculinity and instead proposed the idea of multiple masculinities. This idea of multiple masculinities includes a hierarchal structure with hegemonic masculinity holding the highest-ranking position and considered the form of masculinity culturally esteemed at any one time (Connell, 1995). Hegemonic masculinity is rooted in the hegemony idea of Gramsci (1971), which is based on the notion that certain groups of people claim and sustain power and positions of dominance in social life through coercion and consent rather than force (Connell, 1987). The incorporation of the hegemony Gramscian concept together with masculinity generated Connell's (2005, p.77) following definition of hegemonic masculinity 'the configuration of gender practise which embodies the currently accepted answer to the problem of legitimacy of patriarchy, which guarantees (or is taken to guarantee) the dominant position of men and the subordination of women'. This dominant male status, coupled with women's subordination, provides men with an institutional and economic advantage (Ralph & Roberts, 2020). However, access to these societal advantages is not inclusive of all men and depends on a person's ability to wield power and thus successfully engage with hegemonic masculinity (Waling, 2019).

Although there is an associated link between hegemonic masculinity and power, 'visible bearers of hegemonic masculinity are not always the most powerful' (Ward, 2015, p. 9). Subsequently, hegemonic masculinity is not associated with a fixed character type, yet it is often 'characterised by numerous attributes such as domination, aggressiveness, competitiveness, athletic prowess, stoicism and control' (Cheng, 1999, p. 298). Conversely, Messner (1992) argues that men avoid the appearance of vulnerability, weakness, fear, and compassion because these characteristics are often associated with women and femininity.

Along with women's oppression, discrimination against gay men is also built into hegemonic masculinities (Gough, 2018). Subsequently, homophobia is an additional central tenet in the production and reproduction of hegemonic masculinity (Anderson, 2009). Hegemonic masculinity is categorically heterosexual, whilst homosexual masculinities are subordinated (Connell, 2000). This subordination often involves the oppression of gay men and the policing of non-hegemonic behaviour often regulated through homophobic taunts, which are used as a gender policing tactic and means of ensuring that boys and men avoid actions and practices deemed to be effeminate and homosexual (Connell, 2000; Martino, 2000; Pascoe, 2007). Subsequently, some men avoid engaging in physical or emotional support acts out of fear of being deemed emasculated and homosexual (Haywood & Mac an Ghaill, 2003; Mac an Ghaill, 1994). Collectively, hegemonic masculinity's associated features have led to its affiliation with the endorsement of sexism, homophobia, misogyny, a breadwinner ideology, and suspicion of anything implying femininity (Ralph & Roberts, 2020).

Hegemonic masculinity and its dominant, powerful position rely on consent and persuasion (Connell, 1987). Carrigan et al. (1985) argue that one of the main promoters of this coercion is the mass media and the circulation of idealised images of men and a masculine stereotype often found in sports imagery, films, and advertisements (Connell, 2000; Connell & Messerschmidt, 2005; Messner, 2007, 2013). This visual representation subsequently generates an idealised form of masculinity that filters throughout society, thus becoming the internalised accepted norm within societal institutions such as family, employment and schools (Mac an Ghaill, 1994). Despite this societal pressure, Carrigan et al. (1985, p. 592) argue that only a small percentage of the total population of men actually embody hegemonic masculinity. However, many men are complicit in maintaining this model of masculinity because 'most men benefit from the subordination of women, and hegemonic masculinity is centrally connected with the institutionalisation of men's dominance over women'. Through this idea of complicity, Carrigan et al. (1985) and Connell and Messerschmitt's (2005) notion of multiple masculinities begins to reveal itself fully.

Within Carrigan et al. (1985) and Connell and Messerschmidt's (2005) hierarchal notion of multiple masculinities, sitting directly below hegemonic masculinity is complicit masculinity. This form of masculinity is the category where most males find themselves (Roberts, 2018) and refers to men who do not enact hegemonic masculinity, are not militant in defence of patriarchy, but do benefit from a 'patriarchal dividend' (Connell, 2009, p. 142) – the advantage men gain from maintaining an unequal gender order. Often positioned below complicit masculinity is subordinated masculinity, a category primarily used to refer to gay men (Pascoe, 2007).

The final form of masculinity is marginalised masculinity which refers to men who are powerful in terms of their gender position yet weakened concerning race, class, and ethnicity (Connell, 2005). These features – race, class, and ethnicity – lead to decreased access to economic resources and institutional authority (Connell & Messerschmidt, 2005). Subsequently, due to the reductive nature of these features and the weakened position of power, Connell (2005) presents the notion of protest masculinity. Connell (2005, p. 114) defines protest masculinity as a 'marginalised masculinity, which picks up themes of hegemonic masculinity in the society at large but reworks them in a context of poverty'. This reworking includes trying to obtain power with limited means. Connell (2005, p. 110) argues that this power retrieve is often exercised through various gender practices, including 'school resistance ... heavy drug/alcohol use, occasional manual labor, motorbikes or cars, short heterosexual liaisons', whilst also being associated with 'hypermasculine, aggressive displays of violence and criminal behaviour' (Maguire, 2020, p. 20).

Furthermore, protest masculinity is 'a pattern of masculinity constructed in local working-class settings' (Connell & Messerschmidt 2005, p. 847) and has thus become commonly associated with working-class men (Elliott, 2020) and synonymous with laddish behaviour, which is often linked to macho values including courage, toughness and physical strength (McDowell, 2003). However, as Haywood and Mac an Ghaill (2003) indicate, some of the values and behaviours often attributed to protest masculinity are similar to those associated with hegemonic masculinity (Cheng, 1999). These similarities potentially blur the distinction between protest masculinity and hegemonic masculinity and may complicate identification and classification.

Additional analysis of protest masculinity reveals further ambiguity. For example, Connell (2005) initially associates protest masculinity with violence, crime and drug/alcohol use, all acts that have become commonly associated with the phrase 'toxic masculinity', 'the mainstream term for hegemonic masculinity' (Whitehead, 2019 p. 47). Conversely, in the latter parts of the discussion relating to protest masculinity, Connell (2005, p. 112) argues that protest masculinity 'is not simply observance of a stereotyped male role. It is compatible with respect and attention to women ... egalitarian views about the sexes, affection for children, and a sense of display which in conventional role terms is decidedly feminine'. These aspects of protest masculinity – particularly affection for children – contradict the former characteristics of protest masculinity and align themselves with caring masculinities, defined as types of masculinities 'that reject domination and its associated traits and embraces values of care such as positive emotion, interdependence, and relationality' (Elliott, 2016, p. 240). Subsequently, these conflicting characteristics of protest masculinity potentially create con-fusion (Walker, 2006) and make this form of masculinity challenging to define and identify conclusively, especially considering the contextual societal epoch of Connell's (2005) original definitions, coupled with recent changes that have chal-lenged original notions of class identity (Savage et al., 2013) and working-class status (Ainsley, 2018). Therefore, although this book incorporates the notion of protest masculinity, its adoption is mainly a means of comparative analysis and working within the established and recognised understanding of working-class masculinity.

Connell's (1995) protest masculinity offers an economically associated inter-pretation of working-class masculinity. However, Walkerdine and Jiménez (2012) offer a somewhat alternative understanding of working-class masculinity in the form of heavy industrial masculinity. As opposed to the economic determinism of protest masculinity, industrial masculinity is a form of working-class mascu-linity that is place-based, historically produced, born out of necessity, associated with heavy industry and 'served to keep the community safe through hard-won practices … [and] assuming the bodily strength and fortitude to withstand heavy, dangerous work' (Walkerdine, 2016, p. 701). Due to the centrality of industrial masculinity and its necessity for survival, this masculine mode of being is claimed to be intergenerationally transmitted and 'passed down through generations' (Walkerdine & Jiménez, 2012, p. 94) and potentially cause issues around educa-tion and employment (Jimenez & Walkerdine, 2011; Walkerdine & Jiménez, 2012) due to characteristics that oppose individualism. Although industrial masculinity offers a cultural place-based understanding of masculinity it somewhat overlooks the possibility of external cultural influences beyond the immediate proximity, similar to Connell and Messerschmidt's (2005) locally constructed notion of pro-test masculinity.

Connell's (2005) models of masculinities and the possible static nature have become a notifiable critique, with critics arguing that this masculinities framework has been used to create stationary typologies (Anderson, 2009; Demetriou, 2001) with male research participants merely placed into the masculinity categories of hegemonic, complicit and marginalised (Pascoe, 2007). However, in response to this critique and a reworking of the original concept, Connell and Messer-schmidt (2005, p. 852) state that 'masculinities are configurations of practice that are constructed, unfold, and change through time'. This response suggests that hegemonic masculinity is malleable and susceptible to change, potentially due to alterations in accepted societal and cultural norms and beliefs. Additionally, Connell and Messerschmidt (2005) also argue that the construction of masculin-ity is often place and space specific. Thus, there is the possibility for localised variations of hegemonic masculinity constructed through face-to-face interaction within societal institutions, including families, schools, and peer groups.

The potential multifaceted application of hegemonic and multiple masculini-ties has meant that it has been significantly influential and used as a theoretical template for numerous studies across several academic disciplines ranging from sport (Messner, 1992) to crime (Tomsen & Gadd, 2019) through to domestic vio-lence (Lisco et al., 2015). However, this extensive use highlights an additional critique of hegemonic and multiple masculinities. McCormack (2012, p. 40) argues that the definitions of hegemonic and complicit masculinity are vague and thus 'appear to work as catch-all statements that encompass a large and diffuse range of gendered behaviours'.

Furthermore, I stress that this criticism is particularly applicable to protest masculinity due to the associated extensive range of contradictory characteristics that capture almost all aspects of masculinity, both those considered to be negative or 'toxic' (Whitehead, 2019) along with attributes considered to be progressive and positive (Elliott, 2016). Additionally, some academics have suggested that an over-dependence on hegemonic masculinity may equate to restrictive accounts of masculinity and decreased lines of enquiry (Pringle, 2005; Sparkes, 1992). Moller (2007) substantiates this claim by arguing that some academics identify patterns of hegemonic masculinity even when the social dynamics are often much more complicated. Anderson (2009) also adds further critique by stating that Gramsci's hegemony theory potentially overemphasises a top-down approach to power, thus implying that the hegemonic masculinity theory may exclude human agency and its potential ability to influence gender practices.

Hybrid Masculinity

The notion of agency features in the concerns of Demetriou (2001), who argues for a greater acknowledgement of agency and the way that hegemony is achieved by incorporating elements from subordinated masculinities instead of merely oppression through force or shame. These concerns subsequently led Demetriou (2001, p. 337) to argue that 'hegemonic masculinity is not a purely white or heterosexual configuration of practice, but it is a hybrid bloc that unites practices from diverse masculinities in order to ensure the reproduction of patriarchy'. Essentially, the masculine bloc refers to a hybridised form of hegemonic masculinity that involves incorporating and appropriating selective elements of other masculinities – particularly subordinated masculinity – to adapt to societal changes and maintain systems of power, control, and inequality.

The idea of masculinity hybridity has become a common feature of contemporary masculinities research and used to explore the flexibility, plurality, and fluidity of contemporary masculinities (Gough, 2018). Pivotal to the hybrid masculinity debate and often heavily cited is Bridges and Pascoe's conceptualisation (2014). Drawing on Demetriou's (2001) original notion of the hybrid bloc, Bridges and Pascoe (2014, p. 246) refer to hybrid masculinity as the 'selective incorporation of elements of identity typically associated with various marginalised and subordinated masculinities and – at times – femininities into privileged men's gender performances and identities'. Essentially, hybrid masculinities suggest that some men (particularly those that occupy privileged social categories) display softer masculine characteristics in an attempt to distance themselves from a hegemonic masculine position whilst simultaneously reinforcing dominance and obscuring inequality and gender differences (Eisen & Yamashita, 2017). Subsequently, Christofidou (2021) argues that softer masculine expressions do not challenge systems of gender or sexual inequality.

Despite the notion of hybrid masculinities and the growing popularity in contemporary masculinities research, Connell and Messerschmidt (2005) remain unconvinced that hybrid masculinities represent anything other than a transformation of hegemonic masculinity at a regional level. However, the notion of refashioned masculinity is also evident in additional contemporary masculinities literature. Gough (2018) argues that some men engage in traditionally associated feminine behaviour. However, rather than demonstrating a decline in conventional masculinity, these behaviours are merely a reworking and repackaged form of traditional masculinity that corresponds with a more image-conscious, consumer-orientated society. Fundamentally, these ideas propose that recent changes in male behaviour and masculinity are merely stylistic, and rather than being an indication of progressive change, they are actually 'mechanisms of how hegemonic forms of masculinity perpetuate themselves in the face of challenges' (Elliott, 2020, p. 34) and thus reassert power and dominance. Despite these assertions, Roberts (2018) argues that research on contemporary masculinities needs to consider the possibility of change and resistance beyond the reproduction of dominance – an alternative that hybrid masculinity and hegemonic masculinity fail to permit. It is within this statement that the concerns of myself and this book reside.

The discussed masculinities theoretical frameworks demonstrate a commitment to the ideas of power and dominance, even those that engage with the identification of 'progressive' forms of male behaviour (Whitehead, 2019). There is minimal consideration regarding the possibility that resistance and change may coexist, and that change may be an indication or the possibility of progress rather than a 'covert' tactic. Thus, similar to the argument made by Pringle (2005) and Sparkes (1992), by continually observing male behaviour through a fixed analytical lens, lines of enquiry are diminished, and we negate the possibility of identifying and considering behavioural changes that may be indicative of genuine progressive changes in masculinity and thus denying any hope of fostering positive forms of male behaviour that are beneficial to all. This shortcoming almost has an element of 'complicity' and is particularly damaging for working-class young men on the margins of society whose life chances, education and employment opportunities may be further diminished due to 'regressive' forms of masculine behaviour.

Inclusive Masculinity

Hegemonic masculinity and the associated notions of power, dominance, and inequality are central features that guided much of the previously discussed research. However, some recent masculinities studies have diverged from these ideas and presented a contrasting understanding of contemporary masculinities – primarily through the inclusive masculinity theory (IMT). Unlike hegemonic masculinity, IMT argues that masculinities are no longer stratified and hegemonic. Instead, Anderson (2009) argues that there are two different types of masculinity in contemporary society, sharing equal societal power and neither holding a hegemonic position. These two forms of masculinity include orthodox masculinity, which is comparable to hegemonic masculinity (Anderson, 2005), and inclusive masculinity – a more expressive and tactile version of masculinity. Furthermore, dissimilar to hegemonic masculinity and its associated notions of emotional detachment and the avoidance of actions and practices deemed to be effeminate and homosexual (Connell, 2000), the body of research related to IMT suggests that:

> many young straight men: reject homophobia; include gay peers in friendship networks; are more emotionally intimate with friends; are physically tactile with other men; recognise bisexuality as a legitimate sexual orientation; embrace activities and artefacts once coded feminine; and eschew violence and bullying. (Anderson & McCormack, 2018, p. 548)

The basis for these claims and divergence from previous notions of men and masculinity is essentially underpinned by Anderson's (2009) contested assertion (see, for example, de Boise, 2015) that contemporary Western cultures have experienced a decrease in overt homophobia and what he refers to as 'homohysteria' – 'defined as the cultural fear of being homosexualised' (McCormack, 2011, p. 338), or in other words, viewed as being gay. Subsequently, due to these decreases, the controlling power of homophobic discourse – which has often been used as a central tool for policing male behaviour and maintaining hegemonic masculinity (Anderson, 2009; Pascoe, 2007) – weakens. Thus, heterosexual men can engage in emotional and physical intimacy without fear of being stigmatised.

Despite the significance of homohysteria, Anderson and McCormack (2018, p. 549) argue that additional aspects have also been instrumental in the transformation of contemporary masculinities, including societal and structural changes such as changes in law, greater access and an increased percentage of sexual minorities in a diverse range of social institutions, along with labour market changes and the shift away from an industrial economy, growth of the internet and 'processes of individualisation where social institutions have less influence on moral values'. However, interestingly, despite the inclusion of individualisation and its common association with the diminished relevance of social class in contemporary society (Beck & Beck-Gernsheim, 2001; Giddens, 1991), the findings of McCormack (2014) somewhat present a slightly contradictory argument.

McCormack's ethnographic study incorporated Bourdieusian theory to explore working-class young men's behaviour in a school in the south-east of England. The study's findings revealed inclusive (Anderson, 2009) forms of behaviour among the participants, including pro-gay attitudes, emotional closeness, and homosocial tactility. However, when comparing these findings to a similar study on middle-class six form young men in the same region of England (McCormack & Anderson, 2010), the analysis revealed less pronounced inclusive forms of behaviour in the working-class participants, with the middle-class young men engaging in more intimate forms of male behaviour such as kissing, hugging and cuddling. McCormack (2014, p. 132) explains this differentiation by arguing that class acts as 'a dampening but not prohibitive factor on the development of more inclusive attitudes and behaviours'. Subsequently, these findings and comparative analysis reveal that although individualisation (Beck & Beck-Gernsheim, 2001; Giddens, 1991) is associated with the development of inclusive masculinity (Anderson & McCormack, 2018), paradoxically, social class can also have a buffering effect.

Inclusive masculinity has become increasingly recognised and applied in several UK-based studies related to working-class men in the form of education (Blanchard et al., 2017; McCormack, 2014), sport (Magrath, 2021) and employment (Roberts, 2013). These studies essentially focus on young working-class men. Therefore, Christofidou (2021, p. 7) argues that 'the intersections of class and age may be particularly revealing as age, in this case, maybe the main factor encouraging change'. Despite Christofidou's (2021) claim, scholars such as Roberts (2018) have already recognised and acknowledged the importance of age and its potential influence in determining inclusive masculine practices. However, an aspect that Christofidou (2021) overlooks is the regional specificity of the research. Although the studies identify an inclusive masculine perspective among working-class participants, the results refer to specific areas of the UK – predominantly the South of England. Thus, these studies' regional specificity raises questions about the nature of place, space and their potential influential role in gender construction (Connell & Messerschmidt, 2005), along with the generalisability of the findings (de Boise, 2015).

Despite the current association between working-class studies and inclusive masculinity, initial research relating to the IMT predominantly centred on university attending men in a soccer team (Anderson, 2005), a rugby team (Anderson & McGuire, 2010) and a fraternity (Anderson, 2008). Due to these studies' university-based nature, IMT is often critiqued based on study samples that predominantly included white middle-class participants (de Boise, 2015; O'Neill 2015). Subsequently, scholars such as Gough (2018, p. 10) suggest that 'men who enjoy privileged status and embody traditional markers of masculine success … can more easily engage in traditionally feminised practices without having their masculinity diminished' A further critique of the study sample is offered by de Boise (2015), who suggests that Anderson is selective in his use of examples when demonstrating inclusive masculinities.

Additional general criticism of IMT includes O'Neill (2015), who likens IMT to post-feminism and an association with personal choice, which negates gendered power relations. Similarly, Ingram and Waller (2014, p. 39) argue that IMT 'fails to account for or challenge gender inequalities'. The criticism relating to gender power relations/inequalities reveals an important consideration, including the realisation that many of the IMT-related studies focus on homophobia and male-on-male interaction and thus ignore male and female relations and any possible evidence of a power imbalance and gender inequality. Finally, de Boise (2015, p. 334) offers an additional noteworthy critique of inclusive masculinity, stating that IMT is:

> actively dangerous in that it conflates the hard-fought legal rights won by gay rights activists with a mistaken belief that because homophobic speech and violence are less apparent in public

contexts, that we are nearing some historical end-point for gender and sexuality discrimination. This has the potential to close down discussions around how we should be continuing to change attitudes toward gender and sexuality.

Although de Boise offers an important consideration here, there is a potential contrasting perspective that he negates. If one were to even slightly contemplate the findings or changes linked to IMT-related studies, paradoxically, rather than closing down discussion, they potentially create a debate around how these changes can be fostered and thus decrease levels of gender and sexual discrimination, be that possibly only at a micro level, yet still providing wider benefit.

Conclusion

The masculinities literature offers a diverse range of competing arguments spanning relatively static notions of masculinity to ideas of fluid changing forms of masculinity. However, these explanations potentially offer a limited understanding of the masculine identity construction of contemporary marginalised working-class young men in industrial heartland communities. For example, protest masculinity and its association with poverty suggest an economically deterministic masculinity formation that negates external societal and cultural influences. Similarly, by suggesting that protest masculinity is 'a pattern of masculinity constructed in local working-class settings', Connell and Messerschmidt (2005, p. 847) somewhat suggest that influences outside of immediate residency have limited influence. Equally, Walkerdine and Jiménez's (2012) emphasis on locality and the notion of industrial masculinity may be considered somewhat place-based deterministic due to the focus on locally and historically produced ways of being and intergenerational transmission that somewhat dismisses the impact of cultural forces beyond the immediate vicinity.

Moreover, inclusive masculinity, similarly to the notions of the death of social class and individualisation, is largely premised on broad societal changes and ignores the impact of place-based specificities and their ability to shape masculine identity. Therefore, these explanations of masculinity overlook the possibility of a middle-ground position that considers the significance of place-based specificity and communities with stagnant social and economic development, yet a broader society that has seen significant societal development. Essentially, what happens when old and new ways of being collide, and how does it impact identity construction? When these issues also take into account the previous discussion of working-class, education and employment-related studies, together with future of work debates and social class, overall, the literature review identifies the need to refocus on the school-to-work transition and masculine identity of contemporary marginalised working-class young men.

The following chapter is the first of three empirical chapters and explores my research findings relating to the Ladz educational experiences. The chapter demonstrates similarities and dissimilarities between the lads from Willis's study and young men from contemporary studies.

Section Header

The following three chapters of the book present the results of my ethnography and semi-structured interviews. Chapter Four explores the Ladz and education. Chapter Five explores the Ladz and employment and Chapter Six explores the Ladz' social relations and masculinities. All three chapters collectively consider what the young men's findings tell us concerning future work discussions. Overall, the three chapters develop the argument that although the Ladz share some similarities with prior research concerning marginalised working-class young men, education, employment and masculinity, there are also notable changes in the young men's views and behaviour, which allow us to consider employment futures other than low-skilled manual employment and thus potentially increase the life chances of marginalised working-class young men.

Chapter Four

The Ladz and Education

Introduction

This first findings chapter explores the Ladz' education in the light of Willis's lads (1977) while also considering findings from more contemporary post-industrial studies of the school-to-work transition. It discusses the Ladz' school behaviour, demonstrating their association with Willis's (1977) lads through nonconformist conduct linked to protest masculinity (Connell, 1995), which is amplified by issues including learning difficulties, mental health problems, and disaffection with teachers. However, the association between the two groups of young men becomes somewhat fragmented through a discussion of the Ladz' attitudes towards school and academic credentials. Unlike Willis's lads, the Ladz believe that some academic credentials are important to their employment aspirations. Therefore, this chapter's central argument is that despite the historical association between laddish culture and anti-learning, the Ladz no longer entirely reject education, and there is no indication that undertaking academic work is feminine or cissy (Jackson, 2006, 2002; Willis, 1977). Although these marginalised working-class young men are still 'dossing, blagging [and] wagging' (Willis, 1977, p. 26) and experiencing schooling difficulties; they do not disregard the significance of academic credentials.

'I fucking threw a chair at one of them!'

Akin to their lads' predecessors, 'dossing, blagging [and] wagging' (Willis, 1977, p. 26) and demonstrations of resistance to authority were generally central features of the Ladz' school conduct. The following section presents this behaviour and confirms the participants' laddish association. However, the reasoning and meaning are explored in later sections due to the complex nature

The 21st Century Ladz: Continuity and Changes among Marginalised
Young Men from the South Wales Valleys, 47–67
doi:10.1108/978-1-83797-631-720251005

that extends beyond a macho rejection of educational values (Mac an Ghaill, 1994; McDowell, 2003).

The Ladz were forthright about their laddish school behaviour – they did not try to disguise it, and there even seemed to be an element of bravado and pride attached to some of their descriptions. For example, when I initially asked Ian about his school experience, he responded: '*I was a troublemaker in school. I was always the black sheep in school'*. Similarly, Lewis offered the following response: '*I was a naughty boy in school. I wasn't concentrating; I was always distracting others. I was always messing about'*. In both excerpts, the two young men display a sense of macho agency and personally distinguish themselves as disruptive instigators.

Truancy was an additional feature of the young men's nonconformist school behaviour. Billy's discussion on truancy further demonstrates an element of agency through his selective approach to class attendance and his refusal to engage: '*Like school, like I mitch [play truant from school] sometimes, like I only go to certain lessons, and I play up an tha, like I refuse to do work in school'*. However, this individualist rhetoric did not entirely encapsulate all the truancy-related data.

As previously stated, many aspects of Cole's laddish association were imposed on him due to his adverse childhood experiences and negative ramifications. Due to the involuntary negative features of Cole's childhood, he became a victim of extensive acts of violent school bullying. Cole stated that the school failed to intervene and offer him support against this behaviour, and he was subsequently forced to remove himself from school. Correspondingly, some of the Ladz themselves also committed acts of violence, aggression and bullying towards teachers and fellow students.

Stan, Tommy, Lewis, and Dan's school behaviour extended beyond verbal disruptive and self-detrimental conduct and expanded towards intensified acts of aggression and physical confrontation. Tommy and Stan both openly confessed to their displays of rage-related behaviour, with Stan's extending to acts of violence towards teachers: '*I fucking threw a chair at one of them!*'. Stan then went on to explain how he had to be continually restrained by teachers:

Stan: Restrain me and that. I bet you didn't know you are allowed to restrain kids, did you?

RG: They restrain you in school, do they?

Stan: Fucking right, they do, boy! There were four of them on me!

Here we see a verbally constructed display of machismo. Stan recognises that restraint and the need for four teachers are excessive forms of prevention and seems to use this awareness to portray his threat level and physical strength.

Dan also engaged in physically aggressive acts of violence, yet these were targeted at fellow pupils rather than teachers:

It was just all building up, to be honest – mainly just mitching and fighting, really. Obviously, there are loads of people there [secondary school]. You're not going to get along with everyone. It wasn't that bad.

This excerpt demonstrates a sense of masculine meaning-making. Dan seems to suggest that violence is a natural consequence when individuals are incompatible and dismisses the significance of his behaviour.

Some of the young men's laddish, nonconformist school behaviour was also motivated and determined by peer group pressure and friendship association. Lewis identified his friendship group and the influential role it played in determining his school behaviour, drug use and attitude towards school:

> I would wake up, go to school, mess around and go home and go to bed. I didn't really think of anything 'cos the boys I used to hang out with just used to go down the shop like and smoke weed and chill out like.

In a later discussion, Lewis reconfirmed peer influence and its effect on his performative laddish behaviour (Ward, 2015).

> That's the thing I dun wanna do in class. I'd rather working, work by myself. Cos, do you get me? I work off other people's energy. So then they're full of energy, and tha boosts me up like. So I'm always bouncing around, distracting everyone like.

Craig's data also identified the strength of friendship and the collective importance of group formation. The following excerpt demonstrates that 'the essence of being one of [the Ladz] lies within the group' (Willis, 1977, p. 23).

Craig: I can be naughty sometimes for a bit of a laugh.

RG: What do you mean?

Craig: Like I mess around and all the boys they tell me to do stuff and see if I will do it. If they tell me to run up to the front of the class, I'll just do it.

RG: Why don't you just not listen to them then?

Craig: It's just sometimes they call me a pussy or anything, so then I'd just do it. I just like wanna prove that I'm not scared to do it. And because sometimes I think hanging around with mates is better than school. Even though school is more learning and everything, I know it's a bit boring, but it's actually more educational to take in. Cos I prefer like hanging around with my mates than going to school.

This discussion demonstrates the importance of having a laugh and/or 'laff' (Willis, 1977). This behaviour is influenced by collective identity and a necessity to conform, enforced through gender policing (Butler, 1990) and a sexualised slur

– pussy – which encourages normative gender expressions (Pascoe, 2007; Pascoe & Stewart, 2016). Craig's loyalty to the group seems to be reinforced by educational difficulties and subsequent alienation: *'more educational to take in'*. Essentially, the group seems to offer Craig a sense of male solidarity (Sennett & Cobb, 1972) and ontological security (Giddens, 1991). Furthermore, Craig's responses resonate with O'Donnell and Sharpe's (2003, p. 14) notion of macho masculinity, which is 'characterised by reciprocal loyalty and support among the in-group of 'mates' or lads, and frequently by suspicion and mockery of the 'bosses' and outsiders'.

This section somewhat confirms the participants' association with laddish conduct and identifies a continuation of the behaviour previously expressed by the lads from Willis's (1977) study. However, the following section demonstrates a noticeable significant contrast that distinguishes the Ladz from their predecessors and exposes a view of school that somewhat contradicts their behaviour.

'It's alright, but it's not the best'

The previous section revealed a correlation between the school behaviour of the lads from Willis's (1977) study and the young men in this research. Despite a 43-year time period between both pieces of research, 'dossing, blagging [and] wagging' (Willis, 1977, p. 26) and acts of nonconformist behaviour are features that connect the two study samples. However, this section begins to reveal a contrast and a departure from previously associated laddish qualities.

Although *Learning to Labour* (Willis, 1977) offers a detailed account of the lads' school-to-work transition and their active rejection of school based on its perceived irrelevance, there is relatively limited data on the lads' 'specific' view of school. However, the subsequent two quotations do reveal Spanksy's and Joey's (two members of the lads) relatively negative attitudes towards school:

Spanksy: I mean, what will they [ear'oles] remember of their school life? What will they have to look back on? Sitting in a classroom, sweating their bollocks off (Willis, 1977, p. 14).

Joey: I don't think school does fucking anything to you (...) It never has had much effect on anybody I don't think [after) you've learnt the basics (Willis, 1977, p. 26).

Jackson (2006, p. 10) argues that '"laddish" masculinity is the positioning of schoolwork as uncool'. Although it may be slightly disingenuous to suggest that these quotations demonstrate complete disregard for school, they do present a negative perspective which is further evidenced by the following quotation: 'The total experience of school is something "the lads" most definitely want to escape from' (Willis, 1977, p. 77). Similarly, in Mac an Ghaill (1994, p. 56) post-industrial study, 'The Macho Lads' viewed school as 'a system ... of meaningless demands'. Therefore, based on these perceptions, the following excerpts include the Ladz' responses when asked about their view of school:

Billy: I gotta be honest. I'm not really a fan of school, but I don't completely hate it.

Craig: I don't mind it; it's just sometimes it is really hard.

Cole: School was a nightmare for me. The pressure – I couldn't cope with it anymore. I had people in school on my case.

Ian: It was good.

Dan: I quite disliked it. It wasn't my thing.

Tommy: Ummm, yeah. It's not the best. It's alright, but it's not the best. It's good but boring at the same time like.

Wesley: It was alright. It wasn't bad, as people might say, but it's still quite bad.

Stan: Shit! Fucking hell, school is fucking smelly as fuck.

Despite the Ladz nonconformist school behaviour documented in the previous section, generally, the young men did not demonstrate a total disregard for school as one might expect. There are obvious deviations in the data, including Stan and Cole's potentially predictable responses. However, most of the views represent a middle-ground perspective epitomised by Tommy: *'It's alright, but it's not the best'*. This centre position is often affiliated with ordinary Kids – working-class young men who 'neither simply accept nor reject school' (Brown, 1987, p. 31) or the 'missing middle' (Roberts, 2018) as they have become more commonly known. However, the Ladz rebellious, aggressive and violent hyper-masculine (Mac an Ghaill, 1994) school conduct disaffiliates them from the missing middle category (Roberts, 2018). Therefore, this section, coupled with the previous behavioural discussion, reveals irregularity in the Ladz' school experience, behaviour, and attitude. This section has established that most of the Ladz neither like nor entirely dislike school. The following sections explore this ambivalence and assess the motives for these differing views, initially by providing important contextual, theoretical information.

Teaching Paradigm

One of the core theoretical concepts that underpins *'Learning to Labour'* (Willis, 1977) and the assessment and explanation of the lads' school experience is the teaching paradigm. Essentially, the teaching paradigm – or education paradigm as it is sometimes referred to – distinguishes 'schooling as a series of transactions or exchanges' (Walker, 1985, p. 75). This exchange is based on the idea that teachers can provide important, meaningful knowledge that will lead to qualifications that can potentially facilitate social mobility and rewarding jobs. In return for these credentials and knowledge, students are expected to provide teachers with respect and conform to the rules and social relations of the schooling system (Feinberg & Soltis, 2009). This process and the teaching paradigm can be summarised through the words of Willis (1977, p. 64): 'The teacher's authority must be won and maintained on moral, not on coercive grounds'.

Although most pupils invest in the teaching paradigm and bargaining exchange, the lads did not, which Willis refers to as differentiation. Influenced by their working-class cultural experience and their subsequent preference for masculine-associated manual work, the lads did not see the worth in theoretical knowledge, which was viewed as 'cissy' (Willis, 1977), feminine and irrelevant to their future career orientation (Mac an Ghaill, 1996). Therefore, the lads reject the school paradigm and the expectation of respect and consequently engage in unruly count-school culture behaviour.

Essentially, this discussion suggests that the lads' rebellious school behaviour derives from their rejection of the teaching or educational paradigm and the devaluation of the knowledge exchanged in this relationship. Subsequently, based on this perspective and the previous discussion that detailed the Ladz' display of laddish nonconformist school behaviour, one may reasonably assume that the Ladz also reject the school paradigm and the information and qualifications provided in this transaction. However, as the following sections demonstrate, this assumption would be untrue. The Ladz do place value on some, but not all, knowledge.

'*You need them, you mad head*'

Tommy and Stan's interviews were conducted together at their request. I was initially apprehensive about undertaking a joint interview with these two young men due to their friendship, behaviour and potentially volatile dynamic. This fear was realised by Stan jostling for attention, attempting to smoke out of the window, and breaking a pool cue. Despite this complication, the dynamic between the two young men was equally advantageous and led to revealing conversation and rich data. Stan referred to school as shit, and the following three-way discussion occurred:

RG: Tell me why school is shit [Stan]?

Stan: Everything about school is fucking shit!

Tommy: I don't think that. I think school is alright.

Stan: Shut up!

Tommy: Only, only to get like, like tidy GS, GCSEs.

Stan: Fuck GCSEs.

Tommy: You need them, you mad head.

Despite Tommy's disruptive, aggressive school behaviour that has led to him being excluded from school, Tommy recognises the relevance of GCSEs and does not discard the importance of these credentials. The relationship between Tommy and Stan and their responses to each other are equally important in demonstrating Tommy's commitment to qualifications.

During their interview, Stan offered the following comment: '*I'm the fucking leader of the pack*'. This comment reflects Stan's social standing among the other young men in the youth centre. Stan presented himself as the group alpha male and asserted this status through excessive displays of hyper-masculinity (Mac an Ghaill, 1994), aggression and physicality. Subsequently, Tommy's unwillingness to be submissive and align himself with Stan's negative views of GCSEs potentially reflects the strength of Tommy's views and the importance he places on these credentials. Additionally, through this response: *'Only, only to get like, like tidy GS, GCSEs',* Tommy seems to try to divide school between a societal institution and a credential provider (Walker, 1985).

Apart from Stan, this commitment to qualifications and some theoretical or practical knowledge is a feature that connected all of the young men, evidenced by the fact that they had either gained some level of formal qualifications or had aspirations to obtain these through school and further education.

This section and the Ladz recognition of qualifications demonstrates a partial commitment and understanding of the teacher paradigm. However, conversely, the young men's challenging and unruly school behaviour reveals contradictory conduct through the omission of respect and submissiveness. The following sections explore the factors that generate this contradiction and influence the young men's attitudes and school behaviour. This exploration includes a dissection of the teaching paradigm and an individual assessment of its two essential components, including an analysis of the Ladz' attitude towards school subjects – knowledge, followed by an analysis of the young men's view of teacher – respect.

'Just good knowledge, isn't it'

Like many aspects of the Ladz' data, their attitudes towards school subjects are complex with some irregularities. Although some aspects connect most of the young men, some features only relate to one or two members. However, this information helps provide a broader understanding of the young men's working-class status and their educational meaning-making, thus warranting its inclusion.

The previous discussion demonstrated Stan's working-class masculine laddish qualities through his outright rejection of educational credentials and knowledge (Willis, 1977). The influential nature of masculinity was also distinguishable in Craig's and potentially even Wesley's responses to school subjects. For example, when asked which lessons he favoured and enjoyed, Craig offered the following answer:

Craig: Like in school, the ones I find the easiest lessons are digital technology, home economics and ummm, science. And PE!

In response to this, I asked Craig why he thought these lessons were the easiest:

Craig: Well, because PE – it gets more brain cells working and gets me more energy. Science is kind of alright because we always do practical. And digital, I don't mind doing work for stuff for a practical because I'm making something. I don't know what it's called, but I'm making like a car kit thing.

In his initial reply, Craig predominately identifies associated masculine subjects – physical education (Kehler, 2010) and science (Archer et al., 2012) – and suggests that these are the most manageable and straightforward. When making sense of this easiness, Craig suggests that these subjects trigger biological responses, including increased cognitive ability and vitality. Additionally, there is an apparent masculine sway towards practical subjects with a material outcome (Nixon, 2018).

As mentioned in Chapter One, Wesley was the group's outlier in some ways. Nevertheless, there is also a possible suggestion of masculine meaning-making in Wesley's preference for school subjects. When discussing his educational experience, Wesley provided the following responses:

> I picked media for GCSE. I knew I wanted to do it since year nine. I just liked it because it's really different from GCSE. I'm in college doing media – in the course we do like loads of different stuff, like we're doing photography when we go back after break, and we do like filming and stuff like that.

Although a direct association with masculinity may initially be conceived as a manufactured link, there are elements of this response that are suggestive and warrant consideration. Firstly, Wesley distinguishes media studies from GCSEs, or potentially interpreted as formal traditional theoretical learning. Secondly, photography and filming may be understood as practical processes, not in a complete traditional masculine sense (Willis, 1977). However, they are hands-on (Nixon, 2009) activities that predominantly exclude writing and 'pen-pushing' (Mac an Ghaill, 1994; Willis, 1977).

Despite the slightly individualistic aspects of the young men's data, Maths, English, and the mentioning of these subjects were a feature that connected the majority of the Ladz, yet for varying reasons. Craig and Billy both experienced difficulties with these subjects. Craig offered a response that potentially reflects the hidden injuries of class (Sennett & Cobb, 1972) and a damaged working-class learner identity (Reay, 2017):

> English and Maths, they're hard cos all my life, I've never been good at maths. And English – I'm not the best reader and everything. Like I can read, but it's just, I know I can't read proper.

This excerpt reveals that Craig has struggled with maths and English for the entirety of his life and places specific emphasis on reading. Similarly, Billy struggled with writing together with maths. However, Billy makes sense of these difficulties by suggesting that they are inherent deficiencies and neglects structural failing: *'With maths, it's like I don't enjoy it. I like, struggle ini, that why I don't listen like, do you know what I mean. It's like you got weak points and strong points haven't you'*. In contrast to these responses, Dan and Tommy place significant emphasis on maths and English. The following section includes a lengthy discussion between Dan and me. However, the data distinguishes a critical theme that is essential to almost all of the young men's views of school subjects and their school experience:

RG: Are there any subjects you enjoyed?

Dan: Maths, I didn't mind it, but I didn't like it, but I done it cos it was relevant. You got to know things for exams.

RG: So why did you think Maths was relevant? What was it relevant to?

Dan: Cos I want to be a plumber, and you need a D in Maths GCSE, so I tried to get a D in Maths. Not only that, but it just helps in life, doesn't it. I don't know – simple things. If I never done Maths all my life, I probably wouldn't even go to the shop with a tenner because I wouldn't know how much change I would have. Some people moan about Maths and say we don't need it, but you are going to need it sooner or later in your life in you. So I just get my head down and do it. Sometimes I don't like it, and sometimes I just moan and get sent out, but most of the time, I'm alright like.

This discussion reveals a central theme of the Ladz' school experience and what I refer to as a 'pragmatic approach to education'. These young men are somewhat dissimilar from their laddish (Willis, 1977) counterparts and are no longer completely anti-learning (Jackson, 2006; 2010) and do not entirely reject education and its significance, and there is mainly no association between academic work and femininity (Jackson, 2002) or the notion of it being 'cissy' (Willis, 1977, p. 149). Furthermore, the Ladz also differ from some of their post-industrial study counterparts, who demonstrated a '"don't much care" [attitude] to school' (McDowell, 2003, p. 118), a rejection of 'formal school knowledge and the potential exchange value it has in the labour market' (Mac an Ghaill, 1994, p. 65) and whereby school was perceived to have little importance to the future (Nayak 2003b, 2006). Instead, the Ladz selectively engage in topics that they feel are particularly relevant to their chosen career path – *'Maths and English. Just good knowledge, isn't it. I need them to be a mechanic in it.'* (Tommy), *'Biology's interesting, so I wen tha one. About the body and tha and part of paramedics I wanna do'* (Lewis) – or have real-world value as further demonstrated by Ian:

> ASDAN [Award Scheme Development and Accreditation Network[1]] is something I liked. They actually taught us instead of getting put in front of a book and learning from that. They taught us

---

[1]Award Scheme Development and Accreditation Network provides a variety of nationally recognised certifications focused on enhancing personal, social, and employability skills. The programs and qualifications for high schools aim to help students transition successfully to secondary education, increase participation and motivation, improve fundamental skills, and enhance academic achievement.

> basic skills. Like, one lesson they taught us how to learn to do tax
> and stuff like that. That's what people need more because, yeah,
> they just need it more.

Here again, we see that linkage between education and practicality and skills
and knowledge that have value beyond merely a theoretical use (Willis, 1977).
Additionally, Ian seems to suggest that this knowledge is transmitted through
a 'traditional' teaching style as opposed to the contemporary neoliberalist
approach that is target-driven and where 'students are required to memorise and
repeat received facts and concepts in exchange for certified skills' (Brown et al.,
2020, p. 154).

This notion of practicality transcends the young men's school experience and
also seems to continue into further education, as evidenced by the following quotation from Lewis:

> That's the whole point of being in college. You gotta learn stuff
> like. You just don't. Fuckin' math, we're doing stuff you learnt in
> year 6. Or in English, you just do the same mock tests you done in
> year seven like, so it's not like I'm learning anything.

This suggests that Lewis believes that the standard of education he receives
in college is below his cognitive ability level and offers limited practical benefit.
However, Lewis' successful completion of his college course is potentially determined by productive engagement with these topics and a positive outcome.

Superficially, the Ladz pragmatic approach to education seems to reveal a
method that does deliver some benefit and engagement with education. However, as the following discussion demonstrates, further analysis of this approach
reveals equally detrimental implications.

Dan: It was mainly science we mitched all the time.

RG: Why Science? Why don't you like science?

Dan: I don't care about science. I just wasn't interested at all. I don't feel like I
need it in my life, so I just didn't do it.

As this excerpt demonstrates, the young men's pragmatic approach to education also has negative consequences. Here we see Dan rejecting science based
on its perceived irrelevance and its everyday life benefit. Subsequently, the pragmatic approach to education and the hierarchical selective process reduces the
Ladz' engagement with education to perceived essential subjects, with supposed
unnecessary topics being rejected. This process reduces the young men's ability
to achieve the considered positive educational benchmark of five GCSEs at A-C
(MacDonald & Marsh, 2005). This eventuality may negatively affect the young
men's future life chances (Weber, 1948).

Seemingly, this section shows a departure from the anti-learning laddish culture (Jackson, 2006; 2010; Willis, 1977) through the Ladz' pragmatic approach to

education that is driven by an awareness of the significance of educational credentials: '*You need them [GCSEs], you mad head*' (Tommy). Although contemporary marginalised working-class young men's engagement with education is not unique (Ward, 2015), the Ladz selective involvement resonates with the 'ordinary kids' and what Brown (1987, p. 100) refers to as alienated instrumentalism, which may be understood as viewing school 'as a 'means' of obtaining credentials to compete for certain types of employment'. However, as previously stated, the Ladz' hostility towards teachers and their aggressive macho laddish displays demonstrate contradictory behaviour that disassociates them from the ordinary kids. Brown (1987, pp. 93–94) states that the ordinary kids 'attempt[ed] to avoid conflict and hostility with authority'. Subsequently, the Ladz' attitude towards school and challenging, unruly school behaviour generates a contradiction that complicates the Ladz' true identity and subsequent categorisation. However, additional consideration potentially reveals a reconfigured association with the lads.

The lads from Willis's (1977) study rejected education based on its perceived irrelevance to their future career orientation. The Ladz' pragmatic approach to education is almost identical yet reconfigured in line with contemporary social and economic changes and manifestations of neoliberal culture, including credentialism, which has increased the significance of qualifications (Patrick, 2013). Essentially, the Ladz seemingly recognise the significance of credentials concerning training and job opportunities and, therefore, selectively choose to engage in subjects believed to facilitate their progression into working-class jobs – skilled but still predominantly working-class – whilst actively rejecting school subjects and knowledge perceived as irrelevant to their future career orientation.

'It all depends on the teacher'

The previous section demonstrated the Ladz' partial commitment to the teaching paradigm (Willis, 1977) through their pragmatic approach to education and selective school engagement. This commitment generates questions about the Ladz' unruly laddish behaviour and why they do not fulfil the teaching paradigm requirements by providing teachers with respect and conforming to the rules and social relations of the schooling system (Feinberg & Soltis, 2009). These questions and the fragmentation of the teaching paradigm are explored in the subsequent sections, initially by assessing the young men's view towards teachers and the notion of respect.

When exploring the young men's view towards school, teachers were one of the overriding influential factors. In all interviews, some negativity was aimed at teachers, be that partially or outright disdain. Several factors determined this opposition, yet the notion of respect – in some form or another – is a feature that connects most of the participants' data.

Outright disdain for teachers was associated with Stan. When I initially asked Stan why he did not like school, he responded: '*I despise school. They're cunts*'. Although Stan demonstrates an intensified dislike of school, his use of 'they're' at the end of this statement is particularly revealing. By utilising this word, Stan seems to suggest that it is not the school itself but those within it. I responded to this by asking Stan if there were any aspects of school he liked, and the following discussion proceeded:

Stan: Depends on the teachers and tha, whether they hit me or restrain me and tha.

RG: Why did they restrain you?

Stan: Cause I fucking threw a chair at one of them!

RG: Why did you throw the chair?

Stan: Cause he fucking laughed in my face!

Stan's association with teachers evidently influences his relationship with the school. Although it is important to recognise Stan's hyper-masculine (Mac an Ghaill, 1994) violent laddish behaviour, equal significance is the triggering of this conduct because it resonates with many of the Ladz and inversely connects with the teaching paradigm.

The triggering point for Stan's behaviour is the teacher laughing in his face. One may reasonably assume that Stan feels belittled and disrespected. This notion of being undermined by teachers and a violent reaction is also evident in a response offered by Lewis:

> One teacher, I threw a chair at him. Cos, he told me to fuck off under his breath. So I said go on, say it again. And he smiled, so I lobbed a chair at him. Don't piss me off [laughs].

In these two excerpts, we begin to see the motives behind the Ladz' unruly, challenging school behaviour. Whenever these young men feel undermined, disrespected, or have a sense of powerlessness, they seem to draw upon their hyper-masculine (Mac an Ghaill, 1994) identity and violent behaviour to reclaim self-worth (Jackson, 2002). This response resonates with Dan's earlier rationale for violence, suggesting an instinctive, natural reaction to '*[Not getting] along with everyone*'. Billy also identified teachers as crucial in determining his negative school experience and behaviour: '*I don't mind the education bit, but I can't stand the teachers. They think they can belittle us. They think they're all better*'. This response corresponds with the above excerpts and the notions of disrespect and powerlessness.

The responses of these three participants reveal a contradictory fragmentation in the teaching paradigm. As previously mentioned, the success of teaching paradigms entails pupils providing respect based on the knowledge teachers provide. However, conversely, the Ladz' replies suggest that they unconditionally desire respect from teachers or at least want to be respected. Furthermore, although the teaching paradigm proposes a mutual exchange – knowledge for respect – arguably, it also has undertones of the traditionalist ideas of respect where 'children are taught to respect their parents, elders, people in positions of authority and law' (Elliot et al., 2013). Based on these ideas and perspectives, I decided to further explore the notion of respect in Billy's interview:

RG: Billy, do you think teachers should get respect or do you think they should earn respect? What's your thoughts on that?

Billy: It's 50/50 like ini? Some teachers like, if they did treat me with respect, I'll be the same with them. But like most teachers like, just won't settle down with me like. In my report, they always say I'm lovely kid ana, they say I need to focus on my attention but like it's hard, and them um like, yeah if they treat me with respect I'll treat it with them back, but if I treat them with respect, I can't always expect it back.

Billy suggests that respect is a reciprocal process and neglects the traditionalist ideas that elders and those in authority should freely be awarded dignity based on social status (Elliot et al., 2013). Billy's perspective challenges the very foundations of the teaching paradigm due to his noncompliant offering of unconditional respect based on the knowledge exchange value.

Teachers were also a defining feature of Tommy's school experience, and he also felt that the teachers picked on him and stated: *'They're [teachers] irritating! They pick on me. They piss me off! I hate them'*. Furthermore, based on Tommy's previously mentioned middle-ground school perspective (It's alright, but it's not the best), I asked him what was good about school. He replied: *'Some lessons and sometimes the teachers have a laugh, but sometimes they can be dickheads'*. Tommy's response additionally reconfirms his pragmatic approach to school (some lessons). It also reveals an additional disparity between himself and the lads (Willis, 1977). Tommy's response suggests that if teachers have a laugh or establish a positive relationship, then school is potentially good. Conversely, Willis (1977, p. 83) observations revealed the following:

> Techniques which attempt to get too close to 'the lads' are simply rejected because they come from 'teachers' and are embued with what 'teaching' already stands for in the institution.

Despite Tommy's laddish behaviour, unlike the lads, Tommy seems willing to accept a teacher-pupil relationship based on humour. Tommy's response correlates with Simpson's (2021) study of a state primary school in a former mining community in the north of England. This research revealed that humour helped create and maintain positive relationships between pupils and staff.

Even Wesley, with his seemingly conformist demeanour, identified the significance of teachers. When I asked whether he engaged in school, he responded: *'It depends - sometimes. It all depends on the teacher'*. And Ian talked about how he took advantage of the precarious nature of supply teachers: *'Supply teachers you can just muck around'*.

This section shows that the Ladz' engagement with education – whether negative or positive – is significantly determined by the pupil and teacher relationship. The young men's nonconformist behaviour and lack of unconditional teacher respect may reflect their working-class protest masculinity (Connell, 2005) and the idea of sticking up for oneself, speaking one's mind, and challenging authority (Mac an Ghaill, 1994; McDowell, 2003; Willis, 1977). However, Billy's notion of reciprocal respect and Tommy's compliance based on a sense of humour potentially compromise the idea of outright ingrained anti-authority qualities.

Furthermore, although the data does not evidence it, it is worth considering whether humour has the ability to lessen the hierarchal relationship between pupil and teacher and create a foundation whereby the young men perceive themselves as equal or respected by the teacher.

'I'm fucking autistic'

The previous sections have collectively identified a disparity between the Ladz' alienated instrumentalism (Brown, 1987) or pragmatic approach to education and their laddish, nonconformist, unruly challenging behaviour. This section contributes to this discussion and highlights an additional catalyst for the young men's 'seemingly' laddish classroom conduct.

Seven of the nine young men openly admitted to some form of learning disability and/or mental health condition. Out of the two remaining participants – Dan and Stan – Dan made no mention of these issues. Conversely, although Stan never outright confessed to learning disabilities, he did refer to issues with dyslexia when he was asked to do certain things at the youth centre. For example, on one occasion, Martin, the senior youth worker, asked Stan to engage in a survey, and Stan responded by saying: *'I can't. I'm fucking dyslexic'*. Additionally, in his interview, Stan talked about his junior educational years and said: *'I was good at Maths and English. I am good at everything. It's just. I'm fucking autistic – joking!'* Stan's use of the word 'joking' may potentially mean one of two things. Firstly, this may be a display of his masculine piss-taking behaviour (Collinson, 1988; Nixon, 2009). Alternatively, this term may be a defence mechanism that allows him to evade or conceal difficulties that he may feel demonstrate weakness, especially considering his hyper-masculine (Mac an Ghaill, 1994) qualities and laddish behaviour (Francis, 1999).

Besides Stan and Dan, the other seven members of the Ladz were forthright about their learning difficulties and talked freely about their impact on their educational engagement. A previous section revealed that Billy disliked writing. When I questioned him about this displeasure, Billy offered the following response:

> I dunno. It's just I have, um, ADHD [Attention Deficit Hyperactivity Disorder], so I can't concentrate, and then I'm writing, and I'll be in a mood, then someone catches my attention, then it takes a good 5 minutes to settle then.

In this excerpt, Billy suggests that his ADHD hampers his concentration and writing, affecting his mood and classroom behaviour. Lewis' data also shows this notion of affective negative classroom behaviour due to a learning disability. As the previous section showed, Lewis confessed to being a *'naughty boy in school'*. When making sense of this status, Lewis provided the following rationale:

> I was always messing about. I could never concentrate because, in school, I could never understand the work. And like when people try to give me help, they would give me the wrong help. I didn't

get diagnosed with it, dyslexia, until the end of school. So, I was a bit distracted in school, so then I would mess around. And I was always getting in trouble. And then, when I was getting stressed, I was always working out for a fag. I'd get caught by the principal.

Akin to Billy, Lewis's learning disability also impedes his concentration, leading to disruptive classroom behaviour. However, in an additional response, Lewis contradicts this notion of affective disability behaviour and suggests that some of his adverse school conduct – that verge on sexual harassment – was determined by sexual attraction:

One teacher was my favourite; I was only nice to her because I found her fit. I remember her like. I messed around too much with her, see. I was like, you could say I was very flirtatious with her. In the class, I would slap her arse and walk out. Bearing in mind, I was like 14-15 at the time. I just didn't care. I still don't now.

This excerpt undermines Lewis' initial 'victimhood' response and reveals negative classroom behaviour motivated by sexual desire, and reinforces his hyper-masculine (Mac an Ghaill, 1994) status and laddish qualities. Additionally, through *'I just don't care. I still don t now'* Lewis seems to attempt to normalise his behaviour through a sense of macho (McDowell, 2003) meaning-making. Lewis's sexual objectification of the female teacher may be understood as an attempt to seize 'power through constituting her as the powerless object of sexist discourse' (Walkerdine, 1993, p. 209) and, in doing so, taking the position of a sexualised man and changing the power dynamic.

Within the scope of learning disabilities and mental illnesses, Cole's story and his disaffected school experience become illuminated. As previously stated, the lads' culture and its adverse outcomes are almost imposed on Cole due to his disturbing childhood experiences. The following excerpt demonstrates Cole's disengagement from education due to mental health issues:

Depression come around, and that hit me off. I didn't really know what I wanted from the start of year ten till the end of year eleven. I just give up sort of thing. I didn't have any plans, no dreams, no roles. I just shut down and locked myself away most of the time. Give up with everything like – just wanted to be there and not bothered.

This quotation demonstrates the adverse impact of depression and its negative effect on Cole's learning experience. The magnitude of this depression also threatened Cole's well-being due to self-harm and extensive periods in the hospital.

Tommy also had ADHD and frequently and openly talked about his problems with anger. On one occasion, Tommy arrived at the centre with a black eye. When I asked him about it, he said he had got very angry and punched himself in the face. Tommy's issues with anger were a significant contributor to his school exclusion (discussed in the subsequent section).

Conversely to the negative learning disability and/or mental health affective behaviour, Ian and Wesley demonstrated a functionalist learning disabilities perspective that determined their educational engagement. For example, during their interview together, I asked Ian why he liked certain subjects, and the following conversation proceeded:

Ian: I think that's why I like creating stuff.

RG: Why's that Ia?

Ian: I've got dyslexia. That's why my imagination is running wild.

Wesley: Yeah, my sister is really creative – she has dyslexia and she like the art type, but me I'm just like – I've got dyspraxia and my art skills are not really good.

This excerpt demonstrates a sense of learning disability meaning-making. These two young men seem to determine their academic strengths, weaknesses and subsequent engagement according to their learning disabilities. The Ladz' learning disability and/or mental health issues are features that continue into the employment-related data. Therefore, although these issues are only briefly touched on in this chapter, they are more extensively explored through the notions of medicalisation and individualisation (Ashurst & Venn, 2014) in the following chapter.

'It's like behaviour school'

The previous sections have demonstrated the complexity of the Ladz' schooling experience, including a pragmatic approach to education and negative laddish school behaviour ranging from truanting to violent conduct. This final educational section deals with the ramifications of this negative school behaviour and explores one of the sanctions used on the young men while tying in a few final bits of important education related data.

As stated in previous chapters, I share a connection to the Ladz due to my laddish history and lack of youthful educational engagement. Although I never physically assaulted teachers, and I am not proud of my school behaviour, I was commonly truant, extremely disruptive in class and spent a large portion of my youthful school years engaged in drug-taking and smoking. As one might expect, this behaviour was deemed unacceptable, and I was penalised for it. The sanctions imposed included being repeatedly made to stand outside the class, having my classroom behaviour monitored and reported on by teachers, and eventually being demoted to the lowest ability group in all lessons. Despite the negative school behavioural similarities between myself and the Ladz, the sanctions imposed on them differ significantly from mine.

Due to their negative school behaviour, Tommy, Stan, Dan, and Lewis had all been excluded from school and had spent extended periods in pupil referral units (PRU). Cole had also been referred to a PRU due to his enforced educational difficulties. The Ladz are almost an exact fit with the type of child excluded from school. Their characteristics and vulnerabilities place them at significant risk of being excluded and sent to PRU's. Overwhelmingly, those excluded from school include males, young people associated with poverty and those with special educational needs and/or poor mental health problems (Ashurst & Venn, 2014; Gill et al., 2017). Additionally, the permanent and fixed-term exclusions from schools in Wales records, 2017/18, indicate that persistent disruptive behaviour and verbal abuse/threatening behaviour against an adult were the most common reasons for school exclusion (Hughes, 2019).

Due to the high proportion of the study sample associated with PRU's, I decided to interview the manager of the PRU that the Ladz attended. Therefore, this section includes data from the young men together with Tony, the PRU manager.

The findings relating to the Ladz' experience at a PRU vary and potentially reflect the difficulties of dealing with these young men and catering for their education needs while accounting for their challenging behaviour. For example, Tommy was excluded from school because of his anger issues which sometimes led to violent outbursts: *'It's just my behaviour when I like get pissed off. I just get angry and frustrated when the teachers wind me up'* (Tommy). However, the PRU seemed to be an equal source of frustration for Tommy:

> If I sit there and do fuck all because I've done all the work, they're like, 'Do your work', but I've already done it, and then they're just moody at me then. I always do my work. I'm the first one to do it. When I've done my work [laughs], they go in a mood with me then and blame loads of things on me. I just piss them [teachers] off then.

Tommy suggests that the academic work he is given at the PRU is not challenging enough. Subsequently, we potentially see a clash of frustration between Tommy, who finds the work too easy, and a teacher who cannot complete the teaching paradigm and maintain Tommy's attention and compliance academically.

An additional aspect of noteworthiness is Tommy's physical reaction and laughter after saying: *'When I've done my work'*. This seems a peculiar laughter point? Is Tommy lying about doing his work and being purely disruptive? His previous responses and the importance he places on qualifications suggest otherwise. Additionally, is Tommy's laughter a divergence technique that reflects his complex character of being torn between a laddish masculine avoidance of schoolwork (Connell, 1995; Francis & Archer, 2005) and a pragmatic approach that recognises the importance of qualifications?

Tommy was desperate to return to mainstream education. At the time of his interview, his parents were in talks with his previous school about the possibility of him going back. Returning to mainstream education was also a feature of Tony's interview data:

> Ultimately, I think our goal should be to get everyone back into that kind of environment. I understand that we're needed, but the

ones that are capable of going back to mainstream, we should push to go back to mainstream. All those social exposures that are part of growing up and maturing, are taken away from them just because they come to us. I will try very, very hard to get them back in mainstream school, but it is down to the school's appetite to have them back because, more often than not, once they're done, they're done, and that's it. There's no way back.

Tony's response and the keenness he demonstrates around returning young people to mainstream education reflect the passion for students he demonstrated in his interview. However, this excerpt also highlights his acknowledgement and recognition of the hindering effects of PRU's. Additionally, his notion of 'no way back' correlates with Gill et al. (2017) findings. They suggest that schools have operated on a system that rewards students' academic outcomes since the onset of new public management. Under this system, schools are pressured to improve and sometimes use exclusion to enhance their critical criteria.

My previously documented reflection on my school experience, sanctions and comparison between the Ladz inspired me to ask Tony about this disparity – Tony provided the following response:

I don't think, for many of my kids, I could not put them outside of a classroom for ten minutes to reflect on their behaviour without them wanting to smash and break something, which is unfortunate - but it is concerning.

In this response, Tony arguably suggests a behavioural shift, with contemporary young men being more aggressive and having complex needs. Correspondingly, Gill et al. (2017, p. 19) suggest that the increase in school exclusions can be explained by the rising number of 'children experiencing the intersecting vulnerabilities' – including poverty, learning needs and mental illness – and schools' financial difficulties dealing with these problems.

Contrary to Tommy's negative perspective on PRU's, Dan offered a favourable view of this educational setting:

It's like behaviour school. Just for people who have been in the same situation as me and kicked out of school, but they **help**[2] you a lot more – they've got more **time** for you as well. It's much better, I think. They've just got more **time** for you, and they **help** you a lot more if you're stuck or something. They just **help** you a lot more. Smaller classes plus two teachers in one class.

---

[2]Phrases in excerpts are bolded to highlight their significance and demonstrate wording patterns.

In this short response, the crucial words that are repeatedly used include help and time. Therefore, PRUs, with their smaller classes and more teachers, are beneficial in providing Dan with the support he seems to require. Additionally, despite Dan's laddish school behaviour that led to exclusion, this excerpt arguably further evidences his commitment to 'some' educational engagement.

Despite Dan's recognition of support, this particular PRU boasts that 2020 was its most successful year, with 85% of its pupils achieving five GCSEs of D-G. This attainment level is well below the recognised standard of 'good' educational achievement of five GCSEs at A-C (Roberts, 2018) and places these pupils in danger of becoming NEET (Not in Education, Employment, or Training) (Simmons et al., 2014). Correspondingly, Ian and even Wesley – the apparent school conformist – also left school with qualifications well below the recognised 'good' educational benchmark.

The notion of support was also evident in Dan's discussion about his career advisor: *'I talk to him, and if I need anything, I've got his number. He's sound like'*. The career advice offered to Dan corresponded with his chosen career path, plumbing. Tony referred to this process as a *'career match'*, which in Tony's words, was: *'you tell us what you want to do, and she [career advisor] will get an employer in to talk about how you can get with him'*. Essentially, the Ladz' expectations were married to an equivalent employer. This 'career match' process corresponds with the method used in the Ladz' mainstream school. For example, when Lewis attended an open day at college organised by the school, he was shown construction courses. Therefore, he did not realise that the college offered an access to nursing course, which he is interested in pursuing. Furthermore, when I asked Billy about career advice, he provided evidence of a similar experience:

> People come in for careers and talk about construction an tha, but it doesn't interest me. And oh, was it called? It's in college, and they go to different countries and that, I think its army an tha, the forces and all tha.

Stan's data on his experience at the PRU is limited and potentially reflects his negativity towards school, which often led to sharp responses like: *'school is shit'*. However, his PRU school experience was once mentioned during an ethnographic observation of him talking to a group of girls:

> I'm allowed to do **anything**. I threw a chair at a teacher and still didn't get thrown out. I can literally get away with **anything,** and the teachers won't do **anything**. The best thing is I get to do dull work, colouring and stuff [laughter].

Akin to his previous excerpts, we see Stan's hyper-masculine (Mac an Ghaill, 1994) posturing and desire for attention. Notably, he is talking to a group of girls and claiming he is untouchable – *'anything'* – yet this claim is untrue, as evidenced by the fact that Stan has previously said that teachers restrain him. Therefore, arguably, Stan seemingly tries to impress these girls through a masculine verbal display of strength and superiority. Additionally, he seems to recognise the stigmatisation around PRU's and deflects this by stating that the *'dull work'* is the *'best thing'*.

Unlike Dan's positive experience of PRU's, Cole's encounters with these types of institutions echoed his adverse childhood and consisted of a collection of unfavourable experiences. Due to his forced self-removal from school, Cole was assigned to a PRU where he was provided with two hours of education five days a week, which led to, in Cole's words: *'nothing except for a C in Maths, E in English and RE – that's all I had'*. As stated previously, this attainment level places Cole in significant danger of becoming NEET.

After his GCSEs, Cole could not go to local mainstream colleges out of fear of bullying and reoccurring episodes. Subsequently, Cole was provided with further education through alternative provision (AP), defined as an educational institution 'for children of compulsory school age who do not attend mainstream or special schools and who would not otherwise receive suitable education, for any reason' (DfE, 2018, p. 5). However, this institution could not cater to Cole's career aspiration – funeral directing, explored in Chapter Five – and provide him with the necessary education and training requirements. Therefore, Cole stated that:

> All I was doing was going there to sit there, to fall asleep in the corner and get paid £50 a week for it. I didn't really have much learning there at all. But they wouldn't say no because obviously, we got £50 a week, but they are also earning money because we're there. I weren't stupid – I know why they didn't say no and just left me there.

Essentially, Cole was used as a 'cash cow'. The AP could not meet Cole's education or career training needs yet registered him due to financial rewards. Cole's experience with AP's reveals many failings that compound the severity of his adverse childhood and existing decreased life chances (Weber, 1948).

Cole's experience at PRU's and the lack of opportunity echo Tony's honest account of his centre and the educational institution that the Ladz attended:

> I think firstly, if you come out of a really good mainstream school and you come to us, there's a huge raft of support that's taken away. So the school's pastoral support, education welfare, school-based counsellors, the school nurses, education psychology - all of that is taken away.

As this excerpt shows, although Tony was passionate about providing pupils with the best possible educational outcome, this objective was constrained due to a lack of provisions and financial support. Therefore, and as I critically explore and argue in the final chapter, although the Ladz make life difficult for their teachers in mainstream school (Delamont, 2000), whose benefit do PRU's serve? Because although the smaller classes provide some advantages, the reduced level of provisions often equates to an inadequate educational experience (Ashurst & Venn, 2014) that arguably reinforces a disaffected relationship with education and leads to decreased academic outcomes.

Conclusion

This chapter has demonstrated that although the Ladz share some education related consistencies with Willis's lads, including nonconformist protest masculinity (Connell, 1995) associated behaviour, which is intensified by mental health problems, learning difficulties and disaffected relationships with teachers, the chapter equally shows that the Ladz do not entirely reject education. In contrast to lads from Willis's (1977) study, the Ladz believe that some academic credentials are important to their employment aspirations and adopt what I refer to as a pragmatic approach, meaning they selectively identify and partake in educational topics considered necessary to their employment aspirations whilst rejecting those deemed irrelevant. Therefore, despite the Ladz' nonconformist protest masculinity (Connell, 1995) associated behaviour and connection to the lads, these young men demonstrate relative change and are no longer entirely anti-learning and do not seem to perceive academic work as feminine or cissy (Jackson, 2002; Willis, 1977). Instead, the Ladz partially recognise the necessity of academic credentials, which derives from employment aspirations. The following empirical chapter explores the Ladz' employment orientations and how these are constructed and influenced.

Chapter Five

The Ladz and Employment

Introduction

This chapter presents the Ladz' employment-related data and explores aspects including what jobs the Ladz want to do and why, the jobs they disfavour, and their view towards service sector employment. The main arguments of this chapter are that almost all of the Ladz reject service sector employment based on the perceived inability to engage in emotional labour (Hochschild, 1983), and several of the Ladz demonstrate a continued laddish attraction to manual and physical hands-on forms of employment (McDowell, 2002; Nixon, 2006; Willis, 1977), that largely derives from socialisation or the intergenerational transmission of masculine modes of being (Walkerdine & Jiménez, 2012), often through prominent family and male figures (Tolson, 1977; Veness, 1962; Willis, 1977). However, among some of the Ladz, the intergenerational transmission process has become destabilised through specific social circumstances, leading to an employment orientation other than manual employment. Therefore, this chapter demonstrates both continuity and change among this group of contemporary marginalised working-class young men.

'Anything to do with building'

The lads (Willis, 1977) view towards employment was guided by their masculine working-class cultural and social background, which led them to believe that social mobility and the possibility of 'good' jobs were unattainable (Roberts, 1995). Subsequently, unlike the Ladz from this study, academic qualifications were deemed irrelevant and thought to offer an illusory promise (Willis, 1977). Furthermore, the lads placed minimal emphasis on 'specific' career choices and instead committed themselves to a 'future of generalised labour' (Willis, 1977, p. 100). This commitment was driven by the belief that work offered minimal

The 21st Century Ladz: Continuity and Changes among Marginalised
Young Men from the South Wales Valleys, 69–95
Copyright © 2025 by Richard Gater. Published by Emerald Publishing Limited.
This work is published under the Creative Commons Attribution (CC BY 4.0) licence.
Anyone may reproduce, distribute, translate and create derivative works of this work
(for both commercial and non-commercial purposes), subject to full attribution
to the original publication and authors. The full terms of this licence may be seen at
http://creativecommons.org/licences/by/4.0/legalcode
doi:10.1108/978-1-83797-631-720251006

intrinsic reward, and what mattered was the 'potential particular work situation holds for self and particularly masculine expression, diversion and 'laffs' as learnt creatively in the counter-school culture' (Willis, 1977, p. 100). Essentially, Willis's lads demonstrated a commitment to unskilled and semi-skilled masculine forms of employment and recognised that they did not need qualifications for these jobs (Roberts, 1995).

Despite the initial behavioural similarities between the two study samples, contrary to Willis's lads, most of the Ladz' data does demonstrate a preference towards specific forms of employment other than unskilled and semi-skilled work. For example, when asked what form of employment they would like to do, the Ladz offered the following replies. Craig responded with: *'The most job I would like in the world is a roofer or like a plumber. That is all I would like to do'.* Additionally, Craig also mentioned the possibility of joining the army, doing carpentry and being a chef or a scrap metal collector.

At the time of the study, Ian was employed as a plumber's assistant. In response to the following question: *'Did you ever think about what kind of jobs you wanted to do when you were in school?'* Ian replied: *'Anything to do with building or something. Carpentry, bricklaying or plumbing'.* Correspondingly, Dan also had a strong preference for plumbing. In response to Dan's attraction to plumbing, I asked him the following question: *'So plumbing is the job you favour. Do you think you would like to do any other jobs, Dan?'* Dan offered the following response:

> I put a secondary choice of plastering, and if plumbing doesn't go well, sport. Like going into the local schools and coaching rugby or football, things like that. Mainly rugby – I wouldn't really want to do tennis or anything like that.

In this excerpt, we possibly see the strength of Dan's masculine working-class identity. Notably, Dan rejects involvement in tennis, a sport associated with a middle-class status (Bourdieu, 1984), includes individualistic participation, and involves distance between opponents (Falcous & McLeod, 2012) and thus omits masculine, physical, and bodily contact. Conversely, Dan favours rugby – a game that Bourdieu (1984) links to a working-class identity and is traditionally associated with masculinity (Anderson & McGuire, 2010; Ward, 2015) and involves collective involvement. Evidence of an employment-related masculine working-class identity was also potentially evident in Tommy's job preference data.

Like Craig and Dan, Tommy's preferred choice of work included mechanics, plumbing, and scrap collecting. My ethnographic discussions with Tommy revealed that he had very fixed and rigid ideas about his employment ambition. As the choices demonstrate, Tommy's work preferences exclusively include traditionally associated working-class manual forms of employment (Shildrick & MacDonald, 2007) and exclude any mention of middle-class professions. This exclusion and the rigidity of Tommy's employment aspiration led me to ask him: *'Tommy, ever thought about being a lawyer, or something like that, butt?'* Tommy replied: *'Fuck that, too much paperwork. They gave me a huge paper test in school, and I said, fuck that. I chucked it in the shredder and walked out'.*

Notably, akin to the lads (Willis, 1977) before him, Tommy strongly rejects the possibility of employment-related upward mobility and the middle-class profession of a lawyer and demonstrates resistance to paperwork and an inclination to manual work.

Craig, Ian, Dan, and Tommy's employment preference data reveal a strong connection with traditionally associated working-class forms of skilled manual employment, particularly construction work (Shildrick & MacDonald, 2007). However, this connection was less distinct and rigid among the other five participants.

Being 20 years old, Cole had already reached employment age and worked for the local council as a memorial mason. Being slightly unsure of the job specification for a memorial mason, I asked Cole what the job entails. Cole provided the following response:

> A Memorial Mason is where you check the safety of grave headstones. I look after ten cemeteries and the headstones all over the borough – that's 55000 headstones. I've got to hand test every single one of them in a year to meet the safety specifications.

Although Cole seemed relatively happy in his current form of employment (explored in later sections), this was not his preferred job choice. From the age of eight, Cole had been drawn to funeral directing and also favoured mechanical engineering in the army, yet he was dissuaded from this career choice due to family concerns and disapproval.

Lewis' job preferences included a contrasting mismatch between masculine-associated skilled working-class manual employment, including bricklaying and plumbing (Ness, 2012; Thiel, 2007), and frontline healthcare work in the form of a paramedic, which requires emotional labour (Hayes et al., 2020; Hochschild, 1983) and associated feminine qualities (Leidner, 1993; McDowell, 2003). Lewis' career orientation data reveals a partial deviation from the traditional working-class masculine form of manual employment; this departure is more pronounced in Billy's job preference data.

As was revealed in Chapter Four, unlike the previous six participants, Billy stated that he had no attraction to skilled working-class employment: *'Construction an tha … doesn't interest me'*. Contrary to the other Ladz and the two that follow, Billy's job preference was cooking. In making sense of this preference, Billy offered the following response:

> Cooking is something I enjoy, like with math; it's like I don't enjoy it. I like, struggle ini, that why I don't listen like, do you know what I mean. But with cooking ana, it's something I enjoy. It's like you got weak points and strong points, haven't you.

Cooking seems to provide Billy with a sense of intrinsic reward facilitated by his ability to engage in this activity successfully. The last two participants – Stan and Wesley – reveal further dissimilarities compared to Craig, Ian, Dan, and

Tommy whilst also demonstrating comparative contrast in job preference. However, they equally share a connection that links them together.

Chapter Four revealed Stan's strong association with the lads' category (Willis, 1977) through his rejection of education and volatile displays of hyper-masculine (Mac an Ghaill, 1994) behaviour. Stan's link to the lads' category was additionally evident in his employment preference data. When asked what job he would like to do, Stan offered the following response:

> I don't know! I want to dig graves up, and tha or maybe play rugby. Or do you know wha, I might actually work in a motorbike shop! What would you get more money off – motorbike shop or fucking. I'd probably do grave digging cos it's probably the easiest job. You don't need GCSEs or anything – it's literally easy as fuck!

There are several parts of this excerpt that require an explanation and analysis. Firstly, *'I don't know'* – a response Stan used frequently – was always delivered in an angry and aggressive tone. However, I never once felt threatened by this verbal display of aggression. Instead, I always felt that Stan was angry and frustrated at himself because he could not offer a definitive answer, epitomised by the multiple choices in his response. Furthermore, unlike the previous Ladz and akin to the lads – whose choice of a specific job could be 'quite random' (Willis, 1977, p. 101) – Stan's job preference response is relatively indecisive and ultimately based on the non-requirement of GCSEs.

Although Stan and Wesley had dissimilar personalities – Stan, hyper-masculine (Mac an Ghaill, 1994) and volatile. Wesley, shy and timid – their employment preference data reveals similarities:

> I like television stuff. TV – stuff like that, but I don't know. I might change my mind and find something else that I am good at. I haven't thought like what type of job that much. I'll just give things a try, and then if I think that's not for me or that's not really my kind of thing. I like trying stuff like experimenting with like different jobs. (Wesley)

Akin to Stan and unlike the other seven Ladz, Wesley also had a somewhat ambiguous sense of employment preference. There is no fixed career ambition. We also see the use of the phrase *'I don't know'*, which is missing in most of the Ladz employment preference data and only identifiable in Stan's data.

A 'Lagging' Labour Market

Collective analysis of the Ladz' employment preference data reveals a relatively strong connection to masculine working-class-associated skilled manual employment, yet with some deviations, including funeral directing, healthcare work, cooking, and media. Notably, unlike their laddish predecessors (Willis, 1977), unskilled and semi-skilled manual work and manufacturing are omitted from the Ladz' preferred choice of employment. However, this exclusion potentially reflects the historical changes in the UK labour market.

The 1970s, and the period in which Willis conducted his research, was a time of relatively high rates of manual work, with many working-class young men choosing to leave school at the earliest opportunity (McDowell, 2003) and often finding employment in manufacturing, heavy industry, and jobs constructed as masculine because of their hard, physical, and dangerous nature (Nixon, 2018). However, as stated in Chapter Two, the 'Thatcherite Revolution' (Nayak, 2003a, p. 149), Conservative Government policy, and the onset of modern neoliberalism led to a move away from industrial work, a decline in manual jobs and a shift towards service-sector employment (Simmons et al., 2014). Subsequently, 'the types of work that most of Willis's lads had walked into in 1977 – unskilled manufacturing work with relatively good rates of pay and some prospect of security – [have] virtually disappeared' (McDowell, 2003, p. 2). As a result, service sector work currently accounts for 82% of all UK employment (Brien, 2022), with manufacturing and construction making up around 7.3% and 6.3% of jobs (ONS, 2022), respectively

The historical changes in the UK labour market and demise of heavy industry and manufacturing potentially reflect the Ladz' partial commitment to the teaching paradigm and the recognised significance of 'specific' qualifications that were identified in Chapter Four, especially considering that the mentioning of qualifications and their preferred choice of subject was always attached to their employment preference, for example: *'Maths and English … just good knowledge, isn't it. I need them to be a mechanic in it.'* (Tommy), *'Biology's interesting so I wen tha one. About the body and tha and part of paramedics, I wanna do'* (Lewis). Furthermore, when considering the current UK labour market structure, the exclusion of service sector work in the Ladz' job preferences data is noteworthy. However, as Brown (1987, p. 140) states, 'to understand the transition from school, we need to be aware of the range of occupational opportunities which are available in the local labour market'.

Startlingly dissimilar to the current UK labour market structure, yet relatively comparable to the UK labour market conditions of 1977 – manufacturing 24.3%, construction 6.4% (Syed, 2019) – within the borough in which the Ladz are situated, as of 2020, manufacturing accounted for 20.4% of employment and construction accounted for 5.6% of jobs (ONS, 2021c). The labour market conditions of the Ladz surrounding employment area reveal a disparity compared to the UK figures, with nearly three times more manufacturing than the overall UK statistics. The Ladz' local employment opportunities are also dissimilar to Wales's employment conditions, consisting of 11.2% manufacturing and 5.5% construction, thus resembling the overall UK figures. Although some contemporary UK working-class young men are employed in service sector work (Roberts, 2018) and 'learning to serve' (McDowell, 2000, 2003), considering the relatively high percentage of manufacturing work in the Ladz surrounding employment area, it may be plausible to suggest that many low-skilled working-class young men in this locality are still 'learning to labour' (Willis, 1977). However, the labour market conditions reflect the Ladz surrounding employment area and not the employment structure of their immediate place of residency. Therefore, the actual visibility of manufacturing jobs or the young people's exposure to opportunities for such employment and the subsequent impact may be somewhat questionable.

'It all goes back to family'

The previous two sections explored the Ladz' job preferences and then discussed these concerning the national, regional and local labour market. The Ladz' job choices mostly revealed – with some deviation – a relatively rigid attraction to traditionally masculine-associated working-class forms of skilled manual employment, particularly construction work (Ness, 2012; Shildrick & MacDonald, 2007; Thiel, 2007). The following two sections explore the social, cultural, and individual factors that influence the young men's choice of employment.

When discussing their employment orientation, the influence of family and kin was overwhelmingly apparent in most of the Ladz' replies. These social connections played a crucial role in the young men's understanding of employment and their work choices. For example, when I asked Craig why he favoured specific jobs, he gave the following reply:

> My brother was a plumber, and he went to the army, and he said it's hard, but you have loads of fun there. He says [brother] like 'try and do everything I've done'. So I'm going to try and go to the army.

At further points in the interview, Craig also talked excitedly about how his father took him scrap collecting with him while also mentioning that his grandfather had been employed as a coalminer. Notably, all the jobs that Craig favours are those associated with his immediate male family members, and there is a legacy of manual labour in his family. In the classical studies on working-class young men and employment, this legacy of manual labour is often attributed to a father's influence (Tolson, 1977; Veness, 1962; Willis, 1977). However, as the excerpt and data show, although Craig demonstrates an attachment to his father, this influence is less prominent and replaced by a strong attraction to his brother's employment trajectory. An explanation for this deviation is potentially found in the structure of Craig's immediate family. Although I never wholly explored the Ladz' family structure – because I felt it was inappropriate and was not the focus – Craig and several of the other young men occasionally talked about living in single-parent households headed by their mothers. The influential effect of a brother was also evident in Dan's data:

RG: Why plumbing, Dan? What is it about plumbing?

Dan: It's along the lines of fixing a bike with my brother when I was younger. Ever since he was ten [brother], he's been fixing motorbikes, so I've been brought with it. I've always thought proper work was building walls, bricklaying, plastering, carpentry and plumbing.

RG: Why do you think they are proper jobs, Dan?

Dan: Cos I've always seen people working outside and looking like they're working, all dirty instead of sitting in an office all clean and smartly dressed.

In this discussion – without explicitly using the term – Dan almost effectively explains socialisation: 'the acquisition of values, attitudes and behaviours through exposure to cultural beliefs and values during childhood' (Chesters, 2021, p. 4). Dan seems to have been raised in an environment where traditional working-class masculine forms of manual employment are the norm, and other types of employment are less visible. This process seemed to have determined his employment understanding and what he considers 'appropriately masculine work' (Roberts, 2018, p. 126) or what Dan terms *'proper work'*.

Ian's job motivation also reveals a deviation from the 'traditional' father social reproduction idea (Tolson, 1977; Veness, 1962; Willis, 1977), yet reconfirmed the influence of male relatives: *'My uncle is a carpenter, and I just like what he does and what he works as. He said he likes his job so I gave it a try, and I love it'*. The uncle's employment-related persuasion is potentially explained by Ian's father's prolonged sickness-related unemployment and his mother's ill health and incapacity to work due to an eating disorder.

Craig, Dan, and Ian's employment data demonstrate the significance of male family members or Veness's (1962, p. 69) notion of tradition-direction, which 'refers to the situation in which the choice [of employment] is predetermined by family or neighbourhood traditions because no other choice would be thinkable to the young person', or what we might consider as intergenerational transmission (Ivinson, 2014a; Jimenez & Walkerdine, 2011).

Although Billy and Cole's corresponding findings reveal some connection to male relatives, other influences, including female kin and pivotal life moments, are equally instrumental. Billy's employment aspirations revealed an attraction to cooking. When asked to explain why he favoured this type of work, the following discussion occurred:

Billy: Cos, my nan and family members helped me cook over the years. It just makes them proud to see me do something with what they have taught me.

RG: So it's the influence from your nan?

Billy: It's like my uncle, he loves Liverpool, and when I was younger, he used to buy me all the Liverpool kits. Then, I supported Liverpool. It all goes back to family, like where you start, they teach you things. It's like school, really.

Akin to Dan, Billy also demonstrates an interpretive understanding of socialisation (Chesters, 2021) and highlights the career-determined nature of family members. However, unlike the previous Ladz, rather than male kin, this impact predominantly relates to a female member, who influences a career direction other than traditional masculine-associated working-class forms of employment.

Billy's mother was a single parent, potentially explaining the significant female influence.

As stated in Chapter Four, Cole experienced a traumatic childhood that dramatically negatively affected his educational experiences. However, it equally had a significant effect on his career aspiration. Cole grew up in an abusive household and was a victim of physical and verbal abuse at the hands of his father:

> I couldn't look at him [father] the wrong way. I was made a slave, coffee, food - I was cooking from the age of ten onwards. If I done it wrong, I would have it thrown at me. I had a cup of black coffee thrown at the back of my head once. I had a knife thrown at me in the kitchen, an axe in the garden.

This abuse led social services to award custody of Cole to his grandparents. Cole's brother also died at a young age. These two traumatic childhood experiences caused Cole to suffer from post-traumatic stress disorder (PTSD): *'I sufferer from PTSD. That's through obviously my father and all the abuse and my brother in my arms at the age of six dead'*. Despite the magnitude of these two life events, an additional pivotal moment in Cole's life essentially determined and solidified his career aspiration. At age eight, Cole's aunty passed away in front of him. Being close to his aunt, Cole was allowed to visit her at the funeral parlour. The following words are Cole's depiction of this event:

> I went to see her in the chapel of rest and to see her in a completely different place, looking healthier than she did in life, with brand new clothes on lying in a wooden box, as an eight-year-old that triggers a lot of questions. A lot of curiosity struck me, and I had access to the internet. I wanted to know what it was. I was just google searching, found out about these people, found out about who does this sort of job. The people that sort it and put it into the box, and then I realised what I wanted to do [for employment].

In this excerpt, we see what Thomson et al. (2002, p. 339) refer to as 'critical moments': events depicted in narrative 'considered to be important or to have had important consequences'. However, there are also some indicators of Giddens (1991, p. 113) notion of 'fateful moments' described as: 'times when events come together in such a way that an individual stands, as it were, at a crossroads in his existence'. Although 'fateful moments' are considered to be potentially 'empowering experiences', and I would not in any way want to describe Cole's childhood experiences as 'empowering', far from it, they rigidly determine his career preference, as Cole later explained in his interview: *'I had a hard upbringing, and I knew after that, I couldn't go into like an ordinary type of job'*. However, objective analysis reveals aspects of Giddens' notion of 'fateful moments' (1991), including reflexivity, identity work, and undertaking research. Essentially, the passing of Cole's aunty and the experience of seeing her in the chapel of rest triggers Cole's curiosity and causes him to research funeral directing, which influences his career aspiration. Furthermore, this event, coupled with his childhood experiences, generates reflexivity – *'I knew after that, I couldn't go into like an ordinary type of job'* – strengthening his commitment to this profession.

The Ladz employment preferences revealed a departure from the 'traditional' father intergenerational transmission concept (Invinson, 2014a; Jimenez & Walkerdine, 2011; Tolson, 1977; Veness, 1962; Willis, 1977). However, Tommy and Lewis's corresponding data re-establish the significance of this notion.

Similar to Stan, Tommy's responses were, at times, sharp and short. However, concerning this discussion, this method of response by Tommy potentially reveals the influential strength of his father:

RG: Tommy, why do you want to do mechanics, butt?

Tommy: Cos, my dad done it!

RG: So you want to do it because your dad did it. Is that the only reason?

Tommy: Obviously! And I've always liked cars.

Tommy's responses were delivered with a 'matter of fact' attitude that almost questioned my intelligence. The sharpness and manner in which these responses are delivered demonstrate the influential role of Tommy's father and reconfirms Veness's (1962, p. 69) idea of traditional-direction and notion that 'no other choice would be thinkable to the young person'. However, interestingly, when I questioned how he might achieve employment, Tommy suggested that he would draw on family networks and social capital (Bourdieu, 1986) and ask his father's friend.

The influence of a father figure was also evident in Lewis's responses. When I asked him why he wanted to do construction, he responded: *'Because I go with my dad because he's always building shit. I dunno, he's always buying shit to build. So we are always doing tha'*. However, there is equal job preference influence by his stepfather. When asked why he wanted to be a paramedic, Lewis answered: *'I like helping people and keeping people safe from the world. I've always wanted to be a paramedic since I was six'*. I responded with: *'Why do you think that is?*' Lewis replied: *'My stepfather. He's a paramedic.'* As stated previously, there is a difference in job skill requirements or associations between these two jobs. Construction – masculinity (Ness, 2012; Thiel, 2007) and paramedic – emotional labour (Hayes et al., 2020; Hochschild, 1983) associated with feminine qualities (Leidner, 1993; McDowell, 2003). Lewis seems to have inherited both of these job-associated skills from influential male figures.

Stan was also asked about his job preference and why he wanted to work in a motorbike shop and he provided the following response: *'It's cos we've grown up around bikes and tha!'*. Akin to Tommy's previous response, this reply was delivered in a matter-of-fact manner. Although this response potentially demonstrates the influence of cultural reproduction and link to protest masculinity (Connell, 1995), sometimes, it is important to consider aspects that do not come 'up in the discussions in order to make sense of those that did' (Sennett & Cobb, 1972, p. 45). Notably, unlike the previous Ladz, there is no mention of family members and employment, and there is no mention of these aspects in Stan's ethnographic data.

As stated previously, I did not interrogate these young men about their families. I did not feel comfortable or think it was ethical to dig into the family lives of marginalised young men with somewhat difficult upbringings. If they chose to speak about their families, then I explored those topics. However, because there is a strong association between kin and employment among the other Ladz, we have to consider whether Stan's family, particularly his father, are not prominent in his life and therefore have a less influential effect on employment orientation.

Chapter Four established Wesley's job preferences for media and television. This career choice seemed external from social or cultural influence. Wesley stated that he was drawn to these professions because of the enjoyment he got from his media studies course or interpreted as what Veness (1962) refers to as Inner-direction, whereby the choice of employment is made with reference mainly to a person's interests and talents. Furthermore, when asked how he might gain employment in these professions, unlike Tommy, who mentioned family friends or what we might consider social capital (Bourdieu, 1986), Wesley talked about looking on websites. Therefore, although many of the Ladz demonstrate a masculine working-class orientation to work and mainly reject social mobility, considering the strength of their social capital (Bourdieu, 1986), coupled with the local labour market structure (ONS, 2021c), their chances of employment are arguably more significant than Wesley's, especially considering his low level of academic school achievement.

Unlike the other Ladz, the source of Wesley's media and television career orientation was never wholly revealed beyond intrinsic reward and a liking for these activities. However, Wesley was heavily involved in many media projects at the youth centre. Therefore, we could speculate whether this involvement coupled with Inner-direction (Veness, 1962) may also have contributed to Veness's (1962) notion of 'other-directed', whereby external sources influence a young person's career orientation or at least helped foster Wesley's internal attraction to media and television.

'Older generation type of boy'

The previous section demonstrated how many of the Ladz' preference for certain jobs was developed from a young age and connected to their relationships with significant family members. This section builds on that contribution and explores the Ladz' occupational self (Nixon, 2006) and the individual employment aspects that appeal to the Ladz and thus contribute to their orientation to certain forms of work.

When identifying the Ladz' preferred aspects of work, there were some individualistic elements, yet various factors connected several group members. Craig, Ian, Dan, and Cole all highlighted the importance of working outside, coupled with the masculine-associated notion of dirty work (Ivinson, 2014b; Slutskaya et al., 2016; Walkerdine & Jiménez, 2012) and the idea that 'practice is more important than theory' (Willis, 1977, p. 56).

Ian: I wanted to be something like productive, like doing something outside or anything to do with building or something. Because I'm not very bright in maths or anything like that, so it makes more sense for me to do like anything else. I like to do stuff with my hands. That's why I like the work because I wouldn't want to be stuck in an office typing away, just stuck doing the same stuff over and over.

Cole: I love being outside. I would rather be outside than stuck in an office. It would drive me insane looking at the same four walls every day. I can't sit down. I'm out in all weathers – I don't mind getting dirty. I don't mind getting wet.

These excerpts epitomise Craig, Ian, Dan, and Cole's job environment and role preferences. We see a traditional working-class commitment to manual hands-on (Nixon, 2006) 'practical' forms of employment. Ian's adherence to this type of employment is initially based on a lack of mathematical ability. Additionally, the Ladz make a natural distinction between this form of work and office work, and their replies and inability to be stationary bear a resemblance to a response given by Joey, one of the lads from *Learning to Labour*: 'I got to be moving all the time, too energetic to have a fucking desk job' (Willis, 1977, p. 104). Furthermore, although some working-class jobs have traditionally been associated with a monotonous, unrewarding experience (Beynon, 1973; Goldthorpe et al., 1969; Willis, 1977), conversely, the Ladz have an unfavourable view of middle-class professions based on their perceived repetitive and stationary nature.

When making sense of his preference for traditional working-class manual, physical employment, Cole offered the following response: *'Obviously, I grew up with my grandparents more than my parents, so I'm more older generation type of boy who would rather be out and about'*. In this reply, Cole suggests that his employment orientation would reveal generational disparity due to being raised by his grandparents. However, the data indicates otherwise, with several of the young men having a similar work preference for outdoor physical employment.

The notion of practical contrasted with theory is also evident in Billy's data, yet not in the conventional understanding of manual labour versus mental labour (Willis, 1977). As previously documented, Billy's preferred choice of employment is cooking. When making sense of this orientation, Billy stated that:

It'll [cooking] be more practical than theory, won't it. I couldn't sit in an office all day. I wouldn't have the patience for it, but with cooking these so many things on your mind, oh I done the dough, have I taken it out of the fridge, all that stuff, is more practical needs than theory, well writing down, in cooking I reckon.

In this excerpt, we yet again see the traditional working-class distinction between 'practical' work, office work/mental labour and an associated masculine necessity for active forms of employment (Roberts, 2018). However, more interesting is Billy's ability to retraditionalize (Adkins, 1999) or redefine cooking – work that has traditionally been defined as feminine (Kenway & Kraack, 2004) – within the historical working-class masculine employment meaning-making of practical versus theory (Willis, 1977). Billy's ability to redefine this form of employment is potentially supported by television programmes 'that are hosted by male chefs (e.g. Gordon Ramsey, Heston Blumenthal, Jamie Oliver) [which] may have defeminised the kitchen and allowed men to participate in cooking without compromising their masculinity' (Roberts, 2018, p. 155).

Lewis's data also shows the notion of retraditionalization (Adkins, 1999) and a redefined understanding of hands-on work. The following discussion between Lewis and me is lengthy. However, the findings potentially highlight the blurred nature of Lewis's masculine meaning-making.

RG: Why plumbing Lew?

Lewis: I dunno, it's just all in the category of getting your hands dirty ini.

RG: What is it about getting your hands dirty?

Lewis: I dunno its hand on shit like ini.

RG: What does that mean? Explain that one to me?

Lewis: Like fucking, how can I explain it? Um, I like to use my hand a lot like. My hands gotta be doing something. Cos that like the way I been brought up like to show respect, work and yeah be caring an tha. Because my mother and father broke up at a young age, well, when I was young, so I've just been brought up by my mum cos my father is a bit of a prick. When I was growing up like he left. So I've been brought up by my mother, but she's brought me up the right way.

Traditionally, a working-class inclination to practical manual and 'hands-on' (Nixon, 2006, 2017) work has been theorised and understood through protest masculinity (Connell, 1995). Although protest masculinity 'is compatible with … a sense of display which in conventional role terms is decidedly feminine' (Connell, 2005, p. 11), generally, this form of laddish-associated masculinity (Haywood & Mac an Ghaill, 2003) is often linked to values and characteristics including courage, toughness, stoicism, risk-taking and violence (Connell, 1995; Johansson & Haywood, 2017; Kimmel et al., 2005; McDowell, 2003). However, conversely, in this excerpt, Lewis associates his preference for hands-on work with respect and caring for others, a feature that Elliott (2016) affiliates with caring masculinities, which are defined as alternatives to hegemonic dominant forms of masculinity and include values that have traditionally been associated women (Elliott, 2020).

Correspondingly, when I asked Lewis why he wanted to do construction, hands-on and dirt were also mentioned: *'I just like getting my hands dirty ini. It helps my concentration because I got ADHD'*. Although this is a relatively short response, considering some of the educational data in Chapter Four, it is a reply with important significance, especially considering Tommy also offered a relatively similar response: '*I like taking things apart. It helps with my ADHD'.* (Tommy).

As stated above, whereas an attraction to 'hands-on' work and manual labour has previously been associated with a working-class identity (Nixon, 2006; Willis, 1977) and protest masculinity (Connell, 1995), Lewis and Tommy now associate their attraction to this employment with their learning disability. Therefore, akin to aspects of the Ladz' educational data, there is an indication of learning disability meaning-making. In other words, the young men make sense of their decisions and behaviour in accordance with their learning disabilities. Furthermore, the Ladz' learning disabilities and their subsequent explanation for their behaviour result from a medical diagnosis. Consequently, although I do not want to disregard this diagnosis and the difficulties that these young men face, collectively and arguably, there is a possible case for understanding the Ladz' behaviour and disability meaning-making within the context of medicalization (Rose, 2007), defined as: 'interpreting newer and newer aspects of reality, including human behaviour, in medical terms, and treating them as medical problems rather than e.g. social, political or existential ones' (Kaczmarek, 2019, p. 119). For example, protest masculinity and the behaviour commonly associated with it, including disruptive classroom behaviour and a preference for manual hands-on work (Connell, 1995), is/was considered to arise from a position of powerlessness and condition of poverty (Connell, 1995). Essentially, protest masculinity and the associated behaviour are deemed to be cultural and structural consequences. Conversely, the Ladz' disability meaning-making attached to a medical diagnosis negates the previously associated social, political, and cultural issues and treats their behaviour as an individualistic medical problem, thus corresponding with the definition of medicalization (Kaczmarek, 2019).

Dan's work orientation findings additionally indicate socialisation (Chesters, 2021) and how his 'preferences for particular types of work develop[ed] from classed and gendered experiences from a young age' (Nixon, 2006, p. 210): '*I like fixing things. I don't know – it's weird. It's like Lego – connecting Lego but with pipes and that. I just find it fun'.* Conversely, as the following discussion shows, Tommy and Stan prefer to be destructive.

Tommy: I've always liked breaking stuff and taking things apart.

Stan: Yeah, boy! I love taking things apart.

Tommy: Exactly!

Stan: But it's fucking weird putting things back together.

Tommy and Stan's destructive preference is potentially explained by their hyper-masculine (Mac an Ghaill, 1994) identity and physical actions that facilitate a masculine bodily display of strength, toughness, and aggression. In distinct contrast to Tommy, Stan and the rest of the Ladz, Wesley demonstrated an additional intrinsic association with work and favoured an employment experience that made him proud of himself.

'Everyone knows each other'

The previous sections have explored the Ladz' career orientation and the factors that influence this. Generally, the young men demonstrate a preference for employment that will require academic achievement and training. However, considering the Ladz' challenging school behaviour, there is a likelihood that some of the young men will fail to achieve this career aspiration, especially considering their pragmatic approach to education. Take Tommy, for example, the Level 1 motor vehicle maintenance course he favours requires 3 GCSEs at grades A*-E, including Maths/Numeracy and English/Welsh. However, his selective, limited school engagement reduces his likelihood of achieving these necessary grades.

Furthermore, although the Borough has disproportionately high manufacturing rates, this form of employment may be negatively affected by projected future employment changes towards automation due to its predictable physical nature, making it easier to replicate by machines and thus more susceptible to automation (Frey & Osborne, 2017). In collective consideration of these factors, the following section explores the Ladz willingness to commute and consider relocating for employment.

For most of the Ladz, when questioned and discussing the possibility of moving out of the community to find employment, a sense of commitment to their family and the notion of ontological security was evident. Giddens (1991, pp. 38–39) defines ontological security as a:

> person's fundamental sense of safety in the world and includes a basic trust of other people. Obtaining such trust becomes necessary in order for a person to maintain a sense of psychological well-being and avoid existential anxiety.

Simply put, ontological security refers to continuity in a person's life and environment. These notions of continuity, trust and security were particularly noticeable in most of the Ladz' data. However, there was equal recognition of the limited opportunities in the area and the necessity to find employment outside of the immediate locality. For example, when asked if he would leave the community, myself and Billy engaged in the following discussion:

> Say towards Cardiff or something. But like, I wouldn't wanna move out of the valley, but if I got the opportunity to take my career path further, if they asked me to move out, I'd probably say yeah. It's just, cos in the valleys, it's not boring. It's just. It's just limited amount of things you can do really ini.

In response to this reply, I offered the following question: *'Ok, why would you think about staying in the valley? What would keep you in the valley, butt?'*. Billy gave the following answer:

> The amount of **family** I've got in the valleys so. I got loads of **family** members in the valleys, and it's like **everyone knows each other**

here. You see someone on the street, and it's like, 'alright butt'. **Everyone knows each other**. It's like a little **community** like ini. **Everyone's got each other back** ini.

This excerpt is riddled with the fundamental features of ontological security. There is trust and continuity: *'Family', 'everyone knows each other',* and security: *'Everyone's got each other back'.* Essentially, Billy still identifies with the norms and values – solidarity, community – commonly associated with working-class communities, particularly those related to heavy industry (Ivinson, 2014a; Walkerdine & Jiménez, 2012; Ward, 2015).

A reluctance to relocate, the importance of family, and a commitment to remaining spatially close to these social connections echoed in Tommy, Stan, Craig, Cole and Dan's findings: *'I wouldn't move away for fucking anything!'* (Tommy). *'I'd go to England for two hundred grand a year'* (Stan). *'I wouldn't move too far away because I love my family to bits'* (Craig). *In a reasonable distance like – I wouldn't go miles. family are everything'* (Cole). *'Cardiff is probably the furthest. Just because I've got loads of family here, I wouldn't want to start in a new place'* (Dan). Family was also evident in Lewis's data:

> I don't think I would actually work away from family. I'd rather be where my family cos if I'm not with my family, I feel like I'm **letting them down**, so I'd rather be around my family to **stick up for them** just in case anything happens. I've always been family is everything in life, thas what I know, respect your family like. **I've always stuck up for my family**. I've been in trouble so many times for people having a go at my family.

Notably, although there is a continuation of family importance in this excerpt, there are additional interesting aspects. The traditional notions of the breadwinner ideology (Williams, 2008) refer to a sole male economic provider. However, this idea also assumes a male head of the household that takes care of and protects his family. Even though the excerpt excludes any mention of financial support, Lewis does demonstrate features associated with a breadwinner ideology, including a masculine emphasis on protecting and supporting his family.

In contrast to the other seven Ladz, Ian and Wesley did demonstrate a favourable view of moving away from the community. However, Ian's view is also inversely related to the community:

> I'd move away in a heartbeat! This place is dragging a lot of people down and stopping people from getting opportunities. Like if you wanted to get a job in London and you say you live in this area, they put a bad mark on you because you live here.

Ian's reply echoes Tyler's (2020, p. 8) definition of stigma: 'degrading marks that are affixed to particular bodies, people, conditions and places within humiliating social interactions'. Ian suggests that belonging and being affiliated with his community decreases life chances (Weber, 1948) due to the area's stigmatising ability.

Wesley also favoured moving out of the community, yet for a different reason. Throughout his interview, Wesley continuously emphasised the overwhelming need to be independent. This necessity is displayed in Wesley's reply regarding employment and his community:

> I want to get out. I don't want to be nasty, but I want to get out and move somewhere else. I don't mind where. I just need to get out of this place and survive on my own.

The source of Wesley's desire for independence was never revealed, and due to his timid nature, he was a relatively tricky young man to communicate with. However, I have considered two possible explanations. Firstly, this objective may be linked to a hegemonic masculine identity associated with success, self-reliance and independence (Courtenay, 2000; Rogers et al., 2021). However, I also speculate that this desire might also arguably be linked to Wesley's timid character and a possible need to escape and portray himself differently, thus paradoxically also exposing a commitment to hegemonic masculine values and traits of self-reliance and independence (Courtenay, 2000; Rogers et al., 2021).

'Buy a new car, get a house'

The Ladz' commitment to their family, kinship and associated working-class values of community and solidarity challenge neoliberalist discourse that assumes that these beliefs have broken down, and in the absence of long-term work and due to structural changes in the economy and new labour market conditions, people need to make themselves more competitive (Walkerdine & Jiménez, 2012). The structural changes and accompanying ideas have been supported by a political and cultural shift towards responsibilisation and risk management, where individuals are encouraged to invest in a 'neoliberal project of the self' (Walkerdine, 2003). Furthermore, by investing in this project and 'being adaptable to change, undergoing constant reinvention of the self and risk-taking, individuals are believed to be able to respond to the demands of neoliberal capitalism and become socially mobile' (Folkes, 2021, p. 5). A summary of these ideas can be found in the words of Bauman (1988, p. 62): 'Everyone has to ask himself the question 'who am I', 'how should I live', 'who do I want to become' – and at the end of the day, be prepared to accept responsibility for the answer ... Self-construction of the self is, so to speak, a necessity'. Those who reject this individualist rhetoric, fail to conform to these beliefs, and prefer to be in their home community, are thought to lack bravery and aspiration to compete in the neoliberal labour market (Mannay, 2013). Therefore, within the context of these ideas and the reflexive identity project (Giddens, 1991), the Ladz' commitment to their area and traditional working-class beliefs signify them as having an aspiration deficit. However, all of the Ladz do have clear life goals and ambitions.

Cole, Craig, Wesley, and Dan demonstrated a clear commitment to 'conventional' long-term ambitions (Simmons et al., 2014) of a house, car, wife and family:

Craig: in twenty years, I'm not gonna be as dead rich as I wanna be, but I know I'll at least have like a couple of thousand. So I'll buy a new car, buy a new flat for a bit and then get a house.

Wesley: I'd like a job where I want to go and get loads of money and travel and help stuff like feeding the family and all that. That would be good.

Dan: Hopefully, I earn £1200 or something like that. That's enough to pay your bills, buy food and clothes. I'll maybe have a girlfriend too, and if she had a job as well, it would be sound. We can rent a house and save a bit for a mortgage.

These three excerpts offer an interesting comparative analysis, especially considering the young men's personality traits. Firstly, Craig's emphasis on money stems from an understanding 'that one must earn to make one's way, to live, survive or thrive in the capitalist world' (Roberts, 2018, p. 112). Comparatively and interestingly, despite Wesley's timid and mild demeanour, his ideas around wealth and his notion of *'feeding the family'* possibly align with the hegemonic masculine ideas of a wage-earner and breadwinner ideology (Archer et al., 2001; Connell, 1995). Conversely, Dan, whose hyper-masculine and protest masculine (Connell, 1995; Connell & Messerschmidt, 2005; Walker, 2006) attitude and behaviour have been demonstrated in previous sections, discusses the possibility of sharing bills with his girlfriend, an idea that corresponds with the 'egalitarian family and dual-earner breadwinner model' (Hobson, 2002, p. 16).

None of these excerpts focus on excessive wealth and the neoliberalist ideals of social mobility (Folkes, 2021). However, Reay (2013) suggests that a desire for affluence and power only exists among a few. Conversely, these ladz' responses echo working-class ideas of being ontologically secure and having enough to emotionally and physically survive (Walkerdine et al., 2001).

Despite this notion of being comfortable and secure, some of the Ladz did demonstrate a commitment to becoming socially mobile. For example, Tommy and Stan discussed the possibility of collectively owning their own motorbike shop, but this goal seemed motivated by a protest masculine attraction to motorbikes (Connell, 1995). Billy equally discussed the possibility of having a business, and when questioned about this, Billy offered the following response: *'My ultimate goal is to open my own restaurant'*. I questioned this answer by saying: *'Is this career goal about money or something else'*. Billy gave the following reply:

No **being known** in it. It's a bit about the money, obviously. But it's mainly like **being known**. Like, if a family with like young children an tha or my children my age now and they think, oh there a new restaurant open or he's supposed to be good, like It tha urge of being known in it, the satisfaction of being known, people think positive about my work, praise me.

This response by Billy is interesting and potentially has a couple of explanations. Considering Billy's previous educational data and his notion of reciprocal respect and self-worth (Jackson, 2002), Billy's notion of *'being known'* is possibly an attempt to gain dignity from his employment (Sennett & Cobb, 1972). However, Billy's idea of *'being known'* equally needs to be considered within the context of contemporary society. Youth culture is currently dominated by social media (Lee et al., 2020), including Facebook, Instagram, Twitter, and Snapchat. These forms of social media – particularly Facebook – work on a system where users can 'like' other users' posts. This interaction can and sometimes does deliver social validation and gratification (Sherman et al., 2016). Arguably, Billy's response echoes this process. Billy is driven by external validations, including *'being known'* and people thinking positively about his work and praising him.

Whereas some of the Ladz discussed their future goals, Lewis also spoke about his current employment ambitions. Lewis was in college and received a £30 a week education maintenance allowance[1] and saved this money to pay for motorbike insurance. However, Lewis's mother wanted him to contribute to the family income and pay rent. Therefore, Lewis had attempted to gain employment in a local pub. In the following excerpts, Lewis discusses this experience:

Lewis: I have been trying to get a job. I went for this interview down the pub, and they turned around and said, 'Well, we can't take you on'. I asked why and they said because of who you are. And I was like, wha do you mean? They asked wha my background was and tha, and they said we can't take you on just in case you snap.

RG: What did they ask about your background?

Lewis: How I was growing up like. And I told them about my anger problems. I said I snap really easily when I'm under pressure. They said, look, we can't take you on cos your problems, just in case you snap, which is understandable in a way, but it does have an effect on my self-confidence. That's the biggest issue I got. I haven't got any confidence anyway.

There are a few aspects of this section that are worthy of consideration. Firstly, we see the difficulties of a working-class status whereby Lewis is asked/ expected to contribute to the family income whilst still in education. This predicament is possibly less likely in a middle-class home with a higher income (Reay, 2017). Secondly and more interestingly is the interview experience, the discussion

---

[1]A payment for 16- to 18-year-olds living in Wales, who want to continue their education after school leaving age

and an outcome that arguably reflects contemporary society and issues that some working-class young men may face.

Historically, the traditional markers of hegemonic and/or protest masculinity, including courage, toughness, stoicism, and risk-taking (Cheng, 1999; McDowell, 2003), have prevented many men from discussing their 'psychological health since displaying a concern for one's well-being may be deemed feminine or weak' (Sloan et al., 2015, p. 206). However, conformity to these masculine ideals has been argued to have a harmful effect on the mental health of males (Courtenay, 2000) and is associated with suicidal ideation and suicide in young adults and adolescents (Coleman, 2015). In response to these issues, together with a push for equality and an egalitarian society, contemporary young men have been encouraged to share and express their feelings and emotions (McQueen, 2017). This emphasis has helped generate catchphrases such as *'It's okay not to be okay'*.

When considering the previous section within the context of Lewis's data, there are corresponding similarities. For example, although Lewis associates his anger and aggression with his ADHD, these traits are also associated with protest masculinity and/or hegemonic masculinity (Connell, 1995; Kimmel et al., 2005). Therefore, traditionally, Lewis would have possibly been inclined to suppress emotions (Sloan et al., 2015), especially during an interview process and an employment opportunity. However, Lewis chooses to confess to his issues and adheres to the notion that: *'It's okay not to be okay'*. However, in response to this openness, instead of support and help, Lewis is rejected. This act of rejection intensifies Lewis's emotional distress and further weakens his existing fragile sense of self-confidence. Thus, we arguably see the emergence of a new identity issue where some working-class young men are still inheriting traditional masculine values while also trying to adhere to 'new' contemporary ideas of masculinity (McQueen, 2017) in a society unprepared to deal with this complexity.

As the following excerpt shows, similarly to Lewis, Ian also slightly deviated from a specific focus on career ambition and focused on personal goals.

RG: Have you got any career ambitions, Ian?

Ian: It's just success – that's one thing I want to see because all my family just, most of them have succeeded. I wanna prove everybody wrong that I can succeed.

RG: What does success look like to you?

Ian: Success is a wealthy job – not a wealthy job, a happy job and all that.

Ian seems driven by an internal need to emulate the success of his family members and prove others wrong. Additionally, Ian's data reveals a commonality among the majority of the Ladz. Although Ian seems to recognise the necessity of money, intrinsic reward is also important to him. Conversely, as the following excerpt demonstrates, Willis (1977) lads were purely driven by extrinsic reward and financial gain. The idea that a job itself could deliver intrinsic happiness and satisfaction was dismissed:

Joey: It's just a … fucking way of earning money. There's that many ways to do it (…) jobs all achieve the same, they make you money, nobody does a job for the love or a Job (…) you wouldn't do it for nothing. I don't think anyone would, you need the bread to live (…) there's a difference in the actual ways you do 'em, but it's there like, they all achieve the same end, they all achieve money (Willis, 1977, p. 100).

The notion of extrinsic reward and dead-end jobs (Ashton & Field, 1976) are themes that populate much of the early school-to-work and employment studies based on working-class males. For example, Goldthorpe et al. (1968a) study of male workers from three Luton (UK) based factories found that many workers experienced no reward from work itself and were primarily motivated by extrinsic reward. This notion of financial incentive is equally found in Beynon's (1973, p. 122) classic employment study: 'You work for money. That's what it's all about', and Carter's (1969, p. 166) school-to-work transition study: 'Can't expect much from work – you just have to do it'. In contrast to these studies and despite similarities with Willis's (1977) lads, the Ladz value and desire intrinsic reward.

Craig: It's not all about the money. It's just like getting a job. I just wanna get a job when I'm older and have a happy life and everything.

Dan: Imagine having a really good paid job, but you don't like it – I would hate that. I would just go for something with a lot less pay, but I do like it.

Wesley: I'm not going to a job just for the money. As long as I enjoy it, then I don't care.

Ian: Do a job you enjoy instead of hate. I would rather get £4 a week doing something I enjoy than get a million pounds a day [emphasis] just for doing a job I hate. Money doesn't make the world go round.

Conversely to the above quotation from Joey – one of the lads (Willis, 1977) – and his emphasis on pure extrinsic reward, although Craig recognises the importance of money, these four excerpts demonstrate an almost opposite perspective of employment, where work is first and foremost about intrinsic reward instead of financial gain.

Cole also sought intrinsic reward from his work. However, as the following quotation shows, this intrinsic reward is deeply associated with his life experiences and 'critical moments' (Thomson et al., 2002).

Cole: Work is about enjoyment! The money is just a big bonus. It's a sense of…the responsibilities I just had with burying of a family to dispose of the deceased in a safe and professional manner, I've done it – I've obviously back-filled. I've obviously done my job – they now have got their closure, and they can grieve. So that's like big. Losing my brother, that had a big impact on me growing up, and I didn't get a chance to have [closure], what I give to other people. Do you know what I mean? It makes me feel good about myself. It makes me feel better.

As this excerpt demonstrates, Craig's critical moments (Thomson et al., 2002) have not only shaped his career orientation but also influenced his desire to help others achieve closure, which subsequently provides him with intrinsic reward.

Despite the emphasis on intrinsic reward, Stan offered a response that was almost a duplication of Joey's (lads) previous citation:

Stan: There's no enjoyment in any work really is there. Like waking up in the morning and tha. It's like school but a bit better, probably. You only do it to get money. It depends what job you do, really. If you're a fucking scientist or something, then it's fucking shit!

Not only is this response similar to Joey's above quotation, but Stan mentioning of waking up in the morning also echoes an additional response by Joey: 'No job's enjoyable 'cos of the fact that you've got to get up of a morning and go out when you could stop in bed' (Willis, 1977, p. 102). Furthermore, although middle–class professions – scientist – are perceived to be superior forms of employment due to autonomy, Stan explicitly dismisses this type of work.

'The same stuff over and over'

The previous sections have explored the ladz career orientation and the social, cultural and individual determining factors. These two final sections assess the kinds of work and employment aspects that the Ladz disfavoured and why.

As the data hinted earlier, in contrast to the masculine physical forms of employment that the Ladz favoured, sedentary work was regarded unfavourably, particularly office work:

Ian: My worst job would be working in an office. I hate office working. The same stuff over and over! In the job where I am now, we do the same stuff, but we do it at different times and places. It's like we do tiling one day, but the next time we do tiling, it could be a taller room and a different place.

Cole: I couldn't be stuck in an office. It would drive me insane looking at the same four walls every day. I couldn't sit there all day with that sense of feeling enclosed.

As these two excerpts show, in contrast to the notion that some forms of working-class jobs are dead-end, monotonous (Beynon, 1973), unrewarding, and lack autonomy, Ian and Cole associate these features with office work and employment that has middle-class ties. An aversion to confinement and being seated was also evident in Dan's findings:

Dan: Bus driving is one of the worst jobs I wouldn't want to do. It's just boring sitting down, driving stuck in a little place on your own. Bus driving ain't the worse – I would rather that over the office cos you interact with more people and have a laugh and tha.

This quotation demonstrates Dan's opposition to bus driving due to perceived sedentary, confined working conditions. Although this response correlates with Ian and Cole's office-related responses, Dan's preference for bus driving – as opposed to office work – and the reasoning are particularly significant.

Although Dan dislikes both bus driving and office work, he expresses an inclination towards the former based on greater interaction and the ability to have a laugh. The importance of having a laugh – referred to as 'laff' in *Learning to Labour* – was integral to the lads' school experience and primarily used to 'defeat boredom and fear, and to overcome hardships and problems' (Willis, 1977, p. 29). The use of laughter to overcome certain work conditions – particularly mundanity – is a common feature of working-class employment-related studies (Collinson, 1988; Nixon, 2009; Roy, 1959). Subsequently, Dan's mentioning of laughter within the context of his discussion demonstrates a correlation between these studies. Furthermore, the significance of laughter correlates with Chapter Four's findings, whereby teacher and pupil relationships were strengthened through humour.

The two jobs that Craig disfavoured were a writer and a police officer. The following excerpt shows Craig's rationale:

Craig: Being a writer or a Police Officer – I would hate to be one because you have to fill out ten pages every minute. You have to do it really quick – your hands will be aching at the end of the day. And a Police Officer, I wouldn't be like that because when you catch a guy, you have to get up, write all the things down. And I wouldn't be happy just to sit down – it'd be boring!

Craig's response reinforces the Ladz' dislike of sedentary work and reconfirms the association with boredom. Craig also mentions his aversion to writing and bases this on repetitive strain. However, coincidentally, the education findings revealed that Craig experienced difficulties in English.

Police officers were also mentioned in Tommy and Stan's responses to disliked jobs:

RG: What job wouldn't you like to do, boys?

Tommy: Probably a Police Officer.

RG: Why wouldn't you want to be a Police Officer?

Stan: Or yeah, a Police Officer. Because they are fucking pigs! (aggressive tone)

Tommy: I hate them. I hate their guts! (laughter)

RG: Why?

Stan: Do you know if I got forced to be a Police Officer, Richard! I would fucking (raised voice) commit suicide!

RG: Why don't you like Police Officers Tommy?

Stan: Who the fuck does?

Tommy: Cause they're smelly ugly cunts!

As was evident in their educational data – particularly Stan's – this excerpt is overwhelmingly riddled with a vocal display of antiauthority (Willis, 1977), protest (Connell, 1995) and/or hyper-masculinity (Mac an Ghaill, 1994) that is manifested through an aggressive disdain for police officers. Furthermore, there is terminological use that is additionally noteworthy, particularly by Stan. Firstly, Stan explicitly uses my name. This use reveals a relatively 'clever' feature of Stan's linguistic ability. Whenever Stan wanted to emphasise a point or control the interview, 'Richard' was used loudly and deliberately. Moreover, there is a meaning-making assumption that all individuals dislike the police, thus arguably emphasising his hostility towards this form of authority while also potentially demonstrating a feature of coalfield communities and a historical distrust of the police that often originates from the 1980s mining strikes and police brutality (Bright, 2012; Simpson, 2021).

'I don't take shit off nobody'

Service sector employment often requires emotional labour (Hochschild, 1983). That is, the ability to manage feelings and suppress emotions. Due to the qualities needed to undertake these types of public-facing service sector work, Nixon (2018, p. 64) argues that this form of employment 'may be particularly challenging for [working-class] men, whose embodied masculinity seems particularly at odds with the kinds of skills, attributes and dispositions required'. Nixon's claim has been supported by various studies that demonstrate working-class men's reluctance to engage in service sector work or opting for more masculine roles in distribution and warehousing (Leidner, 1993; McDowell, 2003; Nixon, 2006, 2009; Walkerdine & Jiménez, 2012).

Roberts (2018) offers an additional perspective on working-class men and service sector work and suggests that his 'missing middle' participants no longer fully subscribe to traditional norms of masculinity and are instead modelling a more inclusive form of masculinity (Anderson, 2009) that is more in tune with the emotional labour (Hochschild, 1983) requirements of service sector work.

In keeping with these working-class studies, this final section explores the Ladz' view towards service sector work and their ability to engage in emotional labour (Hochschild, 1983). Although the Ladz' local employment conditions include a relatively high percentage of manufacturing work, similarly to many coalfield areas, the South Wales Valleys also have a significant amount of call centre employment (Beatty et al., 2019). This type of service sector work often requires historically 'prize 'feminized' attributes such as keyboard skills and communication proficiency' (Nayak, 2003c, p. 56). Therefore, based on the Ladz' pragmatic approach to education that makes their preferred employment choice speculative and additional employment possibilities realistic, the young men's attitude towards call centre work was assessed through visual methods.

All of the Ladz were shown a picture of a call centre. They were then asked to identify the work presented in the image and express their thoughts and feelings about the job and the work environment. The following experts are some of the Ladz' responses:

Craig: Nah! [laughs]. Sometimes people rage on the phone, and you have to keep calm and try and hold your anger back, and then you can't, and you just say okay, bye! I'd go round their house and bang them out!

Stan: Fuck that! That's the fucking worst job ever! That's another version of school boy.

Billy: Office work. That's boring! It doesn't interest me. I'm not good with stuff like phones and tha. I can't talk to people like tha. And like, people when they got problems they get angry, and I'd end up getting angry at them, and then I'll lose my job. People need to be calm, don't they? When managing people over the phone, It's just if they were lipping me, I would go nuts.

Tommy: I would never do that because it would be too many people talking at once, and I'd get frustrated and fucking slap them.

Ian: Call centre. Depressing! I would hate to do that. You get spoken to like garbage. Horrible! A lot of people must have a lot of abuse doing that. I would say something back, and I know you're not allowed.

Wesley: If I had to do it and I needed the money, I would. My aunty used to be one, and she said it's all right, but if you're in a bad mood that day, you could get angry, and someone might report you, and you'd be out. People think I'm a really lovely boy, but my anger can go like that sometimes. I could lose my job because of it sometimes.

Lewis: It's a boring man's job. You gotta sit there fucking hours, just speaking shit to people. I don't like talking to people I don't know, and that's what that is ini. I wouldn't do tha job, I know for a fact. I'd fuck up in two minutes. I'd probably tell them to fuck off and end the phone call [laughs]. I don't take shit off nobody!

Although previous studies (Leidner, 1993; McDowell, 2003; Nixon, 2006, 2009; Walkerdine & Jiménez, 2012) have documented working-class men's reluctance to engage in certain forms of service sector work, Roberts (2018) argues that these studies are dated and focus on older or unemployed men. Therefore, the differentiation in his findings may be explained by the recentness of his study and 'young working-class men [that] are not hostage to the traditional predispositions held by their counterparts from previous generations' (Roberts, 2018,

p. 121). Whereas this claim may be valid for Roberts' 'missing middle' study sample, the previous findings of this study do indicate 'traditional predispositions', with many of the Ladz demonstrating an inclination towards traditionally associated working-class forms of employment and displaying protest and/or hegemonic masculine (Cornell, 1995) values and behaviour. This masculine identity is also noticeable in the young men's view of service sector work.

The above five excerpts demonstrate the young men's reluctance to engage in service sector work. One of the crucial factors that makes service sector work unappealing is the possibility of being talked down to or *'spoken to like garbage'* and the Ladz inability to engage in emotional labour (Hochschild, 1983) and manage their feelings and suppress emotions. Instead, the Ladz favour speaking their mind, sticking up for themselves (McDowell, 2003) and 'fronting up' – physically in some instances – when challenged. This notion of defending one's honour and dignity is crucial to expressing hegemonic (Kimmel, 2008) and working-class masculinity (Nixon, 2006; 2009).

The findings indicate that the Ladz are reluctant to engage in service sector work because of their working-class masculine identity, an argument proposed by previous studies (Leidner, 1993; McDowell, 2003; Nixon, 2006, 2009). Although Roberts (2018, p. 145) suggests that this notion is 'damaging and offers a simplistic, almost victim-blaming, rendering of young working-class men's labour market difficulties in contemporary times', it is equally important to identify and highlight the constraining and adverse nature of structural and social inequality and their ability to determine and limit employment outcomes.

An additional aspect and a reoccurring theme that also makes the call centre work unfavourable is the sedentary nature of the work. This theme is also distinguishable in Dan's response to service sector work imagery:

Dan: It's not my thing like. I would find it boring. You are just sitting on a computer. It's just boring like. I like doing more things practical. An office is like smart suits, writing and computers. Offices you have to be smart and all that don't you to get a tidy office job, smart, **clever** like. With a trade, they **give you a chance**. Like my brother, at the age of ten, he just always had it –he learnt himself. But some people try that, and they just can't do it. So you've either got it, or you haven't – that's what I mean by getting your hands dirty. You **either sort of got it, or you haven't.**

Although this excerpt reconfirms Dan's masculine working-class identity and preference for practical, physical forms of employment, there are additional noteworthy aspects. Dan's notion of *'clever'* and *'give you a chance'* potentially reveals the hidden injuries of class (Sennett & Cobb, 1972), whereby Dan does not think he is clever enough or incapable of doing office work. Conversely, Dan seems to suggest that trades and manual work require and draw on inherent or socialised (Chesters, 2021) values or abilities – *'either sort of got it, or you haven't'.*

Unlike the previous Ladz, Cole did not comprehensively discuss the call centre imagery, and although he also offered an adverse response to the call centre picture, his ability or inability to engage in emotional labour (Hochschild, 1983) is relatively unclear in this reply:

Cole: No, thank you. Call office – it would drive me insane. Sat in a rammed room with all them voices and trying to speak to someone on the phone. I don't mind a bit of retail, but it would have to be warehouse work, that sort of thing. I couldn't do shops – the frustration of so many people around me constantly, the fuss – you know what women are like shopping, they are always fussing about.

Although Cole mentions his frustration with noise, it would be disingenuous to claim that this is evidence of emotional labour (Hochschild, 1983) inabilities. However, this excerpt does confirm his protest and/or hegemonic masculinity. Akin to the low-skilled, poorly educated men from Nixon's (2006, 2009) employment study, Cole opts for masculine roles in warehousing where customer interaction and the need for emotional labour (Hochschild, 1983) is minimal. Additionally, there is also a potential element of sexism in Cole's response – *'you know what women are like shopping, they are always fussing about'*. Furthermore, Cole disfavours the predicament of having many people around him, whereas social interaction was identified as an enjoyable aspect of Roberts (2018) respondents' retail employment experience.

Due to Cole's reply and the limited evidence of his ability or inability to engage in emotional labour (Hochschild, 1983), I asked him the following question: *'What are you like dealing with people in your work? Have you ever dealt with angry people?'* Cole gave the following response:

Yeah, I had some guy back a few weeks back threaten to knock my head off my shoulders because he thought our machine had run over his mother's grave. But I promised him it didn't, and I de-fuelled the fire straight away.

Cole's response indicates an ability to engage in emotional labour and begins to reveal a disparity that I found in some of the Ladz' findings and replies.

Together with the call centre imagery, in an attempt to explore the young men's ability to engage in emotional labour and their masculine identity, I also asked them how they would fare taking orders from management or a boss. The following excerpts are some of the Ladz' replies:

Billy: Yeah, not if they were trying to be a twat, but if they were doing it for my benefit, then I'd be comfortable with it. Like you should know, when people are bossing you around, they wanna get the best out of you.

Dan: Yeah, I'll do it. I'll do it easy. Because if they didn't tell me to do this or do that, then I wouldn't know what to do or where to go. There's always someone higher than you to tell you what to do unless you own your company like, which I want to hopefully soon.

Cole: The person I work beside, he's fully qualified. I've got no qualifications really, except for the work experience at the minute. So at the minute, I don't mind taking orders. I would rather someone instruct me and tell me how to do something or show me how to do something, so I can learn and adapt.

Wesley: It depends what it is. It depends what you want me to do. If I'm bad at it, and I know I'm bad, I wouldn't mind because I need how to learn how to do it.

Tommy: You'll have to listen, won't you!

Stan: I'd bang him out! No one is ordering me about!

Apart from Stan, which I have included to demonstrate the difference, these excerpts indicate that some of the Ladz are able and willing to be submissive to authority and accept orders. This notion contrasts with their school data and the Ladz' antiauthority displays of protest masculinity (Connell, 1995) towards teachers. However, additional analysis and consideration reveal a crucial theme identified in the young men's educational data. Excluding Stan, the responses show that the Ladz are prepared to accept orders and commands on the basis that these will enhance their employment capabilities and make them more proficient. This notion reveals a continuation of the pragmatic approach that the Ladz adopted to school. Essentially, certain school subjects and orders are tolerated because of the perceived ability to enhance the Ladz' life chances (Weber, 1948) and employment prospects.

Conclusion

This chapter mainly demonstrates that although some contemporary working-class young men embrace service sector work (Roberts, 2018), the Ladz mainly reject this form of employment due to the perceived inability to engage in emotional labour (Hochschild, 1983). Correspondingly, despite evidence that some contemporary working-class young men are not 'not merely inherit[ing] older generations of men's dispositions towards and understanding of appropriately masculine work (Robert, 2018, p. 126), similarly to the lads (Willis, 1977), some of the Ladz are attracted to masculine manual forms of employment due to socialisation or intergenerational transmission (Ivinson, 2014a; Walkerdine & Jiménez, 2012) that derives from family, friends and prominent male figures (Tolson, 1977; Veness, 1962; Willis, 1977). However, this chapter equally demonstrates that specific social influences have destabilised traditional predispositions towards manual employment among some of the Ladz. In summary, this chapter argues that the Ladz demonstrate both continuity and change and inconsistencies with Roberts (2018) recent findings, thus raising questions about why these contradictions exist and how we might explain them. The following final empirical chapter explores the Ladz' social relations and masculinities.

Chapter Six

The Ladz and Masculinities

Introduction

This final findings chapter is primarily based on my ethnographic observations and discussions with the Ladz at the youth centre. The chapter explores the Ladz' masculine identity within the context of social relations and their relationships with each other, women and their views towards homosexuality while also documenting their open expressions of emotion and compassion. The chapter tries to capture the complexity of the Ladz' masculine identity and show that although these young men do demonstrate behaviour and views that are commonly associated with protest masculinity and display continuities with the lads (Willis, 1977), they equally engage in practices and discourse that may historically be considered as contradictory including same-sex touch, emotional openness, compassion and egalitarian views. Therefore, this chapter raises questions about the construction of contemporary laddish identity and the current understanding of this subgroup of working-class young men and their masculinity.

A Valley Boy Perspective

As previously stated, unlike previous male sociologists 'who worked hard at school, did their homework, passed exams [and] have lovingly chronicled the rebellion and resistance of the hooligans to schooling' (Delamont, 2000, p. 99), my youthful educational years were primarily dedicated to 'dossing, blagging, wagging' (Willis, 1977, p. 26) and tied to a counter-school culture. Subsequently, I arrived at my research site with a lived understanding of the lads (Willis, 1977) category. Although I do not assume that my previous 'laddish' (Francis, 1999; Jackson, 2006; McDowell, 2003) experiences and perceptions are wholly representational of laddish culture, my ethnographic observations were influenced and interpreted through the context of my biography (O'Reilly, 2009). Due to my

The 21st Century Ladz: Continuity and Changes among Marginalised
Young Men from the South Wales Valleys, 97–114
Copyright © 2025 by Richard Gater. Published by Emerald Publishing Limited.
doi:10.1108/978-1-83797-631-720251007

lived understanding of the lads (Willis, 1977) category, behaviour and discourse that were familiar (Mannay, 2010) and unfamiliar to me often drew my attention and subsequent observation, and I believe that 'my personal experience sensitise [d] me to things that others [potentially] wouldn't notice' (Bourdieu, 2001, 0: 44: 10). Consequently, this chapter and its findings and themes are the results of this process and therefore deviates from the trend of the previous findings chapters and the significant focus on interview data and alternatively incorporates a greater proportion of ethnographic findings and my observations of the Ladz' behaviour at the youth centre. This data is discussed and explored through both the context of my laddish biography and relevant literature.

'We don't do it the old-fashioned way'

One of the most strikingly unusual patterns of the Ladz' social behaviour for me was their method of greeting each other. As a lad of the 1990s era, a period when laddish behaviour 'gained renewed prominence in popular and media culture' (Jackson, 2006, p. 4), among my peers and the lads group that I associated with, the method of greeting each other was often verbal in the form of *'Alright, butt'*, and if one wanted to express a more dominant masculine presence, this gesture was sometimes coupled with a nod of the head. My youthful recollection of male greeting practices shares similarities with a response offered by Martin, the lead youth worker at the youth centre who was a similar age to me:

Martin: It was always…I don't know if boys ever really kind of even shook hands or anything like that back then. I've always been old Valleys, like a nod, you know or whatever.

RG: Old valleys as in…? Elaborate on that for me, please.

Martin: Just the old greeting – you know, like; a nod of the head and an 'alright butt'.

Unlike Martin's and my youthful greeting practice that adhered to the traditional masculine 'man code' (King et al., 2021) of emotional inexpressiveness (Courtenay, 2011), the Ladz engaged in a startlingly dissimilar greeting behaviour and hugged each other. For example, one evening, while I was sitting in the youth centre's cafe area and surrounded by a relatively large mixed group of teenage boys and girls, Wesley was leaning against a wall adjacent to me, engaged with his phone. However, this relatively withdrawn practice significantly altered when Ian appeared at the youth centre. Ian had been working overtime and arrived at the centre late on this particular night. Upon arrival at the youth centre and his entrance into the cafe area, Ian spotted Wesley and said: *'Hey, bro'*. The two young men smiled at each other, clasped hands in a tight embrace, and then placed their arms around each other and hugged. This act of tactility between Ian and Wesley was not an isolated incident. It was a form of behaviour that was relatively universal among all of the Ladz and young men at the centre. Even Stan and Tommy engaged in this behaviour, with their embraces and hugs often being the most expressive and sometimes including expressions like: *'I love you, bro'*.

The Ladz' method of greeting each other and hugging practices dumbfounded me. This behaviour contradicted the gender practices that were customary to the lads' culture I was once familiar with. This form of behaviour and physical tactility would have been heresy in my 'laddish' epoch. It would also have made my heterosexuality questionable (Pascoe, 2007) and thus potentially led to ridicule, social ostracisation and even possible acts of gender policing (Martino, 2000; Pascoe, 2007) in the form of physical punishment. Physical tactility and hugging practices were associated with femininity and affection (Frosh et al., 2002) and thus perceived as evidence of homosexuality. Subsequently, we avoided this behaviour and any social activities coded as feminine and subsequently gay (Mac an Ghaill, 1994) out of fear of undermining our masculine identity and retribution.

Due to the disparity between the Ladz' social greeting methods and the traditional laddish code that I once adhered to, including a 'rejection of all aspects that are deemed feminine' (Haywood & Mac an Ghaill, 2003, p. 97), I questioned some of the young men about their conduct. Tommy and Stan were the first two I asked, and the following excerpt is our collective discussion regarding their behaviour:

RG: I've noticed that everyone hugs each other – what's that about then?

Tommy: Best friends.

RG: So you hug each other because you are best friends?

Tommy: Yeah, besties for life! Nah, cos we're all gay together!

RG: You're all gay?

Stan: I'm a homosexual, you dull cunt!

Tommy: Na, joking. To say hello, init. We don't do it the old-fashioned way, do we, Stan.

RG: What's the old-fashioned way?

At this point, Tommy and Stan engaged in a theatrical display. Almost simultaneously, they both raised their hands to form a handshaking gesture, whilst jointly leaning backwards and then meekly shaking each other's hands, whilst Tommy said: *'Good day, good day, boy'*. In response to this demonstration, I asked the following question: *'So what's the new way?'* Subsequently, Stan and Tommy 'fist pumped' and embraced each other with a hug, with Tommy saying: *'Broskies'*. Stan replied with: *'Long-time no see'*.

This excerpt and dramatisation have several aspects that offer interesting evidence. Firstly, there is no attempt to defend or excuse their hugging practice; there is an outright acknowledgement of this behaviour, suggesting it is a normalised practice. Secondly, this behaviour is associated with friendship, or more importantly, *'best friends'* or *'Besties'*, possibly suggesting that this hugging behaviour is not widespread practice and is determined by the strength of the relationship. Thirdly, both young men recognise that male hugging and same-sex touch may be perceived as homosexual behaviour (Blanchard et al., 2017; Ralph & Roberts, 2020), but this does not seem to matter to them. Lastly, we have the theatrical display where the young men identify generational change, suggesting that *'old-fashioned'* greeting methods include shaking hands, distance – the attempt to lean back – and terminology that almost has a middle-class Victorian feel: 'Good day [sir]'. Whereas contemporary greeting methods include a fist pump, tactility and words such as *'Broskies'*. This terminology potentially offers valuable evidential information.

Gough (2018, p. 54) suggests that 'men are hugging each other more so than previous generations, at least in some Western nations like the UK'. This behavioural shift includes the 'man hug' or 'bro hug'. The 'man hug' or 'bro hug' combines both a handshake and a hug and expresses masculinity and affection (Giese, 2018). Although I feel that the young men's hugging practises were slightly more intimate than a 'bro hug', objective reflection of the Ladz' behaviour coupled with consideration of the accompanying terminology – 'Bro', 'Broskie' – does seem to suggest that 'bro hug' is a reasonable explanation. Furthermore, Keith (2020, p. 2) suggests that:

> The term 'bro' is a neologism and abbreviation of the word 'brother' and is thought to have been appropriated by white boys and young men who wanted to emulate what they believed to be cool about black boys and men.

Therefore, similar to Frosh et al. (2002, p. 153) study, which examined 'young masculinities' and aspirations and anxieties of 11–14-year-old boys in London schools, and whereby some of the young men 'adopt[ed] the cultural practices they considered central to 'black masculinity'', the Ladz are also assuming aspects of 'black masculinity' and associated cultural practices including the terminological use of 'Bro' (Keith, 2020), rather than the historical regional working-class associated term of 'Butt' (Ward, 2015). Furthermore, as later sections show, this external cultural influence partially derives from contemporary popular music and seemingly affects the young men's views.

The other member of the Ladz that I questioned about hugging was Billy. The following excerpt is our discussion regarding this behaviour:

RG: Billy, I've noticed that you and the boys in here hug each other. What's that about? What does that mean to you?

Billy: Everyone here is like coming here every day. It's been open for years now, hasn't it. It is a mess about at the end of the day init. It's like when you score a try in rugby, you go over to your teammate and hug them. It's all well done an tha. You see footballers kiss each other on the head an tha. It's just a thing of trust you have ini. It's like they're my best mukkas [friends] an tha ini. And like, it's just weird, it's just. It's not like, like anything weird, it's just, oh, you're one of my best mukkas like. I dunno just close friends.

In this excerpt, Billy suggests that the young men have built up a close, trusting relationship and friendship that enables or facilitates their tactility. Furthermore, mentioning sports and footballers kissing indicates that the media and sports influence behavioural practices. However, conversely to the Ladz' displays of male tactility, media and sport are often perceived to circulate stereotyped gendered images and promote hegemonic masculine ideals (Connell, 2000; Messner, 2007, 2013; Messner et al., 2000), which include a rejection of behaviour coded as feminine and gay (Epstein, 1997; Haywood & Mac an Ghaill, 2003) and the subsequent avoidance of homosocial tactility (Floyd, 2000). Although these notions of sport and media hold some relevance, movements like the '#MeToo ... [have] ushered in a broad cultural examination of masculinity' (Brown, 2022, p. 13), which in turn has led to brands like Gillette releasing the: 'We Believe: The Best Men Can Be' advert which challenges toxic (Whitehead, 2019) and/or hegemonic masculine associated behaviour. Although the Gillette advert received a mixed response – including backlash – the toiletries brand 'Dove' also released the Dove Men+Care adverts series, which features iconic rugby players – including Wales and British Lions rugby captain Alun Wyn Jones – promoting a more expansive representation of masculinity (Levant & Pryor, 2020), showing men as both rugby players and fathers, subsequently demonstrating the notion of caring masculinities (Elliott, 2016; Hunter et al., 2017). The contemporary cultural examination of masculinity has also emphasised the emotional suppressive nature (Courtenay, 2011) of toxic masculinity (Whitehead, 2019) and the detrimental effect on men's mental health. Subsequently, men have been encouraged to become more emotionally expressive (McQueen, 2017). In keeping with this rhetoric and aligned with the theme of emotional expressiveness, the following sections explore some of the Ladz' expressions of feelings and emotions while incorporating reflexive discussion.

'I tried to commit suicide'

Several moments during the data collection brought about profound reflexive moments that caused me to assess my identity, values and beliefs. One of these was the pool incident with Stan that I documented in Chapter One, and Lewis and Cole's interviews caused additional reflexive moments.

Akin to the rest of the Ladz, Lewis and Cole's interviews concentrated on the school-to-work transition and the associated aspects. As stated previously, I never attempted to purposely probe into the young men's personal or family life because I rightly or wrongly felt it was relatively unnecessary and somewhat unethical. However, although I tried to avoid these topics, Lewis and Cole spoke freely and openly about their personal circumstances.

As stated in the earlier description of the Ladz, Lewis independently dedicated significant portions of the interview to discussions about females. However, rather than boasting about sexual conquest – as one might assume based on his hyper-masculine identity (Mac an Ghaill, 1994) – he talked about depression and suicidal thoughts.

Lewis would often weave his depression into the discussion at relatively random points in the interview. Due to this randomness, although I did not entirely want to engage in this discussion (explained below), it seemed clear that Lewis did. Therefore, I reluctantly offered the following question:

RG: Where do you think your depression comes from then? Is there a cause or anything?

Lewis: Yeah. I know wha the cause was, tha relationship with her [girlfriend]. The relationship was way too toxic. She gave me really bad depression. At one point, it was getting too much for me. So I tried to commit suicide. Fuck me, people say things gotta get worse to get better, but I don't want to live because of the depression. It just makes me think like no one wants me, no one cares for me, I'm not worth nothing! This past year it's just been shit cos I been getting into relationships, and they've just been the same. I don't have any luck with girls. I am going to turn into a slag.

Cole also offered a relatively similar response:

Cole: I had mental health. I suffered a lot with mental health because of a bad past. Depression come around and hit me off. I just give up sort of thing. I didn't have any plans, no dreams, no roles. I just shut down and locked myself away most of the time. Give up on everything like. With depression, a lot of it comes at you like, 'you're worthless, you haven't got a meaning, what's the point in you being here?'. I self-harmed – cut my arm up a lot. I ended up in hospital a few times – not eating. I wouldn't want to eat and wouldn't feel hungry. It did have a bad impact on me, like – my health. It did knock me back quite a lot. But I picked myself back up and got myself on the right roads, got myself a job and sorted my own life out.

As stated above, I tried to avoid engaging in these discussions on mental health and self-harm. However, this behaviour reflects my upbringing and socialisation process rather than being unconcerned, and I did report these issues to the staff at the youth centre, who were aware of the problems.

I am the child of an ex-pit miner's son, and I was raised in a family environment with a breadwinner (Williams, 2008) structure whereby traditional (Courtenay, 2011) masculine values were the norms, and I was expected to be tough and courageous (Cheng, 1999). Subsequently, vulnerability disclosures were considered transgression and evidence of weakness and femininity (Connell, 1995). One of my father's 'favoured' methods for regulating traditional masculine behaviour and eliminating potential emotional displays was through the gender policing phrase: *'Stop being a big girl's blouse!'* (Cornwall & Lindisfarne, 2003). Furthermore, in my youthful social surroundings, mental health and depression discussions were relatively unheard of or considered a 'dirty secret'. Therefore, although men's mental health, depression and emotional openness have gained popularity

(McQueen, 2017), unfortunately, due to my socialisation process and the durable nature of my habitus (Bourdieu, 1990a), discussions around emotion, especially male emotion, make me uncomfortable, and I am unsure how to respond or react. Sadly, this uncomfortableness overcame me during the young men's interviews and their expressions of emotional distress. Subsequently, after the interviews, I was compelled to reflect on my identity and awkwardness regarding emotional openness and the differences between myself and the young men.

Although Lewis and Cole's disclosure of mental health, depression, emotions and 'vulnerability' differ from my own experiences and the literature surrounding hegemonic and/or traditional masculinity (Connell, 1995; Courtenay, 2011; Kimmel, 1994), aspects of the two young men's excerpts potentially still indicate attempts to recuperate this masculine status. For example, after he expressed emotional openness and disclosures that would have traditionally been 'considered a sign of weakness for men, resulting in some form of emasculation' (Ralph & Roberts, 2020, p. 97), Lewis says: '*I am going to turn into a slag*' and thus demonstrates sexual promiscuity subsequently recovering a hegemonic masculine status (Paechter, 2018). Correspondingly, at the end of Cole's emotional openness and disclosure, he says: '*I picked myself back up and got myself on the right roads, got myself a job and sorted my own life out*', thus displaying control, independence and self-reliance, features that are consistent with hegemonic masculinity (Messerschmidt, 1993, 2018). Although this analysis potentially establishes a link with hegemonic masculinity, Lewis and Cole's emotional openness equally indicates contradictory behaviour (Haywood & Mac an Ghaill, 2003). The subsequent section demonstrates additional conflicting attitudes through displays of compassion and empathy.

'*Soooo much underpaid*'

As stated in the Introduction, visual methods were incorporated into the semi-structured interviews and used to explore various forms of employment and as a discussion stimulation technique. However, most of the visual methods data offered limited complimentary benefit to the research, and conversation with the Ladz was relatively effortless and fluid, yet some of the pictures provided relevant findings.

Among the selection of photos used was a picture of a male nurse. Akin to the call centre picture, the Ladz were shown the picture and then asked to identify the work presented in the image and express their thoughts and feelings about the job. The following excerpts are the young men's replies:

Billy: I've heard about the, um, the conditions in nursing. It's like I, they're on like 20 thousand a year. That's awful ini If you're saving someone's life every day. Its things shock me; things I hear make my jaw drop.

Ian: Nurse. Underpaid! Soooo much underpaid. They're saving your life, and football players get paid a quarter of a million just for playing football on a football pitch. They're saving your life, and they get paid pennies. It's just horrible! If I had the brains, I would love to do the job. It is something… just helping people.

Cole: I would. I wouldn't mind that – helping people every day of the week. Obviously, I wouldn't want the abuse side of it like when drunks come in, and you're trying to see to them because obviously, it would agitate me. But I wouldn't mind helping someone every day like.

Tommy: Nurse or a doctor, is it? Yeah, actually, I would just to try and figure out the cure for cancer. Just to like help people.

Lewis: Working in the NHS, nursing or doctor. I'd smash tha job. I was looking after my stepfather's Nan because she had dementia, and I was looking after this other old lady who had cancer. I was down their houses after school every day, seeing them, like if they were ok and tha.

Stan: I wouldn't mind being a Doctor. Just sitting on the fucking till in the chemist or something – you get loads of money.

In these replies, initially, through Billy and Ian's responses, we see resentment towards the perceived mistreatment of nurses and the wage allocation that is considered insufficient with respect to the job requirements and responsibility. These responses resonate with the favoured musicians among the youths, including Stormzy and Dave. Simpson (2017) describes Dave as a 'politically charged rapper'. Dave's music was frequently played in the youth centre media room, and one of the preferred songs was 'Question Time' (Dave, 2017). The following lyrics are taken from this song:

All my life I know my mum's been working. In and out of nursing, struggling, hurting. I just find it fucked that the government is struggling to care for a person that cares for a person. So where's the discussion on wages and budgets? … A question for the new Prime Minister.

Comparative analysis of these lyrics and Ian and Billy's response reveals apparent similarity, with all three pieces of data discussing nurses and wages. Although the young men never associated their views with this song, there is an obvious association that again potentially reflects the Ladz' adoption of popular cultural views, as was evident in their terminological use of words such as 'Bro' or 'Broskies'. Furthermore, identity is formed in cultural relations (Willis, 1977), and media and popular culture are often considered to influence and shape the 'common sense of the people, including their taken-for-granted notions of masculinity and femininity' (Hanke, 1998, p. 184). Although the young men's replies superficially offer a limited link to masculinity, the central features of hegemonic masculinity include being unemotional and dispassionate (Collier, 1998; Connell & Messerschmidt, 2005). Conversely, Ian and Billy's responses and consideration of individuals other than themselves possibly indicate open masculinities (Elliott,

2020) or 'new' masculinities characterised by sensitivity, compassion, and empathy (Spector-Mersel & Gilbar, 2021). Moreover, evidence of these traits – sensitivity, compassion, and empathy – are also identifiable in Tommy's response and his desire to *'cure cancer'* and equally through Lewis's caring responsibilities and his *'looking after'* people. Dan's nursing response did not correlate with these excerpts. However, as the following reply shows, despite Dan's previously documented displays of hyper-masculinity, aggression and violence, empathy and compassion were equally evident:

> You learn different pipe sizes, how to fit them in. It's just learning a new skill in general like. So even if you've got a family member who needs something, you can just help them out in it. I don't mind helping people out like.

Despite the young men's documented collective similarities, Stan's nursing reply reveals disparity with no evidence of compassion or empathy, instead contrastingly demonstrating adherence to the hegemonic masculine trait of individualism (Messerschmidt, 1993) and extrinsic reward (Willis, 1977).

'Do you all mix together outside?'

In *Learning to Labour*, documentation of girls is relatively sparse (Carter, 1966). However, Willis (1977, p. 43) states that the lads viewed women 'both [as] sexual objects and domestic comforters', and thus the lads have subsequently been connected with sexism due to their degrading views and behaviour to female teachers and female pupils (Skeggs, 1992). As archaic as this may read, as a lad of the 90s, this was my youthful understanding of women. Subsequently, akin to the young men from Mac an Ghaill's (1994) study, social relations and friendship grouping were single-sex and gender-exclusive, generally involving only males. Conversely, and similarly to the findings of Frosh et al. (2002, pp. 180–181), 'boys who hung around with girls as friends were liable to be constructed as effeminate 'woosies" and at risk of homosexual taunts.

Despite my predominantly gender-segregated male laddish peer friendship grouping, this code was often broken by what we referred to as the 'nine o clock' club, which relates to the time of night when group members were permitted to leave and meet up with girlfriends. However, as Ward (2015, p. 55) mentions in his study of working-class young men in the South Wales Valleys, these members were often met with ridicule through phrases such as 'bros before hoes', meaning male friendship should come before females and sex. Although some readers may find this documentation offensive due to its sexist nature, this is my lived understanding of the lads' culture – warts and all – which correlates with previous research on this subculture of young men.

In contrast to my laddish youthful experiences and to my astonishment, among the Ladz, gender-segregated friendship groupings were non-existent. The Ladz could often be found together with girls chatting, listening to music, dancing or playing pool in what seemed to be an essentially platonic relationship. Further-more, the gender dynamics of these friendship groupings often altered and had irregular formations that sometimes included larger percentages of males and, at other times, a more significant proportion of females.

I often arrived at the centre before opening and saw Tommy walking to the centre with a few girls. Equally, Stan could often be found playing pool in the company of females discussing non-sexualised topics. Although I had observed the Ladz' associating with girls outside of the centre, due to the differentiation between my youthful experiences, initially, I thought the confinement of the youth centre determined this mixed-sex friendship grouping. Subsequently, one night while I was sitting in the pool room surrounded by a few of the Ladz and several girls, I asked the following question: *'Do you all mix together outside of the centre, boys and girls?'*. At this moment, the room went deathly quiet, and everyone turned to look at me with what seemed like a gaze of astonishment. The awkward silence was broken by a girl who responded with *'yes'* in what felt like an aggressive tone as if to say: *'Of course we do, you idiot'*.

Although there was a broadly identifiable platonic relationship among most young males and females at the centre, the friendship between the sexes was not unproblematic and completely egalitarian. Akin to their predecessors, some of the Ladz – mainly Tommy and Stan – often displayed hyper-masculine (Mac an Ghaill, 1994) behaviour and misogynistic tendencies, including calling the girls sluts and physically assaulting and taking their phones off them. However, this conduct was often met with retaliation and physical, aggressive 'laddette'[1] style behaviour (Jackson, 2006), with the girls refusing to be subordinated.

'I should be a barber, boy'

Despite the moments of conflict, there were equal measures of tactility among several members of the mixed friendship group. A particularly noticeable promi-nent form of tactility often practised by both males and females included styling each other's hair. Stan was one of the Ladz members who seemed particularly fond of this activity. On numerous occasions, I observed Stan either letting girls style his hair and placing it in bows or styling girls' hair. Once again, this conduct was particularly puzzling to me. Not so much Stan having his hair done, as this might be considered a flirtatious technique, it was more the fact of him doing the girls' hair. Hairdressing is arguably a feminised profession with an emphasis on effeminate qualities (Hall et al., 2007). Therefore, men engaging in this activity are possibly considered at risk of being perceived as gay (Robinson et al., 2011). Subsequently, based on this notion and Stan's identified hyper-masculine iden-tity that is deemed to fiercely reject all aspects considered feminine (Haywood & Mac an Ghaill, 2003), I closely observed Stan's engagement in this practice. The following excerpt is taken from my ethnographic notes.

---

[1]'ladettes' are [women or girls] presented as crude, loud, bold, (hetero)sexually asser-tive, hedonistic and into alcohol and smoking (Jackson, 2006, p.11).

Tommy and Stan are sitting side by side in the media room with several other young boys playing on the computers in front of them. There is a gap between Tommy and Stan's chairs, and their usual choice of rap music is playing in the background. Chelsea enters the room, grabs a chair, places it between Tommy and Stan and sits on it. They then engage in a three-way discussion, and Stan asks Chelsea: *'Can I do your hair?'* Chelsea smiles and says: *'Go on then'*. Stan then proceeds to plait Chelsea's hair rather proficiently. Stan does not attempt to converse with Chelsea, and there is a large smile on his face, and his tongue is slightly sticking out in what looks like a sign of concentration. After finishing plaiting Chelsea's hair and doing what seems like a relatively good job, Stan gets excited, takes his phone out of his pocket and takes what I later found out is a Snapchat of him and Chelsea. Whilst taking the snap, Stan says: *'Look at this boys, look how mint I've done it. I should be a barber, boy'*.

This scene and general behaviour perplexed me and transgressed all the youthful laddish codes that I was accustomed to, including an apparent friendship involvement with girls (Frosh et al., 2002) and engagement in behaviour that would potentially be considered to have homosexual implications (Robinson et al., 2011). Subsequently, later that evening, I asked Stan about this incident: *Stan, why did you do Chelsea's hair?'*. Based on Stan's prior hyper-masculine (Mac an Ghaill, 1994) and/or hegemonic masculine (Connell, 1995) displays, I expected him to boast about heterosexual desire and attempts at sexual conquest (Connell, 1989). However, Stan merely replied with a smile, so I again said: *'No, serious now, Stan, why did you do Chelsea's hair?'*. Stan replied: *'Chill out, Rich, boy! I'm not going to be a fucking hairdresser'*. At this point, I felt slightly annoyed and angry at myself and had a positionality and ethical crisis, questioning my ability, strengths and weaknesses, including, would a female ethnographer be able to explore these topics better? Would a middle-class 'outsider' (Merton, 1972) do a better job? I felt awkward questioning these young men and continually intruding into a sometimes alien culture. I was questioning them about their taken-for-granted assumptions (Sikes, 2003). What right do researchers have to do this? Do we cross the line when we do this? What impact was I having on these young people by questioning them this way? Was I forcing my traditional masculine (Courtenay, 2011) 'awkwardness' on them? and making Stan masculinely defend his behaviour – *'I'm not going to be a fucking hairdresser'*. Although this was a difficult period for me, and I could not get a clear response from Stan other than his masculine defence, careful consideration of the ethnographic excerpt possibly explains Stan's behaviour.

The apparent explanation is a heterosexuality demonstration, especially considering Stan sends a Snapchat of himself to his male peers. Furthermore, Stan attempts to redefine his behaviour within the masculinised profession of barbering (Ferry, 2020) – *'I should be a barber boy'*. Although Stan's behaviour was peculiar to me and transgressed many of the masculine laddish codes that I adhered to, further consideration of his general behaviour potentially offers an explanation. Stan's behaviour demonstrates the most intensified form of hyper-masculinity (Mac an Ghaill, 1994) among the Ladz based on his overt confessions and displays of aggression, violence, sexism and misogyny. One could argue that Stan has acquired masculine capital (Gough, 2018) or jock insurance (Pascoe, 2003), 'that is, young men who have (in whatever way) "proven" their (heterosexual) masculine credentials [and] can engage in this sort of gender transgression and remain beyond reproach' (Bridges & Pascoe, 2013, para. 5). Despite this explanation, hair styling practises were a generalised form of behaviour, and as previously stated, it transgressed my lived and subsequent taken-for-granted assumptions of laddish behaviour. Therefore, I decided to query this behaviour in my interview with Amy – the youngest youth worker who attended the centre as a teenager herself:

RG: I see lots of boys being slightly intimate, hugging and doing girls' hair. What's your take on this?

Amy: Yeah, they seem more comfortable with male affection, not necessarily homoerotic, but many young men are pretty happy to hug each other or sit on one another's laps and show their affection to one another. I remember we had some young men who behaved quite camply and had many female friends and seemed to be quite flirty with the boys, but they got a lot of girlfriends. I wasn't sure if nowadays if young men have cottoned on a bit to this idea and become more physically affectionate in general.

In this response, Amy suggests that the young men may purposely display associated feminine traits or engage in same-sex behaviour to increase their desirability to females. This idea correlates with Bridges and Pascoe (2014) notion of hybrid masculinities. Hybrid masculinities refer to the 'selective incorporation of elements of identity typically associated with various marginalised and subordinated masculinities and – at times – femininities into privileged men's gender performances and identities' (Bridges & Pascoe, 2014, p. 246). Although this justification is plausible, it offers a relatively reductive explanation. The Ladz' working-class status and behaviour associates them with protest or hyper-masculinity, 'which can be described as a strong exaggeration of certain stereotypical male qualities' (Andreasson & Johansson, 2017, p. 141). Subsequently, by the very nature of them engaging in hybridised displays of masculinity and incorporating softer displays of masculinity, the Ladz partially deviate from the masculine position that has become customary for this sub-group of young men. In other words, even if the Ladz are adopting hybrid masculinities (Bridges & Pascoe, 2014) techniques, this demonstrates a change by itself in relation to how laddish masculinity is commonly understood concerning theory and my lived understanding.

The previous two sections have documented the Ladz engagement with females. Unlike my prior laddish youthful understanding and the single-sex and gender-exclusive male friendship grouping documented in prior related research (Frosh et al., 2002; Mac an Ghaill, 1994), the Ladz demonstrate an association with girls. However, this relationship is not entirely unproblematic, and its meaning is potentially questionable as to whether it is evidence of changing egalitarian views or sexually motivated hybrid masculinities (Bridges & Pascoe, 2014) techniques. Subsequently, the following section assesses the young men's attitudes towards working with females and gay men.

'A boy can be a ballerina'

In *Learning to Labour*, the lads refer to women as sex objects and commodities (Willis, 1977) and use various tropes that identify them as sexist and homophobic (McRobbie, 1991; Skeggs, 1992; Walker, 1985). Furthermore, the lads' sexist and homophobic perspective is associated with their masculine identity that is constructed in oppositional 'relation to various subordinated masculinities as well as in relation to women' (Connell, 1987, p. 183). Subsequently, women are deemed 'inferior and incapable of doing certain things' (Willis, 1977, p. 149), including manual labour and traditionally associated masculine forms of employment. Despite the Ladz' previous findings that have associated them with the lads, the notion of women and inferiority is omitted from many of the young men's data in this section, with some of the Ladz demonstrating an opposing view.

The Ladz were asked about their thoughts and opinions about working with women and gay men. On reflection, this was a blunt approach as I somewhat failed to consider that some of the young men might be gay themselves. Nevertheless, this exploration was intended to assess the young men's views of women, gay men and their masculinity, potentially allowing us to think of an alternative imagined employment future other than male-dominated work. Essentially, are the Ladz capable of working in employment and surroundings besides those dominated by masculine heterosexual males:

Dan: I wouldn't mind – different, but I wouldn't mind it. I'm not sexist; it's just that you don't really see women plumbing, do you? I don't know why. If girls do plumbing, it shows an example and makes others feel more comfortable doing it. There's nothing bad if you're a girl or a boy. A boy can be a ballerina or a dancer – there's nothing wrong with it. It's what you're into in it. I don't care or think anything of it. It's them in it – as long as it's not bothering anyone – let them do what they want. No difference between a man and a woman is there. If anyone thinks there is, it's just sexist in it.

Cole: It wouldn't bother me at all working with women or gays. There are gays in my family. My uncle is gay – happily gay and has been married for 15/16 years. They're no different. Your sexual preference or gender or anything like that doesn't make odds on your personality.

Conversely to Willis' lads, sexist and homophobic discourse, and in contrast to hegemonic (Connell, 1995) and/or hyper-masculine (Mac an Ghaill, 1994) associated ideals, in Dan and Cole's excerpts – particularly in Dan's – we see gender-egalitarian views (Kaplan et al., 2017). Dan states that there is *'No difference between a man and a woman'* and thus disputes the idea that women are inferior (Willis, 1977). Furthermore, Dan's comment demonstrates a sense of naivety, but mild disdain, towards the notion of patriarchy: *'You don't really see women plumbing, do you? I don't know why'*. Cole also deviates from the homophobic position that is often associated with the lads' category and working-class masculinities (Connell, 1995; Epstein, 1997; Francis, 1999; Mac an Ghaill, 1994; Willis, 1977) and states: *'Your sexual preference or gender or … doesn't make odds on your personality'*.

Billy: Yeah, as long as I get my job done. As long as I enjoy what I do, I don't care who I do it with. You have to think dun you, oh, they got the same mindset as me, they wanna do the best, they chose that career for a reason, you let them get on with it ini. Don't judge anyone for who they want to be.

Ian: I don't really care who I work with as long as we get along. If you don't get along with someone, then you can't really work with them, can you?

Wesley: Yeah, I wouldn't mind. I just want a happy relationship with my like…. teammates. As long as I get along, then I can be happy.

Although a gender-egalitarian view (Kaplan et al., 2017) is less prominent in Billy, Ian and Wesley's responses and these young men seem more concerned about being proficient at their job, considering their previously documented hegemonic (Connell, 1995) and/or hyper-masculine (Mac an Ghaill, 1994) disclosures, the exclusion of homophobic and sexist discourse is notable.

Lewis: Really dun bother me tha don't. Even if I was working with fucking any sexuality, it doesn't bother me. They're themselves, shouldn't be judged for who they are. As long as they feel comfortable, it doesn't make me feel uncomfortable. As long as they don't try shit with me, I'm sound.

Craig: I wouldn't mind working with anyone. I wouldn't mind working with gays, it's just like they can't be talking about different weird stuff – cos I can't just like keep listening to it, and it's going in my head, and I'm thinking, am I gay? Like, I'd go to bed, and I'm like, 'Am I gay?'. They might try and make me gay, so that's why I wouldn't like it. I wouldn't mind working with a girl; they just can't be bitchy.

Lewis and Craig's data demonstrates a further departure from the original overt gender-egalitarian views (Kaplan et al., 2017) expressed by Dan and Cole. Similarly, to some of the participants from McCormack's (2014) study of attitudes toward homosexuality among working-class boys in a sixth form in the south of England, Dan and Craig demonstrate ambivalence, particularly towards working with gay men. Initially, both young men offer a positive response.

However, the expulsion and fear of homosexuality curtail this reply and demonstrate the traditional hegemonic masculine expectation of maintaining distance from homosexuality (Mac an Ghaill, 1994).

As stated previously, Stan and Tommy's interviews were conducted together due to their request. The following excerpt is our three-way discussion about working with women and gay men:

RG: Would you work with women, boys? They both respond with '*Yeah*' and laugh. **RG:** What about working with gay men? Both of them laugh and say '*ew*' – an expression of disgust. **Stan:** Fuck that! I'm a homosexual! **RG:** You're what, Stan? **Stan:** I'm a homosexual. **Tommy:** Homophobic? **Stan:** Homosexual! **RG:** So you would you work with gay men then? **Tommy:** No! Cos what if they tried getting on you? Touching your leg and that, trying to touch your cock. **Stan:** I'd be like, 'Fuck you, you fucking'. I'd blow his fucking head off! **RG:** What about working with women then? **Tommy:** Fair enough, we can shag them. **RG:** Would you rather work in a place with all guys or women and guys? **Tommy:** Guys. **Stan:** Women. **Tommy:** Oh yeah – it depends how fit [attractive] they are. **Stan:** Cos guys try and get on women, don't they. **Tommy:** Ooooo yeah (excited tone). **Stan:** I'm the fucking leader of the pack, and I'll fucking shag them all!

Unlike the previous Ladz' responses that have shown a full or partial deviation from the overtly sexist and homophobic position of Willis' lads, Tommy and Stan's data shows a distinct and apparent reconnection with their laddish predecessors through homophobic and degrading discourse (McRobbie, 1991) that sexually objectifies women and verges on a predatory perspective. Furthermore, the language used by Stan: '*I'll fucking shag them all!*' demonstrates a resemblance with the terminology used by Joey, a member of Willis's lads: '*I'm interested in fucking as many women as I can*' (Willis, 1977, p. 199). Additionally, Stan reconfirms his status as '*leader of the pack*' that he has proclaimed in previous replies. There is also a seemingly confused understanding between Stan's anti-gay sentiment and his terminological use. For example, concerning gay men, Stan demonstrates violent disdain and states: '*I'd blow his fucking head off!*' yet Stan refers to himself as '*homosexual*', thus revealing a contradiction between his views and his linguistic use, which Tommy equally identifies and corrects. It is this muddled use of anti-gay terminology and a general complex relationship with homophobia that the subsequent final findings section aims to explore.

'*This game is gay*'

In the previous section, the data evidences Stan's aggressive disdain towards homosexuality. However, in an additional reply, Stan deviated from this contemptuous position and the expulsion of homosexuality often associated with working-class masculinities (Mac an Ghaill, 1994; Willis, 1977) and central to the notion of hegemonic masculinity (Connell, 1995). For example:

Stan: Some gay boys are fit [attractive] as fuck, though, like James Charles.

RG: Who's that?

Stan: It's this fucking gay boy with a fat arse. He got a fatter arse than your sister!

RG: Good looking, is he? Do you think he's good looking, Tommy? (Tommy doesn't reply).

James Charles is an openly gay American YouTube personality, make-up artist and famous social media celebrity. In the excerpt, contradictory to his previous opposition to homosexuality, Stan overtly states that James Charles – an openly gay man – is fit, a term the Ladz use to refer to someone viewed as attractive or good-looking. Furthermore, when I asked Tommy whether he thought James Charles was good-looking, he ignored my question. Comparative analysis between this response and Stan's previous violent disdain towards gay men reveals contradictions that almost epitomise the messy, entangled nature of the Ladz homosexuality-related discourse. An additional example of this is identifiable in Craig's data:

Craig: **There's nothing wrong with being gay** cos my uncle's gay and my brother's gay. **There's nothing wrong with it**. Just cos they talk a bit funny and put a bit of make-up on, it's not really that bad. You can't help it if you're gay or not. **There's nothing wrong with being gay**. It's just nasty when other people make fun of them. **It's not wrong**. It's just kind of sad for the other people because most people now are gay but try and act straight cos they are kind of scared to admit it.

Similarly to Stan's replies, this response by Craig is equally conflicting and confusing. In the previous section, Craig confessed to a fear of working with gay men based on the notion that: *'they might try and make [him] gay'*. However, in this excerpt, he states that: *'There's nothing wrong with being gay'* almost three times. Furthermore, there are additional inconsistencies in this excerpt alone. For example: *'It's just nasty when other people make fun of them. It's not wrong'*. In this response, Craig initially opposes homophobic discourse. However, he then contradicts this by saying: *'It's not wrong'*, a statement that potentially reflects his working-class masculinity (Connell, 1995; Mac an Ghaill, 1994; Willis, 1977) and the notion that challenging anti-gay declarations may lead to homophobic abuse (Nayak & Kehily, 1996). Furthermore, Craig's views have a neoliberalist construction, including the idea that everyone has to create themselves and their own trajectory through life, and everyone should be whom they want to be. We also see that Craig's uncle and brother are gay, yet he does not outright condemn homophobic discourse, nor does he endorse it – there is a muddled construction of views.

This comparative analysis reveals the complexity of the Ladz homosexuality discourse, which was equally evident in the young men's general use of this terminology. Rather than using this language to refer to a person's sexuality or behaviours traditionally associated with this discourse, including same-sex touch, the Ladz also used it to refer to aspects not associated with these categories. The youth centre pool room was a place where this notion was particularly evident. For example, Tommy noticed a girl playing pool left-handed, and he called her gay because she was using that hand. Stan and Craig, on different occasions, both said to their opponents: *'If you miss that shot, you're gay'*. Additionally, Stan and Lewis were playing a football game on the computer. Stan was winning, and Lewis became animated, jumping about, threatening to punch the screen and saying: *'this game is gay'*.

Notably, none of the references to 'gay' relates to same-sex desires or behaviour traditionally associated with this discourse. Thus seemingly, the Ladz' use of 'gay' corresponds with the notion of anti-gay 'banter', which signifies 'behaviours or individuals as stupid, weird, and out of place in the peer group' (Wang et al., 2021, p. 1940). However, although there is no apparent homophobic context in the Ladz' use of the term 'gay', a close reading of the data and additional consideration reveals a contradictory explanation. Tommy initially uses this word to refer to a girl playing pool left-handed. Subsequently, we may understand this use of the term gay to refer to 'different' or 'abnormal'. Additionally, Stan and Craig use the term in reference to the possibility of inept ability and *'missing [the] shot'*, and Lewis uses the term gay towards the computer game in the context of defeat. Subsequently, Lewis arguably uses this term to undermine the game, offset his loss, and thus recoup self-esteem. Therefore, collectively, rather than being anti-gay banter (Wang et al., 2021) or gay discourse where there is 'no intent to marginalise or wound people with this use of language' (McCormack, 2012, p. 119), the term gay is used by the Ladz to associate perceived 'dysfunctionality' and thus used as a gender policing technique (Martino, 2000; Pascoe, 2007) which subsequently reinforces the marginalisation and stigmatisation of homosexuality.

In the interest of the youth centre and its integrity, it is important to state that the Ladz' use of homophobic discourse was challenged and deemed unacceptable. Two youth workers who were particularly prominent in contesting negative gay discourse included Martin and especially Amy. The following excerpt is Dafydd's – the youth centre manager – view of Amy:

Dafydd: Amy brings something…she's stirring things up a little bit, and I think we need that. She's bringing a much younger and diverse perspective to everything, and she has her feminist views.

In this excerpt, Dafydd suggests that Amy brings a diverse feminist perspective and is *'stirring things up'*, challenging the status quo, or what may be interpreted as 'traditional' working-class laddish ways of doing masculinity, which sometimes include sexism and homophobia (Connell, 2005; Mac an Ghaill, 1994;

Willis, 1977). The notion of challenging negative hegemonic or hyper-masculine behaviours is evident in Amy's following response:

Amy: Well, some of it is just sort of saying like, 'That's gay that is', about something that they think is a bit shit. They don't seem to use too much in terms of sort of more hard slurs, but most of the time when I challenge them on it, it's something like, 'Hahaha, this person must be gay', and then you just say, well, 'And what if he was?'.

In this response, Amy substantiates my observations of the Ladz and their use of gay terminology. Furthermore, rather than deeming this language as merely anti-gay 'banter' (Wang et al., 2021) or inoffensive gay discourse (McCormack, 2012), Amy somewhat understands the negative implications and the gender policing qualities (Martino, 2000; Pascoe, 2007) and thus challenges the young men's use of this terminology. This behaviour by Amy summarises my experience at the youth centre, which I found to be an organisation that aimed to provide a welcoming, progressive and gender-egalitarian (Kaplan et al., 2017) environment where young people could feel safe, secure and comfortable.

Conclusion

This final empirical chapter demonstrates inconsistencies with the previous two empirical chapters and the protest masculinity (Connell, 1995), lads association (Willis, 1977) and laddish practices that have been evident throughout the young men's data. The findings in this chapter evidence gender-egalitarian views (Kaplan et al., 2017), physical tactility, sensitivity, empathy and compassion, all aspects that supposedly conflict with hegemonic masculinity (Collier, 1998; Connell & Messerschmidt, 2005). Therefore, this chapter illustrates that the Ladz are experiencing a change in their masculine identity formation and not merely inheriting locally and historically produced working-class protest masculine ways of being. Instead, their understanding of manhood seems to be influenced by sources beyond the confines of their locality, including popular culture, music and media. In essence, this chapter, combined with the previous two empirical chapters, demonstrates that the Ladz masculine identity consists of both working-class laddish dispositions and softer, more fluid displays. How we might understand and interpret this coexistence is part of the source of enquiry in the following final chapter, which attempts to make sense of the Ladz ways of being.

Chapter Seven

Continuity and Change

Refresher

This book aimed to explore the school-to-work transition and masculine identity of a group of marginalised working-class young men from the South Wales Valleys who resembled the lads from Willis's (1977) study in the context of social and economic change after the end of heavy industry. Although there have been numerous research relating to working-class young men, education, employment, and masculinity (Ashton & Field, 1976; Brown, 1987; Carter, 1966; Mac an Ghaill, 1994; McDowell, 2003; Nayak, 2006; Nixon, 2009; Veness, 1962; Walkerdine & Jiménez, 2012; Ward, 2015; Willis, 1977), these studies may be considered somewhat dated in a contemporary context, and recent studies have tended to focus on missing middle participants (Brozsely & Nixon, 2022; Roberts, 2018). Therefore, I have argued that there is a need to return the focus to working-class young men that have commonly been associated with a negative or complex relationship with education, manual employment aspirations and linked to protest masculinity (Connell, 1995; Haywood & Mac an Ghaill, 2013; Willis, 1977), because future employment changes are potentially set to negatively impact low-skilled, poorly educated young men and manual forms of employment (Frey & Osborne, 2013; Mckinsey, 2017; Hawksworth et al., 2018).

Furthermore, concerning masculinities, I argued for the significance of place specificity (Walkerdine & Jiménez, 2012) and recognising that 'the industrial and social history of a place affects [the] identity of its inhabitants' (McDowell, 2003, p. 96). I also argued for recognising the impact of social and economic change and external cultural influences beyond immediate surroundings. Therefore, I suggested considering contemporary marginalised working-class young men's identity construction through a dualistic perspective that considers the significance of local and general influences. Based on these perspectives, this final chapter returns to the findings from this study and compares the Ladz to Willis's

The 21st Century Ladz: Continuity and Changes among Marginalised
Young Men from the South Wales Valleys, 115–136
Copyright © 2025 by Richard Gater. Published by Emerald Publishing Limited.
doi:10.1108/978-1-83797-631-720251008

(1977) lads, along with considering additional studies and knowledge on the laddish (Mac an Ghaill, 1994; Nayak, 2003b; Ward, 2015) working-class young men. I also autoethnographically embed myself within this final chapter, sharing my lived understanding as a self-proclaimed and documented youthful lad (Willis, 1977) who resides in the related study community. Although autoethnography is sometimes criticised for being narcissistic, self-indulgent and individualised (Wall, 2016), I justify my inclusion based on the following citation:

> The freedom of a researcher to speak as a player in a research project and to mingle his or her experience with the experience of those studied is precisely what is needed to move inquiry and knowledge further along. (Wall 2006, p. 146)

While also arguing that 'my personal experience [has] sensitise[d] me to things that others [potentially] wouldn't notice' (Bourdieu, 2001, 0: 44: 10). This discussion section is structured in a specific order (starting with employment rather than education), to present a coherent and rational narrative, providing a better overall understanding of the Ladz' lived experiences.

Employment Preference

The initial self-evident theme related to the Ladz' employment data is the realisation that, unlike the lads (Willis, 1977), none of the young men from this study mentions manufacturing as an employment option. On the face of it, this may seem like an obvious difference considering the significant decrease in manufacturing that has seen this employment sector nationally shrink by 17% since 1977 and now accounts for 7.4% of UK jobs (House of Commons Library, 2022; Syed, 2019). However, these national statistics do not reflect the labour market conditions of the Ladz' surrounding employment area, where manufacturing accounts for 20.4% of employment (ONS, 2021c), a figure similar to the 24.3% UK manufacturing employment rate of 1977 (Syed, 2019). However, despite this, the Ladz seeming dismissal of manufacturing work and comparative analysis somewhat reveals a different conclusion from that drawn by Willis (1977, p. 126) and his claim that working-class culture 'knows' the economic realities of the labour market, or at least concerning the Ladz and their local labour market. However, the lack of recognition of manufacturing work may also indicate reduced visibility, especially when considering that the high manufacturing rates relate to the Ladz surrounding employment area rather than the employment structure of their immediate place of residency, which has minimal job opportunities. Although manufacturing is omitted from the Ladz' responses, among the majority of the respondents, there is equally still an obvious attraction to manual labour employment and traditionally associated working-class jobs, albeit skilled and particularly construction work (Shildrick & MacDonald, 2007).

Although the Ladz' attraction to skilled manual employment somewhat corresponds with relatively contemporary studies of subgroups of a similar nature, including Nayak's (2003b, p. 13) 'Real Geordies' who had 'an appreciation of skilled physical labour' and Ward's (2015, p. 45) Valley Boiz who were drawn to "acceptable' manual occupation', the Ladz' relatively rigid job preferences differ from Roberts (2018, p. 93) working-class 'missing middle' young men that 'remained largely unsure about what forms of employment they ultimately hoped to attain'. Furthermore, a comparison between some of the Ladz and their Laddish predecessor – the lads (1977) – reveals increased aspiration and social mobility through their attraction to skilled labour rather than non-skilled. Moreover, this notion of differentiation is further distinguished among four members of the Ladz: Billy's rejection of manual work and desire to become a chef; Lewis's partial attraction to frontline healthcare work in the form of a paramedic; Wesley's media related preference; and Cole's funeral director career aspiration. Nevertheless, the employment preference data mainly shows the early emergence of the Ladz' protest masculinity and working-class identity through an attraction to manual labour (Connell, 1995) and hands-on work (Nixon, 2006, 2009) whilst equally demonstrating deviation in Lewis, Wesley, Billy and Cole's job choices which somewhat depart from the manual work preference that is commonly associated with this subgroup of working-class young men.

Identity Formation

The previous section began to demonstrate and discuss the emergence of the Ladz' working-class identity and protest masculinity (Connell, 1995) through their job preference, yet also showed some form of deviation among some of the young men. This section extends the job preference discussion by identifying influential factors that determine the Ladz' employment orientation and contribute to the young men's identity construction. Furthermore, I begin to embed myself and my understanding of the area and its residents within this section.

All but two of the Ladz' job preferences and formulations around employment derive from family members and close associations. The findings show that the young men are predominantly raised in an environment where traditional manual forms of working-class employment are the recognised norm: *'I've always seen people working outside and looking like they're working'* (Dan). *'My brother was a plumber'* (Craig), *'Because my dad done it!'* (Tommy). The Ladz' career orientations correspond with Veness's (1962) traditional-direction model, which refers to the situation in which family, friends and community traditions influence a working-class young man's choice of employment. Moreover, consistent with the lads (Willis, 1977) and additional early working-class young men and employment discussion (Tolson, 1977), male influence features strongly in determining the Ladz' understanding of employment and job preference.

An additional response by Dan – *'Ever since he was ten [brother], he's been fixing motorbikes, so I've been brought with it'* – illustrates the extent to which family and community structural and cultural influences help formulate and shape the young men's employment understanding and working-class identity or habitus (Bourdieu & Wacquant, 1992), which includes a specific set of dispositions of thought, action and behaviour acquired during early childhood socialisation which shapes a person's identity, often determining mannerisms, values, morals and beliefs (Bourdieu, 1990a; Reay, 2004) and provide a 'feel for the game' (Bourdieu, 1990b, p. 108) or an understanding of the world and a person's place within it. Furthermore, Bourdieu's notion of habitus and 'feel for the game' potentially help make sense of the employment aspects that the young men dislike and favour because a person's habitus process and content create familiarity and unfamiliarity in social environments and surroundings (Bourdieu, 1990b). Therefore, considering the cultural and structural environments that the Ladz are raised in, whereby active manual labour is the typical job type among family members, the fact that many of the Ladz dislike sedentary employment, such as office work, further demonstrates how the young men's habitus (Bourdieu, 1990a) and protest masculine (Connell, 1995) attraction towards employment are shaped within their primary socialisation environments (Chesters, 2021).

Moreover, a comparative analysis of the work aspects that the Ladz favour is illustrative of the commonly associated link between a working-class masculine identity, dirt, hands-on work and practicality (Nixon, 2006, 2009; Slutskaya et al., 2016; Walkerdine & Jiménez, 2012; Willis, 1977): *'My hands gotta be doing something'* (Lewis). *'I wanted to be something like productive, like doing something outside. I like to do stuff with my hands'* (Ian). The differentiation between the two types of work and job aspects is:

> illustrative of a traditional class-based dichotomy between manual work and mental work, including an aversion to middle-class 'pen-pushing' (Mac an Ghaill, 1994) and an inclination towards employment that provides material worth often valued by working-class males, especially in the former industrial heartlands of Britain. (Gater, 2022, p. 117; Nixon, 2018)

The Ladz' employment-related data and the above argument correspond to previous research I conducted in the Aber Valley in 2018 (Gater, 2022). The research explored the employment experiences and relationships of a group of working-class young men who had rejected school and education based on its perceived irrelevance. The findings indicated that community traditions influenced participants' experiences and relationships with employment and working-class masculinity (Connell, 1995) and led the young men to favour some, but not all, forms of manual employment, while also dismissing sedentary service sector employment (Gater, 2022). Comparative analysis of the two studies' findings demonstrates a remarkable resemblance that potentially reveals generational transmission of an attraction to manual employment among specific members of the Aber Valley and cultural reproduction that stems from community and family cultural and structural conditions, which may be understood by considering the communities history, current conditions and drawing on the ideas and South Wales based study of Walkerdine and Jiménez (2012).

As discussed in Chapter One, coal mining was essentially the bedrock upon which the Aber Valley was founded and was previously a significant and largest source of employment in the area. Within the context of heavy industrial work, Walkerdine and Jiménez (2012) argue that the harsh conditions of this form of employment generated a hardness of body, spirit and a form of hard industrial masculinity that 'served to keep the community safe through hard-won practices … [and] assuming the bodily strength and fortitude to withstand heavy, dangerous work' (Walkerdine, 2015, p. 701) Furthermore, Walkerdine and Jiménez (2012, p. 94) then go on to argue that due to the significance of these modes of being, 'these embodiments [are] passed down through generations. In all their detailed subtlety, the tiny performances of this masculinity were what one learnt to do, to be'. Based on this notion of generational transmission, I want to argue that, concerning employment aspiration, these modes of being have not been ruptured among some of the Ladz and continue to influence employment choices and attract these young men towards manual employment. Although I will further strengthen this argument through the notion of rupture and by returning to outliers in the Ladz group, I first want to discuss the Aber Valley within a neoliberal context and draw on the research of Roberts (2018) and my own personal experiences to support my argument of generational transmission.

The Aber Valley has failed to replace the jobs lost due to the coal industry's demise. Subsequently, in contrast to the location of Roberts (2018, p. 121) study, where the 'young working-class men [were] not hostage to the traditional predispositions held by their counterparts from previous generations' and the locale had 'witnessed profound growth in retail, hotels, restaurants and wholesale' (Roberts, 2018, p. 2018), other than a few schools, community resources, several shops, and takeaways, the Aber Valley offers no significant employment opportunities. Furthermore, as stated previously, the labour market conditions of the neighbouring area and the nearest source of work consist of an employment opportunity structure that shares similarities with the UK labour market conditions of 1977. As noted, manufacturing accounts for a significant source of employment at 20.4%, construction makes up 5.6% and wholesale and retail trade; repair of motor vehicles and motorcycles is the second-largest source of employment below manufacturing at 13% (ONS, 2021c).

As previously stated, the actual visibility of manufacturing jobs or the Ladz exposure to opportunities for such employment and the subsequent impact may be somewhat questionable. However, drawing on and offering my own experience of the Aber Valley, I would argue that the virtually non-existent employment opportunities of this community, coupled with disproportionately high rates of manufacturing and construction in the neighbouring area, are an additional reason why Dan has always *'seen people working outside and looking like they're working'* or what we might interpret as people employed and associated with manual labour.

As mentioned previously, I did not return to education and university until I was 32. However, as you might imagine, I am not the only person in the Aber Valley to have gone to university and not even the first in my family. My brother was the first member of my family to attend university. My best friend also attended university, and several people in my age group in school also went to university. Although this demonstrates that some working-class young men in the Aber Valley are consistent with the notion of the ear'oles and do have middle-class aspirations (Willis, 1977), what is consistent among all of the mentioned people is other than some of them having brief spells living in the Aber Valley, none of them currently reside in this area, and the majority never returned after university, possibly due to the limited amount of employment for degree graduates, which is a theme consistent with coalfield communities as documented by Beatty et al. (2019, p. 31) The State of the Coal fields 2019 report:

> Areas with a high proportion of manual jobs, such as the coal-fields, are unlikely to retain or attract highly qualified workers, who move to the places where higher-grade jobs are more plentiful. One of the main mechanisms through which this occurs is when young people move away to university and then stay away when they move into employment, stripping the coalfields of successive cohorts of bright, well-qualified youngsters.

This is further evidenced by the disproportionately high rates of no educational attainment in the Aber Valley, consisting of 34.6% of the population, and a Level 4 and above qualification achievement of 13.6% compared to the England and Wales rates of 23% and 27%, respectively (ONS, 2011a, 2011b).

The overall argument that I want to make is that, unlike Roberts (2018, p. 121) working-class young men, some of the Ladz' employment-related findings suggest that these young men are 'hostage to the traditional predispositions held by their counterparts from previous generations' and their habitus has remained consistent with previous modes of being that were initially generated through the harsh conditions of heavy industry (Walkerdine & Jiménez 2012). However, rather than 'victim blaming' (Roberts, 2018, p. 145), I am arguing that these young men are victims of discriminatory neoliberal policy that creates winners and losers (Joppke, 2021) and a lack of regeneration, whereby the Aber Valley has seen relatively stagnant social and economic development since deindustrialisation and the demise of coal mining. Essentially, the Aber Valley has almost become structurally frozen in time, with previous modes of being going largely unchallenged and unruptured, thus equating to a continuation and transmission of a specific set of working-class masculine dispositions and subsequent attraction to manual employment. To further strengthen this argument and the notion of rupturing, the following section returns to the outliers in the Ladz' group and the young men who were not attracted or had a partial attraction to manual employment and discusses the developments of this process.

Identity Disruption

The employment aspiration data of Billy and Wesley, and Lewis and Cole, to some extent, differs from the previous Ladz and demonstrates only a partial or complete omission of traditionally masculine-associated working-class forms of skilled manual employment, particularly construction work (Ness, 2012; Shildrick & MacDonald, 2007; Thiel, 2007). Therefore, considering the protest masculinity (Connell, 2005) shared behavioural commonalities among the Ladz and the cultural and structural intergenerational transmission (Invinson, 2014a;

Walkerdine & Jiménez, 2012) related arguments presented above, the questions then are, why and how have these members of the Ladz become outliers and have differing job preferences?

Firstly, Billy rejects traditionally masculine associated working-class forms of skilled manual employment: *'Construction an tha … doesn't interest me'* and instead favours cooking and being a chef. Unlike the previous mentioned Ladz and the male association with their job preference, Billy's employment influence comes from his nan. Therefore, we may understand Billy's different job orientation through a rupturing of structurally established masculine modes of being through female influence. Similarly, although Lewis demonstrates a partial attraction to manual employment and male influence, his job preference also includes being a paramedic, which Lewis largely attributes to female influence:

> I like helping people and keeping people safe from the world … I like to use my hand a lot like. My hands gotta be doing something because that like the way I been brought up like to show respect, work and yeah be caring an tha. Because my mother and father broke up at a young age, well, when I was young, so I've just been brought up by my mum . So I've been brought up by my mother, but she's brought me up the right way.

Additionally, Lewis's stepfather is a paramedic, which Lewis equally identifies as a source of influence for his career choice. Through the transmission of dispositions, including respect and caring, which are aspects affiliated with caring masculinities (Elliott, 2016) and representation, both parent guardians seem to have somewhat destabilised the masculine modes of being and attraction to masculine forms of manual employment. However, additional evidence in these two young men's data suggests that they redefine or retraditionalize (Adkins, 1999) the type of work within traditional masculine working-class ideals. For example, in Lewis's above excerpt, we see a muddled attraction to hands-on work (Nixon, 2006, 2009) that is combined with the ideas of caring and respect. Furthermore, although Billy favours cooking and work traditionally defined as feminine (Kenway & Kraack, 2004), he defines the job role through the traditional masculine dichotomy between mental work and manual work (Willis, 1977): *'It'll [cooking] be more practical than theory, won't it. I couldn't sit in an office all day. Cooking there is so many things on your mind. it is more practical needs than theory'*.

Cole's employment aspiration data bears some of the hallmarks of the established modes of being, including a rejection of sedentary work and an attraction to dirt (Slutskaya et al., 2016; Walkerdine & Jiménez, 2012; Willis, 1977). However, we also see a form of rupturing that derives from the loss of a family member and what Thomson et al. (2002, p. 339) refer to as 'critical moments': events depicted in narrative 'considered to be important or to have had important consequences' that leads Cole to believe that he: *'couldn't go into like an ordinary type of job'* and he is instead predominantly drawn towards funeral directing. Additionally, although Wesley demonstrated several connections to other members of the Ladz, Wesley's

career orientation also omits skilled manual employment and includes job preferences attached to media and television. This employment preference raises specu-
lation about whether Wesley's involvement in media projects at the youth centre
influenced the concept of 'other-directed', wherein external factors shape a young
person's career orientation (Veness 1962, p. 73), or, at the very least, whether it may
have fuelled Wesley's intrinsic interest in media and television.

Place Attachment

The previous two sections concentrated on the Ladz' identity construction, showing how the young men's habitus, modes of being, and subsequent employment
aspirations are constructed in the context of family, community and peer groups,
whilst also demonstrating how a working-class masculine attraction to manual
employment and laddish associated (Willis, 1977) ways of being may be partially
ruptured through particular circumstances. This section demonstrates the reinforcing qualities of community and family and the strength to which these aspects
may potentially determine employment opportunities.

Learning to Labour (Willis, 1977) does not entirely explore the lads' community
attachment, or not in the purest sense. However, among most of the Ladz, place
attachment plays a significant role in shaping the young men's employment-related
views and willingness to commute and consider relocating for employment purposes.

Place attachment is a concept that often comes with various, although sometimes
marginal, differences in how this idea is understood and how it relates. Therefore,
this section defines its use of place attachment according to Hidalgo and Hernandez (2001, p. 274) definition: 'a positive affective bond between an individual and
a specific place, the main characteristic of which is the tendency of the individual
to maintain closeness to such a place'. Although this interpretation is included and
mainly reflects the Ladz' community-related data, as subsequent sections will show,
whether the young men's attachment to their community is positive is open to interpretation and dependent upon how one assesses the impact.

Among the Ladz, although there is a limited sense of place attachment in a
geographical form, there is evidence of a relatively strong social bond to the Aber
Valley among many of the young men. This attachment derives from ontological
security (Giddens, 1991) together with a sense of close-knittedness that stems
from family attachment and the idea that: *'everyone knows each other'* and *'everyone's got each other back'* (Billy). Essentially, in a world that has supposedly
become individualised (Bauman, 1999; Beck, 1992; Giddens, 1991), among the
majority of the Ladz, there is a recognised sense of community belonging that
attaches itself through support networks and a fondness for family and kin. This
attachment gives the young men a sense of ontological security (Giddens, 1991)
that derives from the notion of a secure environment and the company of familiar
unthreatening others. However, this mental state equally helps generate a 'terrified
clinging' (Walkerdine & Jiménez, 2012, p. 75), in a sense that the young men are
torn between a desire to remain rooted in their community whilst acknowledging
limited employment opportunities and the necessity to find work that generates a
restrictive and condition-based spatially close employment approach.

Whilst wishing not to pathologise the young men's cultural adoption and ways of being – for I am also deeply attached to this community for similar reasons as the Ladz – one equally needs to be a realist and recognise the limitation of the young men's community attachment and the structural hindering effect of the area that reduces employment opportunities. As stated previously, the Aber Valley offers these young men a virtually zero work source. Furthermore, the local employment opportunity structure is significantly comprised of manufacturing work (ONS, 2021c). Therefore, if the Ladz' employment ambitions are to be realised, realistically, these young men will be required to at least commute to work outside their local borough and possibly further afield beyond the secure confines of their community. Although some of the Ladz are willing to commute to work, this is often conditionally based on a significant wage and a relatively short travelling distance, further restricting the young men's employment possibilities.

This employment-related section has essentially argued that the Ladz social reality and employment understanding are largely determined by the intergenerational transmission of historically related modes of being (Walkerdine & Jiménez, 2012). The following section demonstrates the education-related effect of these modes of being and employment understanding and their influence on the Ladz' approach concerning school and their level of academic engagement.

Educational Juxtaposition

In several ways, the Ladz' school behaviour demonstrated a relatively static configuration and a combination of practices that echo those of their laddish predecessors, demonstrated through school and social conduct that included 'dossing, blagging, wagging' (Willis, 1977, p. 26), smoking and taking drugs, along with nonconformist performative masculine (Ward, 2015) school behaviour such as classroom disruption and a somewhat unwillingness to engage that derived from educational difficulties, peer group pressure, gender policing techniques (Martino, 2000; Pascoe & Stewart, 2016) and subsequent macho masculine displays (O'Donnell & Sharpe, 2003). Furthermore, some of the young men's behaviour extended beyond the lads (Willis, 1977) and included physical confrontations with teachers and authority figures (Roberts, 1995). However, despite the Ladz' nonconformist school behavioural displays, rather than demonstrating an outright disdain for school, the Ladz essentially adopted a middle-ground perspective epitomised by Tommy's response: *'It's alright, but it's not the best'*. Subsequently, we were left with a seemingly odd juxtaposition whereby the Ladz' nonconformist school behaviour places them within the lads' category (Willis, 1977). Yet, their view of school represents a centre position that is often affiliated with ordinary Kids – working-class young men who 'neither simply accept nor reject school' (Brown, 1987, p. 31) – or the 'missing middle' (Roberts, 2018, p. 78) as they have become more commonly known.

Pragmatism

The source of the Ladz' educational juxtaposition derives from several aspects. The *'alright'* perspective reflects the young men's partial commitment to the teaching paradigm (Willis, 1977), whereby, unlike the lads and Mac an Ghaill (1996, p. 65)

'The Macho Lads' who rejected 'formal school knowledge and the potential exchange value it has in the labour market', the Ladz recognise the importance of educational attainment and its necessity in enabling them to pursue their chosen career path and job aspiration as epitomised by Tommy's excerpt: *'You need them [GCSEs], you mad head'*. The Ladz commitment to education reflects a labour market change whereby during the lads' (Willis, 1977) era, working-class young men who left school with no qualifications were able to find employment with satisfactory rates of pay and some prospect of security with reasonable ease (Roberts, 2020), whereas, contemporary working-class young men who leave education with no qualifications are now likely to find themselves in the precariat class and limited job opportunities in minimum wage employment such as 'hospitality (hotels, bars, cafes, restaurants) and in retail shops' (Roberts, 2020, p. 35).

Furthermore, the educational requirements for further education (FE) courses have also increased. For example, in my youth, entry into FE and the Carpentry and Joiner L2 course at the local college that the Ladz are likely to attend was based on no necessity for GCSEs. However, that same course now requires successful completion of the Foundation Carpentry & Joinery course. The Foundation Carpentry & Joinery course requires 3 GCSEs at grade A*- E, including English/Welsh and Maths/Numeracy, or completing Construction Skills Entry 3. Furthermore, Construction Skills Entry 3 requires an Entry Level 2 in Literacy and Numeracy.

The identification of marginalised working-class young men engaging in education is not unique in a contemporary context (Freie, 2007; Ward, 2015; Weis, 1990). However, the Ladz do not merely engage in education for knowledge in its purest sense; instead, their process is measured, calculated and primarily based on their employment aspiration: *'Maths and English … just good knowledge, isn't it. I need them to be a mechanic in it.'* (Tommy), *'Biology's interesting so I wen tha one about the body and tha and part of paramedics I wanna do'* (Lewis).

> Maths I didn't mind it, but I didn't like it, but I done it cos it was relevant. You got to know things for exams. I want to be a plumber, and you need a D in Maths GSCE, so I tried to get a D in Maths. (Dan)

The Ladz' selective engagement with education resonates with the 'ordinary kids' and what Brown (1987, p. 100) refers to as 'alienated instrumentalism', which may be understood as viewing school 'as a "means" of obtaining credentials to compete for certain types of employment'. However, the Ladz' approach to school is not 'Justified for getting any job rather than the jobs they want' (Brown, 1987, p. 67). Neither is the young men's approach an attempt to engage with a 'normalised discourse of compliance' akin to Roberts (2018, p. 94) missing middle because the Ladz' school behaviour includes non-compliance. Instead, the Ladz approach to education is what I refer to as pragmatic, this being a purposeful and selective approach to education based on employment aspiration that largely derives from the intergenerational transmission and modes of being (Walkerdine & Jiménez, 2012). This pragmatic approach to education somewhat demonstrates the strength of the employment-related intergenerational transmission process (Ivinson, 2014a; Walkerdine & Jiménez, 2012), for subjects deemed irrelevant to the Ladz' employment orientation are primarily disregarded and deemed meaningless knowledge. Furthermore, the pragmatic approach collectively reduces the Ladz' academic engagement to roughly three to four subjects, which is the minimum entry requirement for many of the Further Education courses on which the Ladz hopes to enrol, thus leaving no scope for failure or bargaining power.

Pragmatism Consequences

Within the Ladz' pragmatic approach, educational subjects considered unimportant to career orientation are primarily disregarded, which places a significant strain on the teaching paradigm and the idea that teachers can provide important, meaningful knowledge, and in return, students are expected to give the teachers respect and conform to the rules and social relations of the schooling system (Feinberg & Soltis, 2009; Walker, 1985; Willis, 1977). The rejective side of the Ladz' pragmatism undermines the foundations of the modern capitalist schooling system and the notion of compliance with the young men often refusing to attend or engage in lessons deemed irrelevant, which leads to truancy, classroom disruption and even physical confrontations with teachers. Essentially, when the Ladz' pragmatic school approach is threatened, or when the young men are challenged and feel undermined, they draw on their traditional masculine modes of being and engage in masculine-associated behaviour (Francis, 1999; Jackson, 2006; Willis, 1977) to help cope with the external forces that threaten the practical sense of their working-class habitus (Bourdieu, 1990a).

Fundamentally, as Delamont (2000, p. 99) states, the Ladz 'make life hard for [some of] their teachers, reject the opportunities for [certain] credentials', yet the young men don't 'hate school', they don't 'despise [all] teachers', and they don't see 'boys who do work as effeminate and weak', for they themselves with their masculine modes of being and behaviour equally engage in some school work. Therefore, I would argue that a standoff better explains the disjointed teacher and pupil relationship in the sense that the intergenerational transmission process has produced what, to the Ladz, is a seemingly natural and common-sense approach to education. However, the Ladz' pragmatic engagement and selective approach to knowledge contradict a teacher's understanding of school and the underpinning teaching paradigm notion that all knowledge is meaningful and worthy of respect and conformism (Feinberg & Soltis, 2009; Walker, 1985; Willis, 1977). In essence, neither party understands the other's meaning-making, and each party's practices threaten the other approach, equating to a sense of inferiority and subsequent conflict.

Pragmatism Reinforcement

A pragmatic approach to education demonstrates how intergenerational transmissions are converted to agency. In other words, the Ladz' understanding of employment and their job orientation largely derives from family and community members, which in turn determines the young men's selective individual approach to school, including positive and negative engagement. This section focuses on an aspect that reinforces the young men's pragmatic approach and has educational and employment consequences.

Seven of the Ladz openly admitted to some form of medically diagnosed learning disability and/or mental health condition, and there was also a partial suggestion that one of the other two remaining members also suffered from a similar problem. Therefore, whereas Willis' lads were simply categorised as 'non-conformist' or 'anti-school', the Ladz' learning disabilities and/or struggles with mental health often negatively affect their schooling experience and behaviour. For example:

> I didn't get diagnosed with it, dyslexia until the end of school ... So, I was a bit distracted in school. I was always messing about, and I was always getting in trouble. I could never concentrate because, in school, I could never understand the work. (Lewis)

> I dunno. It's just I have, um, ADHD, so I can't concentrate, and then I'm writing, and I'll be in a mood; then someone catches my attention, then it takes a good 5 minutes to settle then. (Billy)

These excerpts demonstrate that the young men's educational difficulties generate frustration, leading to disengagement and disruptive classroom behaviour. This sequence of events resonates with Jackson's (2002) notion that some young men engage in acts of masculine-associated laddish class clown behaviour in an attempt to protect their self-worth. However, rather than being a means of increasing 'status within [the] peer group' or an attempt to 'deflect attention away from poor academic performance [and] sabotage the efforts and performances of classmates' (Jackson, 2002, p. 47), I would argue that the young men's modes of being and masculinity act as a default position (Ward, 2015) that they return to and draw on in times of difficulty, possibly because they lack the confidence or ability to draw on other techniques, or perhaps their masculine identity makes them reluctant to ask for support and seek help.

The Ladz' learning disability and/or mental health condition have additional education and employment consequences. For some of the young men, the diagnosis of these conditions reinforces their educational pragmatism, for example: *'That's why I like creating stuff. I've got dyslexia. My imagination is running wild'* (Ian). *'My sister is really creative – she has dyslexia and she like the art type, but me I'm just like – I've got dyspraxia and my art skills are not really good'* (Wesley). In essence, these young men adopt a sense of learning disability meaning-making and determine their strengths, weaknesses and engagement through this. The notion of learning disability meaning-making and the idea that the young men make sense of their abilities and behaviour in accordance with their learning disabilities also filter through to their employment understating, for example: *'I just like getting my hands dirty ini. It helps my concentration because I got ADHD'* (Lewis). *'I like taking things apart. It helps with my ADHD'.* (Tommy).

What is notable about these excerpts, particularly the employment-related ones, is the fact that an attraction to 'hands-on' work and manual labour has previously been associated with a working-class identity (Nixon, 2006, 2009; Willis, 1977) and protest masculinity (Connell, 1995), whereas Lewis and Tommy now associate their attraction to this employment aspect with their learning disability.

At this point, and although I knew I could not answer it, I asked myself: did the lads (Willis, 1977) have learning disabilities that went undiagnosed due to a lack of understanding? I asked this because Willis's study shows significant comparative similarities between the behaviour of these young men and the lads. Alternatively, does the Ladz data demonstrate medicalisation (Rose, 2007), defined as: 'interpreting newer and newer aspects of reality, including human behaviour, in medical terms, and treating them as medical problems rather than e.g. social, political or existential ones' (Kaczmarek, 2018, p. 119)? If we consider the periodic shift and the neoliberalist ideologies that have accompanied this change, including individualism, self-determination and self-responsibility (Harvey, 2007), then it becomes slightly coincidental that forms of behaviour and views that were once associated with protest masculinity and structural issues, including a position of powerless and poverty (Connell, 1995), have now become an individualistic medical problem (Kaczmarek, 2018; Rose, 2007), or at least in respect of the Ladz' understanding. I am not for one second disregarding the reality of learning disabilities because I have a lived understanding of them. However, this comparative discussion raises questions about understanding behaviours within a contemporary context and demonstrates the ramifications of learning disability diagnosis and how it affects the Ladz' level of academic engagement.

Pragmatism Incubated

The reality of the young men's school behaviour, which includes classroom disruption and verbal and physical confrontation with teachers, has meant that five have been excluded from mainstream school and attend alternative provisions (AP). Although the young men's behaviour may hinder 'classmates' efforts and performances' (Jackson, 2002, p. 47) and 'make life hard for their teachers' (Delamont, 2000, p. 99), one questions whose benefit this process serves because there are some alarming statistics associated with this strategy. For example, young people with special educational needs, disabilities and those living in poverty are more likely to be excluded and educated in an alternative provision than their peers (Gill, 2017). Furthermore, 'only 1 per cent of excluded young people achieve five good GCSEs including English and maths' (Gill, 2017, p. 22), and the majority of UK prisoners have been excluded from school (Gill, 2017). Based on these facts, it would be easy to present the argument of exclusion and AP's as a state apparatus of social reproduction (Althusser, 1970). However, I would prefer to avoid that potentially deterministic association and instead discuss them within the context of the themes central to this book, including intergenerational transmission and rupturing, combined with my lived understanding of the lads' culture. Therefore, I want to argue that exclusion and AP's act as an incubation chamber.

An incubation chamber is essentially a device that enables organisms to grow by providing optimal conditions. Taking this definition, I argue that APs potentially create a perfect environment for laddish culture (Jackson, 2006; McDowell, 2004) to thrive and develop a continuation of the Ladz' educational pragmatic approach. Firstly, although Dan offered some favourable recognition of AP's, including increased support and smaller classes, which I will return to in the policy approach section, in essence, these educational institutions group together young people with shared difficulties, like-minded school-related beliefs and behaviour, and often, hyper-masculine (Mac an Ghaill, 1994) tendencies. From my experience as a laddish (Jackson, 2006; McDowell, 2004) young man who encountered a similar environment through my classroom disruption behaviour that led to me being placed in the lowest attainment group for several school subjects and surrounded by individuals who shared my school disposition, this grouping process creates a breeding ground whereby hyper-masculinity (Mac an Ghaill, 1994) and a counter school culture (Willis, 1977) is fostered and cultivated, often by young men who are jostling for position and eager to express their identity and self-worth (Jackson, 2006) against an environment that corrodes self-respect (Sennett & Cobb, 1972).

Secondly, APs sometimes provide a limited curriculum and focus on maths, English and vocational options (Mills et al., 2016), a process that mirrors the Ladz' pragmatic approach to education and 'can reinforce marginalisation and disadvantage' (Tate & Greatbatch, 2017, p. 36). In essence, APs potentially provide an environment conducive to 'laddism' (Jackson, 2014; Phipps, 2017; Willis, 1977) and the Ladz' pragmatism and seemingly offer minimal means of rupturing these ways of being, a process identified above as being crucial in altering the young men's mindset, destabilising established modes of being and creating an alternative perspective.

Unspoiled Habitus

The Ladz' employment and educational findings and discussion demonstrate a close association with working-class masculinity (Connell, 1995). This concluding school-to-work transition section confirms the strength of this masculine identity by discussing the Ladz' service sector employment-related data and considering and comparing the young men's findings concerning relevant prior working-class related studies.

The Ladz' service sector employment-related data mostly revealed that the young men were reluctant to engage in service sector work due to concerns about being: *'spoken to like garbage'* (Ian), an inability to *'keep calm and try and hold anger back'* (Craig), *'getting angry'* (Billy) and a reluctance to *'take shit off nobody'* (Lewis). These excerpts are reminiscent of prior employment-related studies of working-class men that have often demonstrated a rejection or reluctance to engage in service sector employment due to the inability to 'put on a smiley face' (Nixon, 2006, 2009), engage in emotional labour (Hochschild, 1983) and the associated features of deference and docility, features that are claimed to be at odds with working-class masculinity (Connell, 1995) and 'the right to stick up for yourself' (McDowell, 2003, p. 176). However, the relatively recent research of Roberts (2018, p. 121) has challenged these claims and identified working-class young men that 'embrace[d] service work, and its attendant demands'.

The disparity between the findings of this study and that of Roberts (2018) raises questions about the source of these differences and how they might be explained and understood. The answer to these questions is potentially found by comparing both studies, location, changes, and labour market conditions. Firstly, Roberts (2018, p. 126) argues that his participants 'had not merely inherited older generations of men's dispositions towards and understanding of appropriately masculine work'. However, some of the Ladz' data does suggest 'intergenerational transfers of knowledge from father to son' (Walker & Roberts, 2018, pp. 10–11) or male kin, which includes an understanding of appropriate forms of employment.

Secondly, Roberts then goes on to argue that his participants 'entered the economy some 25 to 30 years after the process of de-industrialisation began', and thus for his young men, due to locational labour market changes, service sector work 'is all they know' (2018, p. 126) and therefore, their working-class habitus has adapted to this change. Conversely, the Ladz' immediate spatial labour market conditions are dissimilar and resemble the labour market conditions of the 1970s, with comparatively high rates of manufacturing and construction (Syed, 2019) and virtually no substantial service sector work in their immediate community, the Aber Valley. Therefore, rather than the Ladz' habitus remaining 'durable in the face of social and economic change' (Roberts, 2018, p. 126), I argue that these young men's habitus generally has not been subjected to change and challenged or at least in a structural employment-related sense. In essence, the comparison between the two study findings and the regional characteristics strengthens my earlier argument concerning inherited modes of being, and a lack of rupturing, which has caused a continuation of working-class masculinity (Connell, 1995) employment-related orientation towards manual forms of employment.

Contradictory Protest Masculinity Behaviours

I have demonstrated and discussed the Ladz' association with working-class and/ or protest masculinity through some form of school resistance, association with manual labour, and violence through physical confrontations with teachers (Connell, 1995). However, despite this association, several of the Ladz' responses and findings included emotional openness and behavioural practices that contradicted this masculine position and thus raised questions about the young men's masculinity formation and their ways of doing gender (West & Zimmerman, 1987).

The Ladz' working-class and/or protest masculinity (Connell, 1995) contradictory practises and views featured through multiple facets, including a hugging greeting practice and physical tactility that may be perceived as a feminine practice (Frosh et al., 2002) and thus challenging the hyper-masculine notion of a 'rejection of all aspects that are deemed feminine' (Hayward & Mac an Ghaill, 2003, p. 97), whilst also demonstrating same-sex touch which historically may be perceived as homosexual behaviour (Blanchard et al., 2017; Ralph & Roberts, 2020). Furthermore, some of the Ladz discussed mental health issues and expressed emotional openness and disclosures of vulnerability that would have historically been 'considered a sign of weakness for men, resulting in some form of emasculation' (Ralph & Roberts, 2020, p. 97) and contradict the traditional masculine (Courtenay, 2011) values of being tough and courageous (Cheng, 1999). Moreover, the visual methods data and nursing picture revealed sensitivity, compassion, and empathy, aspects that oppose hegemonic masculinity's central features, including being unemotional and dispassionate (Collier, 1998; Connell & Messerschmidt, 2005).

Additionally, dissimilar to prior studies whereby social relations and friend-ship grouping were single-sex, and gender-exclusive (Frosh et al., 2002; Mac an Ghaill, 1994) and women were viewed merely as 'both sexual objects and domes-tic comforters' (Willis, 1977, p. 43), and whereby 'boys who hung around with girls as friends were liable to be constructed as effeminate "woosies"' and at risk of homosexual taunts (Frosh et al., 2002, pp. 180–181), among the Ladz gender-segregated friendship grouping was non-existent, with the young men frequently mixing together with girls chatting, listening to music, dancing or playing pool in what seemed to be an essentially platonic relationship that was not met with ridicule. Similarly, and contrary to Willis' lads' sexist and homophobic discourse (McRobbie, 1991; Skeggs, 1992; Walker, 1985), which deemed women 'inferior and incapable of doing certain things' (Willis, 1977, p. 149), including manual labour and traditionally associated masculine forms of employment, some of the young men expressed gender-egalitarian views, stating that there is: *'No difference between a man and a woman'* (Dan) and thus disputing the idea that women are inferior (Willis, 1977), whilst also deviating from the homophobic position that is often associated with the lads' category and working-class masculinities (Connell, 1995; Epstein, 1997; Francis, 1999; Mac an Ghaill, 1994; Willis, 1977) and stating that: *'Your sexual preference or gender or ... doesn't make odds on your personality'* (Cole).

Amalgamated Masculinities

Although there is some variation in the young men's responses and it would be disingenuous to claim that these working-class/protest masculinity (Connell, 1995) contradictory practices are entirely representative of the Ladz. There are unmistakable masculinity-related behavioural and attitude changes among these young men that somewhat challenge the recognised understanding of laddish cul-ture (Jackson, 2006; McDowell, 2004; Willis, 1977). Therefore, change in itself is not questionable; instead, it is a question of how we explain and understand this change. The following section explores the young men's gender practices, using masculinities theory to explain the Ladz' gender formation whilst also offering my interpretation.

Firstly, we may understand the young men's masculinity practices in terms of Connell and Messerschmidt's (2005, p. 849) hegemonic masculinity theory and through the notion of a locally constructed form of masculinity that derives from 'the arenas of face-to-face interaction of families, organizations, and immediate communities, as typically found in ethnograph[y]', and the idea that 'men can adopt hegemonic masculinity when it is desirable, but the same men can distance themselves strategically from hegemonic masculinity at other moments' (Connell & Messerschmidt, 2005, p. 841).

Similarly, the notion of hybrid masculinities may explain the Ladz' views and opinions. For example, the young men's attraction to manual work and school resistance demonstrates an affiliation with protest masculinity (Connell, 1995) and values including toughness and stoicism (McDowell, 2003). Whereas expressions of physical tactility, sensitivity, compassion and empathy and gender-egalitarian views (Kaplan et al., 2017) may be understood as incorporating 'elements associated with … subordinated masculinities and femininities' (Bridges & Pascoe, 2014, p. 246). Collectively, the young men's views and opinions, which include toughness combined with emotional openness and the admittance of vulnerability, arguably support the notion of hybrid masculinities (Bridges & Pascoe, 2014; Messner, 2007).

However, both these ideas suppose that the Ladz are purposely adopting a sophisticated practice whereby softer masculine characteristics are demonstrated in an attempt to somewhat distance themselves from a protest or hegemonic masculine position (Bridges & Pascoe, 2014). Although I do not entirely dispute this idea and the possibility that the young men may have adopted this approach to present themselves favourably to female peers and me, given the social location of these men, it seems implausible to argue that they are borrowing 'from below', as per hybrid masculinity (Gater, 2024).

Furthermore, we may also assume that, akin to Roberts (2018, p. 2) missing middle, the Ladz' 'working-class young masculinity is itself in a state of transition'. However, transition assumes 'change from one state to another' (Collins English Dictionary, 2012, p. 608) Yet, the Ladz' working-class and/or protest masculinity (Connell, 1995) generally seems to be in a relatively static state, evidenced by the fact that many of the young men have a fairly rigid employment aspiration that almost exclusively includes manual labour or have redefined and retraditionalize (Adkins, 1999) alternative types of work within traditional masculine working-class ideals. However, they equally demonstrate qualities associated with a softer version of masculinity, including 'emotional openness [and] peer tactility' (Anderson & McCormack, 2018, p. 547). Therefore, although I recognise that: 'protest masculinity … is compatible with respect and attention to women … egalitarian views about the sexes … and a sense of display which in conventional role terms is decidedly feminine' (Connell, 2005, p. 112), I want to suggest that some of the Ladz display what I refer to as amalgamated masculinities (Gater, 2024) – a fusion of both working-class/protest masculine (Connell, 1995) characteristics and softer masculine attributes (Anderson & McCormack, 2018).

My explanation for the formulation of the young men's amalgamated masculinities initially derives from employment findings that demonstrate primary gender socialisation (Pilcher & Whelenhan, 2004) and the 'intergenerational transfers of knowledge' (Walker & Roberts, 2018, p. 8), which initially establishes working-class and/or protest masculinity (Connell, 1995) evidenced through the Ladz attraction to manual labour and subsequent school resistance. However:

> Socialisation is ... a life-long process and as individuals grow up
> and older, they continually encounter new situations and expe-
> riences and so learn new aspects of femininity or masculinity
> throughout their lives. (Pilcher & Whelenhan, 2004, p. 160)

Therefore, I suggest that some of the young men are assimilating some ideas
of manhood and masculinity beyond their primary socialisation and immediate community and internalising softer masculine ideals through popular media,
which has included scrutiny upon men and masculinity (Wolfman et al., 2021).
The notion of media influence was evident within Billy's response to explaining
male peer tactility and potentially in the Ladz responses to the nursing picture
that included 'new' masculinity characteristics of sensitivity, compassion, and
empathy (Spector-Mersel & Gilbar, 2021), which were comparable to the contemporary lyrics of Dave's 'Question Time' song which discussed the idea nursing
wage inequality.

What Lies Ahead for the Lodz?

As discussed in Chapter Two, the future of work is a contested terrain with conflicting perspectives and predictions regarding the impact of artificial intelligence
and automation on jobs (Arntz et al., 2016; Frey & Osborne, 2013; Hawksworth
et al., 2018; Leopold et al., 2018; McKinsey, 2017). However, despite the competing viewpoints, there is a consensus that new technologies will cause some
employment disruption (Welsh Government, 2019a) and jobs that were thought
to be resilient to new technologies, including several of the Ladz' construction
work career orientations (Chui & Mischke, 2019; Wallace-Stephens & Morgante,
2021) are likely to be affected by new technologies. For example, a recent Royal
Society for Arts, Manufactures and Commerce report predicts that up to 50 per
cent of some individual construction tasks could be automated (Wallace-
Stephens & Morgante, 2021). This prediction stems from an increased 'trend
towards modular construction, which is manufactured offsite and more easily
automated' (Wallace-Stephens & Morgante, 2021, p. 26). Furthermore, construction work is increasingly incorporating new technologies, meaning 'even the average construction worker will be expected to use a tablet to access building plans or
operate a drone in place of doing a physical site walkthrough' (Chui & Mischke,
2019, p. 5). These changes will transform the skills needed in the construction
industry, and workers will be required to upskill and acquire new technological
and digital skills (Wallace-Stephens & Morgante, 2021).

Aside from the fact that the Ladz' pragmatism lessens their engagement with
education and reduces the likelihood of them achieving the necessary qualifications to facilitate entry into FE and subsequently achieving their employment
goal, the above discussion demonstrates that all of the young men's career orientations are susceptible to new technologies. Even Billy's catering preference is not
immune, with Manyika et al. (2017) suggesting that cooking has a high automation potential. Subsequently, the Ladz are likely to succumb to the upskilling and
reskilling notion surrounding the future of work (Bell et al., 2017; Brown et al.,

2020; HM Government, 2021; Schlogl, 2021; Wheelahan, 2022) and be required to re-engage with some form of education. Based on the young men's educational pragmatism, predicting how they will cope with this requirement is difficult. For example, will they recognise the relevance and necessity of upskilling and reskilling requirements and pragmatically engage? Or will they fail to recognise the importance of this process and underestimate the impact of new technologies? A conclusive answer to these questions is impossible. However, based on the findings about the young men, we can surmise that the Ladz' educational pragmatism will play a pivotal role in determining the outcome.

Along with the importance of upskilling and reskilling, future of work predictions equally anticipate an increased demand for competencies that are currently believed to be hard for robots to replicate, including soft skills and social skills (Brynjolfsson & McAfee, 2012; Davenport & Kirby, 2016; Deloitte, 2016; Goodhart, 2020) and related abilities such as 'emotional intelligence … sympathy and empathy, relationship-building and negotiation skills, resilience and character' (Haldane, 2018, p. 16). The Ladz' masculinities demonstrate the emergence of these qualities among the young men, which suggests that they have capabilities that could potentially help achieve a successful employment future. However, the young men's inherited modes of being and socialisation processes (Pilcher & Whelenhan, 2004) have largely created a career orientation that nullifies the usefulness of these qualities and the possibility of employment options other than those that have become customary to the young men.

Policy Approach

The previous section and those before have identified barriers that could harm the Ladz's ability to achieve a successful school-to-work transition and possibly hinder their chances of employment progress and stability. These barriers include a socialisation (Pilcher & Whelenham, 2004) process or 'intergenerational transfers of knowledge' (Walker & Roberts, 2018, p. 8), which establishes the Ladz' career orientation, which in turn contributes to the young men's pragmatic and selective approach to education, which causes the young men to partly oppose the teaching paradigm (Willis, 1977) and brings them into opposition with the rules and social relations of the schooling system (Feinberg & Soltis, 2009; Walker, 1985). This makes it virtually impossible for them to achieve the educational benchmark of five GCSEs at A-C (MacDonald & Marsh, 2005), reducing the likelihood of them gaining entry into FE and ultimately reaching their career expectation.

The cumulative effects of class inequalities that shape the Ladz experiences of the school-to-work transition, place them in danger of becoming not in education, employment or training (NEET). However, recent UK Government policy discourse aims to prevent this and has centred on the notion of levelling up, which 'means giving everyone the opportunity to flourish. It means people everywhere living longer and more fulfilling lives, and benefitting from sustained rises in living standards and well-being' (HM Government, 2022, p. xii). The levelling up process focuses on deprived areas and includes raising educational attainment and providing young people with the skills employers need. Similarly, the Wales

Well-being of Future Generations Act aims to improve the 'social, economic, environmental and cultural well-being of Wales' (Welsh Government, 2021, p. 9). One of the goals of this Act is to create a: 'society that enables people to fulfil their potential no matter what their background or circumstances (including their socio-economic background and circumstances)' (Welsh Government, 2021, p. 7), which includes a focus on providing school leavers with skills and qualifications, young people developing the right skills and ensuring equal access to decent jobs (Welsh Government, 2021).

Although both of these policy approaches centre around the social mobility agenda and reducing social disadvantage (Ingram & Gamsu, 2022) and aim to enhance the school-to-work transition of marginalised young men, both strategies are relatively generic in their approach and ignore specificity, and the culturally and community founded education and employment perspectives identified in this study. Therefore, I propose the following policy interventions:

1. The Ladz have established a specific approach to education and employment that will be relatively difficult to change due to its primary socialisation origins (Pilcher & Whelenhan, 2004). Therefore, we need to recognise their pragmatic approach to education and consider ways of enhancing and developing this approach. I suggest a collaborative educational strategy whereby these young men select their own subject engagement and construct a personal academic timetable whilst also manipulating this process through career advice around necessary academic credentials and predicted future of work changes. This approach would empower these young men, draw on their protest masculinity (Connell, 1995) and harness the masculine traits of 'autonomy, independence and control' (Messerschmidt, 1993, p. 104) in an attempt to increase their level of educational engagement.

2. Early intervention is needed to increase employment aspiration among the Aber Valley young men. Working-class manual employment orientations are established through kin, community (Veness, 1962) and primary socialisation (Pilcher & Whelenhan, 2004), which in turn determines their pragmatic approach to education. Therefore, early rigid career dispositions need to be challenged, or 'disrupted' in order to broaden the young men's employment orientations and potentially increase academic engagement and outcomes. Subsequently, I suggest that a programme be delivered whereby primary school young people are given talks and introduced to people in employment other than manual labour as a means of demonstrating representation of alternative forms of employment for working-class persons. This notion corresponds with Veness's (1962, p. 73) idea of other-directed, where a young person's career orientation is influenced by external sources of information and stimulated by 'talks, conversations, pamphlets, broadcasts and so on'. However, the people will equally need to be individuals the young men can identify with to make the career option realistic. Consequently, I propose a financially supported community delivered programme whereby residents in the Aber Valley or similar coalfield areas in employment other than manual

labour are recruited to deliver discussions about their employment role and job satisfaction.

3. There is a recognised need for additional support for young men with education and learning difficulties. Subsequently, I propose a relatively radical, possibly divisive approach to these problems. Rather than merely focusing on the challenges and negative aspects of learning disabilities, we should equally identify the strengths of these issues and try to foster them through tailored forms of academic engagement. For example, dyslexia is believed to enhance critical thinking and abstract thinking and dyslexics 'think mainly in pictures instead of words' (Davis & Braun, 2010, p. 5). These qualities need to be spoken about and activated. Subsequently, increasing the young men's abilities whilst also preventing the young men's sense of learning disability meaning-making that decreases their academic confidence and engagement. Similarly, there needs to be increased consideration and effort to integrate these young men into mainstream school and among pupils with differing qualities and aspirations, rather than within the alternative provision incubating echo chamber.

Final Thoughts

This book contributes to the contemporary understanding of marginalised working-class young men's school-to-work transition and their formulation of masculinity in the context of societal and industrial change. My research in the Aber Valley illustrates a degree of compliance to certain traditional cultural values associated with working-class masculinity, including a general orientation to manual labour (Connell, 1995), whilst also demonstrating something of a shift in young men's perception of the relevance of education and masculine identity. Unlike their laddish predecessors (1977), although the Ladz demonstrate a complex relationship with school, they are no longer anti-learning (Jackson, 2006, 2010) and do not reject the relevance of academic credentials (Mac an Ghaill, 1994). Instead, they recognise their necessity in facilitating employment opportunities. However, for several of the young men, their schooling process is still bound up with the theme of 'Learning to Labour' – albeit skilled labour rather than non-skilled – which I argued resulted from intergenerational transmission (Ivinson 2014a; Walkerdine & Jiménez, 2012), and a relatively static regional labour market and minimal regeneration within the Aber Valley.

Nevertheless, although the young men share commonalities, there is some evidence of changes in employment orientation among some of the Ladz, which derived from destabilised and ruptured modes of being (Walkerdine & Jiménez, 2012). Evidence of change is further pronounced in the young men's masculinities discourse and practises through softer displays (Anderson, 2009) of masculinity, that somewhat contradict ideas of protest masculinity (Connell, 1995). Although the strength and understanding of this change are relatively inconclusive, there is undoubtedly change among these young men. Therefore, rather than making marginalised working-class young men the scourge of society and labelling them as regressive (Roberts & Elliott, 2020), I urge policymakers and academics to consider these changes beyond performative masculinities (Ward, 2015) and 'selective incorporation' (Pascoe, 2014, p. 246) and recognise the possibility to harness and develop these changes to help increase working-class young men's life chances and deliver broader societal benefit.

References

Adkins, L. (1999). Community and economy: A retraditionalization of gender? *Theory, Culture & Society, 16*(1), 119–139.

Adler, P. A., & Adler, P. (1987). *Membership roles in field research*. Sage.

Aggarwal, S., & Nash, S. (2018). *Automation trends in 2018: New model of creative thinking through human–machine collaboration*. Newbookhill.

Ainsley, C. (2018). *The new working class: How to win hearts, minds and votes*. Policy Press.

Allas, T., Fairbairn, W., & Foote, E. (2020). *The economic case for reskilling in the UK: How employers can thrive by boosting workers' skills*. McKinsey & Company.

Allen, K., & Hollingworth, S. (2013). "Sticky Subjects" or "Cosmopolitan Creatives"? Social class, place and urban young people's aspirations for work in the knowledge economy. *Urban Studies, 50*(3), 499–517.

Althusser, L. (1970). *Ideology and ideological state apparatuses*. Verso Books.

Anderson, E. (2005). Orthodox and inclusive masculinity: Competing masculinities among heterosexual men in a feminized terrain. *Sociological Perspectives, 48*(3), 337–355.

Anderson, E. (2008). Inclusive masculinity in a fraternal setting. *Men and Masculinities, 10*(5), 604–620.

Anderson, E. (2009). *Inclusive masculinity: The changing nature of masculinities*. Routledge.

Anderson, E., & McCormack, M. (2018). Inclusive masculinity theory: Overview, reflection and refinement. *Journal of Gender Studies, 27*(5), 547–561.

Anderson, E., & McGuire, R. (2010). Inclusive masculinity theory and the gendered politics of men's rugby. *Journal of Gender Studies, 19*(3), 249–261.

Andersson, A., & Beckman, A. (2018). Young working-class men without jobs: Reimagining work and masculinity in postindustrial Sweden. In C. Walker & S. Roberts (Eds.), *Masculinity, labour, and neoliberalism working-class men in international perspective* (pp. 101–124). Springer.

Andreasson, J., & Johansson, T. (2017). Doped manhood: Negotiating fitness doping and masculinity in an online community. In T. Johansson & C. Haywood (Eds.), *Marginalized masculinities* (pp. 139–154). Routledge.

Archer, L., DeWitt, J., Osborne, J., Dillon, J., Willis, B., & Wong, B. (2012). "Balancing acts": Elementary school girls' negotiations of femininity, achievement, and science. *Science Education, 96*(6), 967–989.

Archer, L., Pratt, S., & Phillips, D. (2001). Working-class men's constructions of masculinity and negotiations of (non)participation in higher education. *Gender and Education, 13*(4), 431–449.

Arntz, M., Gregory, T., & Zierahn, U. (2016). 'The risk of automation for jobs in OECD countries: A comparative analysis'. *OECD Social, Employment, and Migration Working Papers, (189)*. OECD.

Ashton, D., & Field, D. (1976). *Young workers: From school to work*. Hutchinson.

Ashurst, F., & Venn, C. (2014). *Inequality, poverty, education: A political economy of school exclusion*. Palgrave Macmillan.

Atkinson, W. (2007). Beck, individualization and the death of class: A critique. *The British Journal of Sociology, 58*(3), 349–366.

Atkinson, W. (2015). *Class*. Polity Press.

Attia, M., & Edge, J. (2017). Be (com) ing a reflexive researcher: A developmental approach to research methodology. *Open Review of Educational Research*, 4(1), 33–45.

Autor, D. (2015). Why are there still so many jobs? The history and future of workplace automation. *Journal of Economic Perspectives, 29*(3), 3–30.

Autor, D., & Handel, M. (2013). Putting tasks to the test: Human capital, job tasks, and wages. *Journal of Labor Economics, 31*, 59–96.

Bauman, Z. (1988). *Freedom*. Open University Press.

Beatty, C., Fothergill, S., & Gore, A. (2019). *The state of the coalfields 2019: Economic and social conditions in the former coalfields of England, Scotland and Wales*. Sheffield Hallam University: Coalfields Regeneration Trust.

Beaudry, P., Green, D., & Sand, B. (2016). The great reversal in the demand for skill and cognitive tasks. *Journal of Labor Economics, 34*(S1), 199–247.

Beck, U. (1992). *Risk society: Towards a new modernity*. Sage.

Beck, U., & Beck-Gernsheim, E. (2001). *Individualisation: Institutionalised individualism and its social and political consequences*. SAGE.

Beck, U., & Lau, C. (2005). Second modernity as a research agenda: Theoretical and empirical explorations in the 'meta-change' of modern society. *The British Journal of Sociology, 56*(4), 525–557.

Bell, M., Bristow, D., & Martin, S. (2017). *The future of work in Wales*. Public Policy Institute for Wales.

Benería, L. (1979). Reproduction, production and the sexual division of labour. *Cambridge Journal of Economics, 3*(3), 203–225.

Berger, R. (2015). Now I see it, now I don't: Researcher's position and reflexivity in qualitative research. *Qualitative Research, 15*(2), 219–234.

Beynon, H. (1973). *Working for Ford*. Penguin Books.

Blanchard, C., McCormack, M., & Peterson, G. (2017). Inclusive masculinities in a working-class sixth form in northeast England. *Journal of Contemporary Ethnography, 46*(3), 310–333.

Boise, S. (2015). *Men, masculinity, music and emotions*. Palgrave Macmillan.

Bonner, A., & Tolhurst, G. (2002). Insider-outsider perspectives of participant observation. *Nurse Researcher, 9*(4), 7–19.

Booth, R. (2017). Robots 'could take 4m UK private sector jobs within 10 years'. *The Guardian* 19 September. Retrieved January 7, 2019, from https://www.theguardian.com/technology/2017/sep/19/robots-could-take-4m-privatesector-jobs-within-10-years

Bottero, W. (2004). Class identities and the identity of class. *Sociology, 38*(5), 985–1003.

Bourdieu, P. (1984). *Distinction: A social critique of the judgement of taste*. Routledge.

Bourdieu, P. (1986). The forms of capital. In J. Richardson (Ed.), *Handbook of theory and research for the sociology of education* (pp. 241–258). Greenwood Press.

Bourdieu, P. (1989). Social space and symbolic power. *Sociological Theory, 7*(1), 14–25.

Bourdieu, P. (1990a). *The logic of practice*. Polity Press.

Bourdieu, P. (1990b). *In other words*. Stanford University Press.

Bourdieu, P. (2001). *la Sociologie est un sport de combat*. Directed by Pierre Carles [DVD]. CP Productions and VF Films.

Bourdieu, P., & Wacquant, L. (1992). *An invitation to reflexive sociology*. Polity Press.

Brannon, R. (1976). The male sex role – and what it's done for us lately. In R. Brannon & D. Davids (Eds.), *The forty-nine percent majority* (pp. 1–40). AddisonWesley.

Breen, L. (2007). The researcher 'in the middle': Negotiating the insider/outsider dichotomy. *The Australian Community Psychologist, 19*(1), 163–174.

Bridges, D. (2001). The ethics of outsider research. *Journal of Philosophy of Education, 35*(3), 371–386.

Bridges, T., & Pascoe, C. J. (2013). *Bro Porn: Heterosexualizing Straight Men's Anti-Homophobia Stances*. Retrieved February 10, 2022, from https://www.huffpost.com/entry/bro-porn-207heterosexualizing-straight-mens-anti-homophobia-stances_b_4386206

Bridges, T., & Pascoe, C. J. (2014). Hybrid masculinities: New directions in the sociology of men and masculinities. *Sociology Compass, 8*(3), 246–258.

Brien, P. (2022). *Service industries. Key economic indicators.* House of Commons Library.

Bright, N. (2012). 'Sticking together!' Policy activism from within a UK coal-mining community. *Journal of Educational Administration and History, 44*(3), 221–236.

Brown, E. (2022). *To raise a boy: Classrooms, locker rooms, bedrooms, and the hidden struggles of American boyhood.* Simon and Schuster.

Brown, P. (1987). *Schooling ordinary kids.* Tavistock.

Brown, P. (1990). Schooling and economic life in the UK. In L. Chisholm, P. Büchner, H-H. Krüger, & P. Brown (Eds.), *Childhood, youth and social change: A comparative perspective.* The Falmer Press.

Brown, P., Lauder, H., & Cheung, S. (2020). *The death of human capital: Its failed promise and how to renew it in an age of disruption.* Oxford University Press.

Brown, P., Lloyd, C., & Souto-Otero, M. (2018). *The prospects for skills and employment in an age of digital disruption: A Cautionary Note.* [PDF] Oxford: SKOPE. Retrieved January 10, 2019, from http://www.skope.ox.ac.uk/wpcontent/uploads/2018/11/Brown-Lloyd-and-Souto-Otero-2018.-The-prospects-forskills-and-employment-in-an-age-of-digital-disruption.pdf

Brozsely, B., & Nixon, D. (2022). Pinball transitions: Exploring the school-to-work transitions of 'the missing middle'. *Journal of Youth Studies,* 1–16.

Bryman, A. (2016). *Social research methods.* Oxford University Press.

Brynjolfsson, E., & McAfee, A. (2012). *Race against the machine.* Digital Frontier Press.

Bukodi, E., & Goldthorpe, J. (2018). *Social mobility and education in Britain.* Cambridge University Press.

Butler, J. (1990). *Gender trouble: feminism and the subversion of identity.* Routledge.

Carrigan, T., Connell, B., & Lee, J. (1985). Toward a new sociology of masculinity. *Theory and Society, 14*(5), 551–604.

Carter, M. (1966). *Into Work.* Penguin Books.

Chan, S. (2016). Robots are coming for your job: And faster than you think. *The Telegraph,* 21 January. Retrieved January 7, 2019, from https://www.telegraph.co.uk/finance/financetopics/davos/12113314/Robots-arecoming-for-your-job-and-faster-than-you-think.html

Cheng, C. (1999). Marginalised masculinities and hegemonic masculinity: An introduction. *The Journal of Men's Studies, 7*(3), 295–315.

Chesters, J., (2021). Gender attitudes and occupational aspirations in Germany. Are young men prepared for the jobs of the future? *Work, Employment and Society, 37*(3), 571–587.

Christofidou, A. (2021). Men and masculinities: A continuing debate on change. *NORMA, 16*(2), 81–97.

Chui, M., & Mischke, J. (2019). *The impact and opportunities of automation in construction.* McKinsey & Company.

Coleman, D. (2015). Traditional masculinity as a risk factor for suicidal ideation: Crosssectional and prospective evidence from a study of young adults. *Archives of Suicide Research, 19*(3), 366–384.

Collier, R. (1998). *Masculinities, crime and criminology: Men, heterosexuality and the criminal(ised) other.* Sage.

Collinson, D. L. (1988). 'Engineering humour': Masculinity, joking and conflict in shopfloor relations. *Organization Studies, 9*(2), 181–199.

Connell, R. W. (1987). *Gender and power: Society, the person, and sexual politics.* Stanford University Press.

Connell, R. W. (1995). *Masculinities.* Polity.

Connell, R. W. (2000). *The men and the boys.* Allen & Unwin.

Connell, R. W. (2005). *Masculinities* (2nd ed.). Polity.

Connell, R. W. (2009). *Gender: In world perspective.* Polity Press.

Connell, R. W., & Messerschmidt, J. (2005). Hegemonic masculinity rethinking the concept. *Gender & Society, 19*(6), 829–859.

Cornwall, A., & Lindisfarne, N. (2003). *Dislocating masculinity: Comparative ethnographies.* Routledge.

Courtenay, W. (2000). Constructions of masculinity and their influence on men's wellbeing: A theory of gender and health. *Social Science and Medicine, 50*(10), 1385–1401.

Courtenay, W. (2011). *Dying to be Men: Psychosocial, environmental, and biobehavioral directions in promoting the health of men and boys.* Routledge.

Crompton, R. (1996). The fragmentation of class analysis. *The British Journal of Sociology, 47*(1), 56–67.

Crompton, R. (2008). *Class and stratification.* Polity Press.

Crompton, R. (2010). Class and employment. *Work, Employment and Society, 24*(1), 9–26.

Dave. (2017). *Question Time.* Retrieved January 19, 2021, from https://open.spotify.com/track/0UYKSIjIUiO1T3BBuCeTVF

Davenport, T. H., & Kirby, J. (2016). *Only humans need apply: Winners and losers in the age of smart machines.* Harper Business.

Davis, R. D., & Braun, E. M. (2010). *The gift of dyslexia: why some of the brightest people can't read and how they can learn.* Souvenir Press.

Delamont, S. (2000). The anomalous beasts: Hooligans and the sociology of education. *Sociology, 34*(1), 95–111.

Deloitte. (2016). *Talent for survival Essential skills for humans working in the machine age.* Deloitte.

Demetriou, D. Z. (2001). Connell's concept of hegemonic masculinity: A critique. *Theory and Society, 30*(3), 337–361.

Devine, F. (1998). Class analysis and the stability of class relations. *Sociology, 32*(1), 23–42.

DfE. (2018). *Creating opportunity for all our vision for alternative provision.* Department for Education.

Dick Cavett Show. (1980). PBS, 25th July.

Dorling, D. (2014). Thinking about Class. *Sociology, 48*(3), 452–462.

Dwyer, S. C., & Buckle, J. L. (2009). The space between: On being an insider-outsider in qualitative research. *International Journal of Qualitative Methods, 8*(1), 54–63.

Eisen, D., & Yamashita, L. (2017). Borrowing from femininity: The caring man, hybrid masculinities, and maintaining male dominance. *Men and Masculinities, 22*(5), 801–820.

Elliot, M., Pitchford, A., & Brackenridge, C. (2013). Young people, football and 'respect'? In A. Parker & D. Vinson (Eds.), *Youth sport, physical activity and play: Policy, intervention and participation* (pp. 83–95). Routledge.

Elliott, K. (2016). Caring masculinities: Theorizing an emerging concept. *Men and Masculinities, 19*(3), 240–259.

Elliott, K. (2020). *Young men navigating contemporary masculinities.* Palgrave Macmillan.

Epstein, D. (1997). Boyz'own stories: Masculinities and sexualities in schools. *Gender and Education, 9*(1), 105–115.

Esping-Andersen, G. (2009). *The incomplete revolution: Adapting to women's new roles.* Polity Press.

Falcous, M., & McLeod, C. (2012). Anyone for tennis?: Sport, class and status in New Zealand. *New Zealand Sociology, 27*(1), 13–30.

Feinberg, W., & Soltis, J. (2009). *School and society.* Teachers College Press.

Ferry, P. (2020). *Beards and masculinity in American Literature.* Routledge.

Finlay, L. (2002). "Outing" the researcher: The provenance, process, and practice of reflexivity. *Qualitative Health Research, 12*(4), 531–545.

Floyd, K. (2000). Affectionate same-sex touch: The influence of homophobia on observers' perceptions. *The Journal of Social Psychology, 140*(6), 774–788.

Folkes, L. (2021). Re-imagining social mobility: The role of relationality, social class and place in qualitative constructions of mobility. *Sociological Research Online, 27*(1), 136–153.

France, A., & Roberts, S. (2017). *Youth and social class: Enduring inequality in the United Kingdom, Australia and New Zealand.* Springer.

Francis, B. (1999). Lads, Lasses and (New) Labour: 14-16-year-old students' responses to the 'laddish behaviour and boys' underachievement' debate. *British Journal of Sociology of Education, 20*(3), 355–371.

Francis, B., & Archer, L. (2005). Negotiating the dichotomy of boffin and triad: British-Chinese Pupils' Constructions of 'Laddism'. *The Sociological Review, 53*(3), 495–521.

Fraser, N. (2000). Rethinking recognition. *New Left Review, 3*, 107–120.

Freie, C. (2007). *Class construction: White working-class student identity in the new millennium.* Lexington Books.

Frey, C., & Osborne, M. (2013). *The future of employment: How susceptible are jobs to computerisation?* Retrieved September 10, 2020, from https://www.oxfordmartin.ox.ac.uk/downloads/academic/future-of-employment.pdf

Frey, C. B., & Osborne, M. A (2017). The future of employment: How susceptible are jobs to computerisation? *Technological Forecasting and Social Change, 114*, 254–280.

Frey, C., Osborne, M., & Delcitte. (2014). *Agiletown: The relentless march of technology and London's response.* Deloitte.

Frosh, S., Phoenix, A., & Pattman, R. (2002). *Young masculinities: Understanding boys in contemporary society.* Palgrave Macmillan.

Furlong, A., & Cartmel, F. (2004). *Vulnerable young men in fragile labour markets: Employment, unemployment and the search for long-term security.* Joseph Rowntree Foundation.

Gater, R. (2022). 'Dirty, dirty job. Not good for your health': Working-class men and their experiences and relationships with employment. In K. Simpson & R. Simmons (Eds.), *Education, work and social change in Britain's Former coalfields communities: In the shadow of coal.* Palgrave Macmillan.

Gater, R. (2024). Amalgamated masculinities: The masculine identity of contemporary marginalised working-class young men. *Sociology, 58*(2), 312–329.

Geertz, C. (1973). *The interpretation of cultures: Selected essays.* Basic Books.

Giddens, A. (1991). *Modernity and Self-identity: Self and Society in the Late Modern Age.* Polity.

Giese, R. (2018). *Boys: What it means to become a man.* Seal Press.

Gill, K., Quilter-Pinner, H., & Swift, D. (2017). *Making the difference breaking the link between school exclusion and social exclusion.* Institute for Public Policy Research.

Gold, R. (1958). Roles in sociological field observations. *Social Forces, 36*(3), 217–223.

Goldthorpe, J. H. (1980). *Social mobility and class structure in modern Britain.* Clarendon Press.

Goldthorpe, J. H. (2016). Social class mobility in modern Britain: Changing structure, constant process. *Journal of the British Academy, 4*, 89–111.

Goldthorpe, J. H., & Hope, K. (1974). *The social grading of occupations.* Clarendon.

Goldthorpe, J. H., & McKnight, A. (2006). The economic basis of social class. *Mobility and Inequality: Frontiers of Research in Sociology and Economics*, 109–136.

Goldthorpe, J. H., Lockwood, D., Bechhofer, F., & Platt, J. (1967). The affluent worker and the thesis of embourgeoisement: Some preliminary research findings. *Sociology*, *1*(1), 11–31.

Goldthorpe, J. H., Lockwood, D., Bechhofer, F., & Platt, J. (1968a). *The affluent worker: Industrial attitudes and behaviour*. Cambridge University Press.

Goldthorpe, J. H., Lockwood, D., Bechhofer, F., & Platt, J. (1968b). *The affluent worker: Political attitudes and behaviour*. Cambridge University Press.

Goldthorpe, J. H., Lockwood, D., Bechhofer, F., & Platt, J. (1969). *The affluent [database] worker in the class structure*. Cambridge University Press.

Goodhart, D. (2020). *Head, hand, heart: Why intelligence is over-rewarded, manual workers matter, and caregivers deserve more respect*. Simon and Schuster.

Goos, M., & Manning, A. (2007). Lousy and lovely jobs: The rising polarization of work in Britain. *The Review of Economics and Statistics*, *89*(1), 118–133.

Gough, B. (2018). *Contemporary masculinities: Embodiment, emotion and wellbeing*. Palgrave Pivot.

Grace, K., Salvatier, J., Dafoe, A., Zhang, B., & Evans, O. (2018). When will AI exceed human performance? Evidence from AI experts. *Journal of Artificial Intelligence Research*, *62*, 729–754.

Gramsci, A. (1971). *Selections from the prison notebooks*. International Publishers.

Griffin, C. (1985). *Typical girls? Young women from school to the job market*. Routledge.

Griffin, C. (2005). Whatever happened to the (likely) lads? 'Learning to Labour' 25 years on. *British Journal of Sociology of Education*, *26*(2), 291–297.

Grow, J. M., & Yang, S. (2018). Generation-Z enters the advertising workplace: Expectations through a gendered lens. *Journal of Advertising Education*, *22*(1), 7–22.

Haldane, A. (2018). *Ideas and institutions–a growth story*. Speech given at the Bank of England. https://www. bankofengland. co. uk/-/media/boe/files/speech/2018/ideasand-institutions-a-growth-story-speech-by-andy-haldane

Hall, A., Hockey, J., & Robinson, V. (2007). Occupational cultures and the embodiment of masculinity: Hairdressing, estate agency and firefighting. *Gender, Work & Organization*, *14*(6), 534–551.

Hammersley, M., & Atkinson, P. (2007). *Ethnography: Principles in practice* (3rd ed.). Routledge.

Hanke, R. (1998). Theorizing masculinity with/in the media. *Communication Theory*, *8*(2), 183–202.

Harvey, D. (2007). *A brief history of neoliberalism*. Oxford University Press.

Hawksworth, J., Berriman, R., & Goel, S. (2018). *Will robots really steal our jobs? An international analysis of the potential long term impact of automation*. PricewaterhouseCoopers.

Hayes, C., Corrie, I., & Graham, Y. (2020). Paramedic emotional labour during COVID-19. *Journal of Paramedic Practice*, *12*(8), 319–323.

Haywood, C., & Mac an Ghaill, M. (2003). *Men and masculinities: Theory, research and social practice*. Open University Press.

Hebson, G. (2009). Renewing class analysis in studies of the workplace. *Sociology*, *43*(1), 27–44.

Hidalgo, M. C., & Hernandez, B. (2001). Place attachment: Conceptual and empirical questions. *Journal of Environmental Psychology*, *21*(3), 273–281.

HM Government. (2021). *National AI strategy*. HM Government.

HM Government. (2022). *Levelling up the United Kingdom*. HM Government.

Hobson, B. (2002). *Making men into fathers: Men, masculinities and the social politics of fatherhood*. Cambridge University Press.

Hochschild, A. (1983). *The managed heart: Commercialisation of human feeling*. University of California Press.

Hopkins, P. E. (2013). *Young people, place and identity*. Routledge.

House of Commons Library. (2022). *Manufacturing*. Retrieved February 10, 2022, from https://researchbriefings.files.parliament.uk/documents/SN05206/SN05206.pdf

Hughes, S. (2019). *Permanent and fixed-term exclusions from schools in Wales, 2017/18*. Statistics for Wales.

Hunter, S. C., Riggs, D. W., & Augoustinos, M. (2017). Hegemonic masculinity versus a caring masculinity: Implications for understanding primary caregiving fathers. *Social and Personality Psychology Compass, 11*(3).

IFR. (2018). *The impact of robots on productivity, employment and jobs*. [online] Retrieved January 14, 2019, from https://ifr.org/img/office/IFR_The_Impact_of_Robots_on_Employment.Pdf

Ingram, N. (2018). *Working-class boys and educational success: Teenage identities, masculinities and urban schooling*. Palgrave.

Ingram, N., & Gamsu, S. (2022). Talking the talk of social mobility: The political performance of a misguided agenda. *Sociological Research Online, 27*(1), 189–206.

Ingram, N., & Waller, R. (2014). Degrees of masculinity: Working and middle-class undergraduate students' constructions of masculine identities. In S. Roberts (Ed.), *Debating modern masculinities: Change, continuity, crisis?* (pp. 35–51). Palgrave Macmillan.

Ivinson, G. (2014a). Ghosts from the past: Exploring community cultures and school cultures in relation to poverty. *Improving Schools, 17*(3), 250–260.

Ivinson, G. M. (2014b). Skills in motion: Boys' trail motorbiking activities as transitions into working-class masculinity in a post-industrial locale. *Sport, Education and Society, 19*(5), 605–620.

Jackson, C. (2002). 'Laddishness' as a Self-worth Protection Strategy. *Gender and Education, 14*(1), 37–50.

Jackson, C. (2006). *Lads and ladettes in school: Gender and a fear of failure*. Open University Press.

Jackson, C. (2010). 'I've been sort of laddish with them… one of the gang': Teachers' perceptions of 'laddish' boys and how to deal with them. *Gender and Education, 22*(5), 505–519.

Jimenez, L., & Walkerdine, V. (2011). A psychosocial approach to shame, embarrassment and melancholia amongst unemployed young men and their fathers. *Gender and Education, 23*(2), 185–199.

Johansson, T., & Haywood, C. (2017). Introduction. In T. Johansson & C. Haywood (Eds.), *Marginalized masculinities* (pp. 1–18). Routledge.

Jones, O. (2012). *Chavs: The demonization of the working class*. Verso.

Joppke, C. (2021). Nationalism in the neoliberal order: Old wine in new bottles? *Nations and Nationalism, 27*(4), 960–975.

Kaczmarek, E. (2019). How to distinguish medicalization from overmedicalization? *Medicine, Health Care and Philosophy, 22*(1), 119–128.

Kanuha, V. K. (2000). "Being" native versus "going native": Conducting social work research as an insider. *Social Work, 45*(5), 439–447.

Kapetaniou, C. (2019). *Becoming Future-Fit: What we know about adult learning across Europe*. Nesta.

Kaplan, D., Rosenmann, A., & Shuhendler, S. (2017). What about nontraditional masculinities? Toward a quantitative model of therapeutic new masculinity ideology. *Men and Masculinities, 20*(4), 393–426.

Kehler, M. (2010). Negotiating masculinities in PE classrooms: Boys, body image and 'want[ing] to be in good shape'. In M. Kehler & M. Atkinson (Eds.), *Boys' bodies: Speaking the unspoken* (pp. 153–175). Peter Lang.

Keith, T. (2020). *The bro code: The fallout of raising boys to objectify and subordinate women*. Routledge.

Kenway, J., & Kraack, A. (2004). Reordering work and destabilizing masculinity. In N. Dolby, G. Dimitriadis, & P. Willis (Eds.), *Learning to labor in new times* (pp. 95–109). Routledgefalmer.

Kerstetter, K. (2012). Insider outsider, or somewhere in-between: The impact of researchers' identities on the community-based research process. *Journal of Rural Social Sciences, 27*(2), 99–117.

Kimmel, M. (1994). Masculinity as homophobia: Fear, shame, and silence in the construction of gender identity. In H. Brod & M. Kaufman (Eds.), *Theorizing masculinities* (pp. 119–141). SAGE Publications.

Kimmel, M. S. (2008). *Guyland: The perilous world where boys become men.* Harper Collins.

Kimmel, M., Hearn, J., & Connell, R. (2005). *Handbook of studies on men and masculinities.* Sage.

King, K., Rice, S., Schlichthorst, M., Chondros, P., & Pirkis, J. (2021). Gender norms and the wellbeing of girls and boys. *The Lancet Global Health, 9*(4), e398.

Lee, H. Y., Jamieson, J. P., Reis, H. T., Beevers, C. G., Josephs, R. A., Mullarkey, M. C., O'Brien, J. M., & Yeager, D. S. (2020). Getting fewer "likes" than others on social media elicits emotional distress among victimized adolescents. *Child Development, 91*(6), 2141–2159.

Leidner, R. (1993). *Fast food, fast talk: Service work and the routinization of everyday life.* University of California Press.

Leopold, T., Zahidi, S., & Ratcheva, V. (2018). *The future of jobs report 2018.* World Economic Forum.

Levant, R. F., & Pryor, S. (2020). *The tough standard: The hard truths about masculinity and violence.* Oxford University Press.

Lindsay, C., & McQuaid, R. (2004). Avoiding the 'McJobs'. *Work, Employment and Society, 18*(2), 297–319.

Lisco, C., Leone, R., Gallagher, K., & Parrott, D. (2015). "Demonstrating Masculinity" via intimate partner aggression: The moderating effect of heavy episodic drinking. *Sex Roles, 73*(1-2), 58–69.

Llywelyn, J. (2013). *Remember Senghenydd.* Gwasg Carreg Gwalch: Llanrwst.

Lockwood, D. (1989). *The blackcoated worker: A study in class consciousness* (2nd ed.). Clarendon.

Lub, X., Bal, P., Blomme, R., & Schalk, R. (2015). One job, one deal…or not: do generations respond differently to psychological contract fulfillment? *The International Journal of Human Resource Management, 27*(6), 653–680.

Mac an Ghaill, M. (1994). *The making of men.* Open University Press.

Mac an Ghaill, M. (1996). *Understanding masculinities.* Open University Press.

MacDonald, R., & Marsh, J. (2005). *Disconnected youth? Growing up in Britain's poor neighbourhoods.* Palgrave Macmillan.

Magrath, R. (2021). Inclusive masculinities of working-class university footballers in the South of England. *Sport in Society, 24*(3), 412–429.

Maguire, D. (2020). *Male, failed, jailed: Masculinities and "Revolving-Door" Imprisonment in the UK.* Palgrave Macmillan.

Malesic, J. (2017). The Year the Robots Came for Our Jobs. *The New Republic,* 29 December. Retrieved January 7, 2019, from https://newrepublic.com/article/146399/year-robots-camejobs

Mannay, D. (2010). Making the familiar strange: Can visual research methods render the familiar setting more perceptible? *Qualitative Research, 10*(1), 91–111.

Mannay, D. (2013). 'Keeping close and spoiling' revisited: Exploring the significance of 'home' for family relationships and educational trajectories in a marginalised estate in urban south Wales. *Gender and Education, 25*(1), 91–107.

Mannheim, K. (1970). The problem of generations. *Psychoanalytic Review*, *57*(3), 378–404.

Manstead, A. S. (2018). The psychology of social class: How socioeconomic status impacts thought, feelings, and behaviour. *British Journal of Social Psychology*, *57*(2), 267–291.

Manyika, J., Chui, M., Miremadi, M., Bughin, J., George, K., Willmott, P., & Dewhurst, M. (2017). *A future that works: Automation, employment, and productivity*. McKinsey & Company.

Martino, W. (2000). Policing masculinities: Investigating the role of homophobia and heteronormativity in the lives of adolescent school boys. *The Journal of Men's Studies*, *8*(2), 213–236.

Marx, K., & Engels, F. (1987). *The communist manifesto*. Pathfinder.

McCormack, M. (2011). The declining significance of homohysteria for male students in three sixth forms in the south of England. *British Educational Research Journal*, *37*(2), 337–353.

McCormack, M. (2012). *The declining significance of homophobia*. Oxford University Press.

McCormack, M. (2014). The intersection of youth masculinities, decreasing homophobia and class: An ethnography. *The British Journal of Sociology*, *65*(1), 130–149.

McCormack, M., & Anderson, E. (2010). 'It's Just Not Acceptable Any More': The erosion of homophobia and the softening of masculinity at an English Sixth Form. *Sociology*, *44*(5), 843–859.

McDowell, L. (2000). The trouble with men? Young people, gender transformations and the crisis of masculinity. *International Journal of Urban and Regional Research*, *24*(1), 201–209.

McDowell, L. (2003). *Redundant masculinities? Employment change and white working class youth*. Blackwell.

McKinsey Global Institute. (2017). *A future that works: Automation, employment and productivity*. McKinsey Global Institute.

McQueen, F. (2017). Male emotionality: 'boys don't cry' versus 'it's good to talk'. *Norma*, *12*(3-4), 205–219.

McRobbie, A. (1991). *Feminism and youth culture: From 'Jackie' to 'Just Seventeen'*. Palgrave Macmillan.

Meo, A., & Parker, A. (2004). Teachers, teaching and educational exclusion: Pupil Referral Units and pedagogic practice. *International Journal of Inclusive Education*, *8*(1), 103–120.

Mercer, J. (2007). The challenges of insider research in educational institutions: Wielding a double-edged sword and resolving delicate dilemmas. *Oxford Review of Education*, *33*(1), 1–17.

Merton, R. K. (1972). Insiders and outsiders: A chapter in the sociology of knowledge. *American Journal of Sociology 78*( ), 9–47.

Messerschmidt, J. W. (1993). *Masculinities and crime: Critique and reconceptualization of theory*. Rowman & Littlefield Publishers.

Messerschmidt, J. W. (2018). *Hegemonic masculinity: Formulation, reformulation, and amplification*. Rowman & Littlefield.

Messner, M. (1992). *Power at play: Sports and the problem of masculinity*. Beacon Press.

Messner, M. (2013). Reflections on communication and sport: On men and masculinities. *Communication & Sport*, *1*(1-2), 113–124.

Messner, M. A. (2007). The masculinity of the governator: Muscle and compassion in American politics. *Gender & Society*, *21*(4), 461–480.

Messner, M. A., Dunbar, M., & Hunt, D. (2000). The televised sports manhood formula. *Journal of Sport and Social Issues*, *24*(4), 380–394.

Mills, M., McGregor, G., Baroutsis, A., Te Riele, K., & Hayes, D. (2016). Alternative education and social justice: Considering issues of affective and contributive justice. *Critical Studies in Education*, *57*(1), 100–115.

Moller, M., (2007). Exploiting patterns: A critique of hegemonic masculinity. *Journal of Gender Studies*, *16*(3), 263–276.

Muro, M., Maxim, R., Whiton, J., & Hathaway, I. (2019). *Automation and artificial intelligence: How machines are affecting people and places*. Brookings.

Nayak, A. (2003a). 'Boyz to Men': Masculinities, schooling and labour transitions in deindustrial times. *Educational Review*, *55*(2), 147–159.

Nayak, A. (2003b). Last of the 'Real Geordies'? White masculinities and the subcultural response to deindustrialisation. *Environment and Planning D: Society and Space*, *21*(1), 7–25.

Nayak, A. (2003c). *Race, place and globalization: Youth cultures in a changing world*. Berg Publishers.

Nayak, A. (2006). Displaced masculinities: Chavs, youth and class in the postindustrial city. *Sociology*, *40*(5), 813–831.

Nayak, A., & Kehily, M. J. (1996). Playing it straight: Masculinities, homophobias and schooling. *Journal of Gender Studies*, *5*(2), 211–230.

Ness, K. (2012). Constructing masculinity in the building trades: 'Most jobs in the construction industry can be done by women'. *Gender, Work & Organization*, *19*(6), 654–676.

Nixon, D. (2006). 'I just like working with my hands': Employment aspirations and the meaning of work for low-skilled unemployed men in Britain's service economy. *Journal of Education and Work*, *19*(2), 201–217.

Nixon, D. (2009). 'I Can't Put a Smiley Face On': Working-class masculinity, emotional labour and service work in the 'New Economy'. *Gender, Work & Organisation 16*(3), 300-322.

Nixon, D. (2018). Yearning to Labour? Working-class men in Post-Industrial Britain. In C. Walker & S. Roberts (Eds.), *Masculinity, Labour, and Neoliberalism Working-Class Men in International Perspective* (pp. 53–75). Springer.

O'Donnell, M., & Sharpe, S. (2002). *Uncertain masculinities: Youth, ethnicity and class in contemporary Britain*. Routledge.

O'Neill, R. (2015). Whither critical masculinity studies? Notes on inclusive masculinity theory, postfeminism, and sexual politics. *Men and Masculinities*, *18*(1), 100–120.

ONS. (2010). *Standard occupational classification 2010*. Palgrave Macmillan.

ONS. (2021a). *Aber Valley Ward (as of 2011)*. Retrieved October 1, 2021, from https://www.nomisweb.co.uk/reports/localarea?compare=W05000720

ONS. (2021b). *Employment in the UK, 2021*. Retrieved October 6, 2021, from https://www.ons. gov.uk/employmentandlabourmarket/peopleinwork/employmentandemployeetypes/bulletins/employmentintheuk/august2021

ONS. (2021c). *Labour Market Profile - Caerphilly*. [online] Nomisweb.co.uk. Retrieved July 10, 2021, from <https://www.nomisweb.co.uk/reports/lmp/la/1946157400/report.aspx#tabempocc>

ONS. (2022). *Labour Market Profile – Great Britain*. Retrieved June 27, 2022, from https://www.nomisweb.co.uk/reports/lmp/gor/2092957698/report.aspx

O'Reilly, K. (2009). *Key concepts in ethnography*. Sage.

Paechter, C. (2018, May). Rethinking the possibilities for hegemonic femininity: Exploring a Gramscian framework. *Women's Studies International Forum*, *68*, 121–128.

Pajarinen, M., & Rouvinen, P. (2014). Computerization threatens one third of Finnish Employment. *ETLA Brief*, *22*(13.1), 1–6.

Parsons, T. (1954). *Essays in sociological theory*. Free Press.

Parsons, T. (1964). *Social structure and personality*. Free Press of Glencoe.

Pascoe, C. (2007). *Dude, You're a Fag: Masculinity and sexuality in high school*. University of California Press.

Pascoe, C. J., 2003. Multiple masculinities? Teenage boys talk about jocks and gender. *American Behavioral Scientist,* 46(10), 1423–1438.

Pascoe, C., & Stewart, L. (2016). Policing masculinities and femininities. In A. Goldberg (Ed.), *The SAGE encyclopedia of LGBTQ studies* (pp. 860–863). SAGE Publications.

Patrick, F. (2013). Neoliberalism, the knowledge economy, and the learner: Challenging the inevitability of the commodified self as an outcome of education. *International Scholarly Research Notices,* 8, 1–8.

Patton, M. (2002). *Qualitative research & evaluation methods* (3rd ed.). Sage.

Phillips, J. (1991). *Abertridwr through the ages.* The Starling Press.

Phipps, A. (2017). (Re) theorising laddish masculinities in higher education. *Gender and Education,* 29(7), 815–830.

Pilcher, J. (1994). Mannheim's sociology of generations: an undervalued legacy. *British Journal of Sociology,* 45(3), 481–495.

Pilcher, J., & Whelenhan, I. (2004). *Fifty key concepts in gender studies.* Sage Publications.

Pringle, R. (2005). Masculinities, sport and power. *Journal of Sport and Social Issues,* 29(3), 256–278.

Proshansky, H., Fabian, A., & Kaminoff, R. (1983). Place-identity: Physical world socialisation of the self. *Journal of Environmental Psychology,* 3(1), 57–83.

Qayyum, A., Ye Zhang, T., Lawrence, F., Yull, J., & Marlow, J. (2020). *Changes in the economy since the 1970s.* Office of National Statistics.

Ralph, B., & Roberts, S. (2020). One small step for man: Change and continuity in perceptions and enactments of homosocial intimacy among young Australian men. *Men and Masculinities,* 23(1), 83–103.

Reay, D. (2013). Social mobility, a panacea for austere times: Tales of emperors, frogs, and tadpoles. *British Journal of Sociology of Education,* 34(5–6), 660–677.

Reay, D. (2017). *Miseducation: Inequality, education and the working classes.* Policy Press.

Reidy, T. (2014). Workers' experience of the Robot revelution. In S. Westlake (Ed.), *Our work here is done: Visions of a robot economy* (pp. 111–118). Nesta.

Rifkin, J. (1995). *The end of work.* Putnam book.

Roberts, K. (1995). *Youth employment in modern Britain.* University Press.

Roberts, K. (2020). Regime change: Education to work transitions in England, 1980s–2020s. *Journal of Applied Youth Studies,* 3(1), 23–42.

Roberts, S. (2011). Beyond 'NEET' and 'tidy' pathways: Considering the 'missing middle' of youth transition studies. *Journal of Youth Studies,* 14(1), 21–39.

Roberts, S. (2013). Boys will be boys... won't they? Change and continuities in contemporary young working-class masculinities. *Sociology,* 47(4), 671–686.

Roberts, S. (2018). *Young working-class men in transition.* Routledge.

Roberts, S., & Elliott, K. (2020). Challenging dominant representations of marginalized boys and men in critical studies on men and masculinities. *Boyhood Studies,* 13(2), 87–104.

Robinson, V. Hall, A., & Hockey, J. (2011. Masculinities, sexualities, and the limits of subversion: Being a man in hairdressing. *Men and Masculinities,* 14(1), 31–50.

Rogers, A. A., Nielson, M. G., & Santos, C. E. (2021). Manning up while growing up: A developmental-contextual perspective on masculine gender-role socialization in adolescence. *Psychology of Men & Masculinities,* 22(2), 354–364.

Rose, D., & Pevalin, D. (2003). *A researcher's guide to the national statistics socioeconomic classification.* Sage Publications.

Rose, N. (2007). Beyond medicalisation. *The Lancet,* 369(9562), 700–702.

Rowlingson, K. (2011). *Does income inequality cause health and social problems?.* Joseph Rowntree Foundation.

Roy, D. (1959). "Banana time": Job satisfaction and informal interaction. *Human Organization,* 18(4), 158–168.

Saidin, K. (2017). Insider researchers: Challenges & opportunities. *Proceedings of the ICECRS, 1*(1), 849–854.

Savage, M. (2010). *Identities and social change in Britain since 1940: The politics of method.* Oxford University Press.

Savage, M., Cunningham, N., Devine, F., Friedman, S., Laurison, D., McKenzie, L., Miles, A., Snee, H., & Wakeling, P. (2015). *Social class in the 21st century.* Pelican.

Savage, M., Devine, F., Cunningham, N., Taylor, M., Li, Y., Hjellbrekke, J., Le Roux, B., Friedman, S., & Miles, A. (2013). A new model of social class? Findings from the BBC's Great British Class Survey Experiment. *Sociology, 47*(2), 219–250.

Schlogl, L., Weiss, E., & Prainsack, B. (2021). Constructing the 'Future of Work': An analysis of the policy discourse. *New Technology, Work and Employment, 36*(3), 307–326.

Seemiller, C., & Grace, M. (2018). *Generation Z: A century in the making.* Routledge.

Sennett, R., & Cobb, J. (1972). *The hidden injuries of class.* Vintage.

Sherman, L. E., Payton, A. A., Hernandez, L. M., Greenfield, P. M., & Dapretto, M. (2016). The power of the like in adolescence: Effects of peer influence on neural and behavioral responses to social media. *Psychological Science, 27*(7), 1027–1035.

Shildrick, T., & MacDonald, R. (2007). Biographies of exclusion: poor work and poor transitions. *International Journal of Lifelong Education, 26*(5), 589–604.

Sikes, P. (2003). Making the Familiar Strange: A new look at inequality in education. *British Journal of Sociology of Education, 24*(2), 243–248.

Simmons, R., Thompson, R., & Russell, L. (2014). *Education, work and social change: Young people and marginalisation in Post-Industrial Britain.* Palgrave Macmillan.

Simpson, I. (2017). Question Time by Dave: A politically charged rapper for right now. *The Guardian*, 20 October. Retrieved January 4, 2021, from https://www.theguardian.com/music/2017/oct/20/dave-question-time-track-ofweek?utm_source=esp&utm_medium=Email&utm_campaign=Sleeve+notes+Collections&utm_term=248832&subid=13184&CMP=sleevenotes_collection

Simpson, K. (2021). *Social haunting, education, and the working class: A critical Marxist ethnography in a former mining community.* Routledge.

Skeggs, B. (1992). Paul Willis, learning to labour. In M. Barker & A. Breezer (Eds.), *Reading into cultural studies* (pp. 185–201). Routledge.

Sloan, C., Conner, M., & Gough, B. (2015). How does masculinity impact on health? A quantitative study of masculinity and health behavior in a sample of UK men and women. *Psychology of Men & Masculinity, 16*(2), 206–217.

Slutskaya, N., Simpson, R., Hughes, J., Simpson, A., & Uygur, S. (2016). Masculinity and class in the context of dirty work. *Gender, Work & Organization, 23*(2), 165–182.

Sparkes, A. C. (1992). The paradigms debate: An extended review and celebration of difference. In A. Sparkes (Ed.), *Research in physical education and sport: Exploring alternative visions* (pp. 9–60). Falmer.

Spector-Mersel, G., & Gilbar, O. (2021). From military masculinity toward hybrid masculinities: Constructing a new sense of manhood among veterans treated for PTSS. *Men and Masculinities, 24*(5), 862–883.

Spencer, D., & Slater, G. (2020). No automation please, we're British: Technology and the prospects for work. *Cambridge Journal of Regions, Economy and Society, 13*(1), 117–134.

Stephenson, J. B., & Greer, L. S. (1981). Ethnographers in their own cultures: Two Appalachian cases. *Human Organization, 40*(2), 123–130.

Stern, A. (2019). *Proud boys and the white ethnostate.* Beacon Press.

Syed, A. (2019). *Changes in the economy since the 1970s.* Office for National Statistics.

Tate, S., & Greatbatch, D. (2017). *Alternative provision: Effective practice and post 16 transition.* Department for Education.

Thiel, D. (2007). Class in construction: London building workers, dirty work and physical cultures. *The British Journal of Sociology*, *58*(2), 227–251.

Thomson, R., Bell, R., Holland, J., Henderson, S., McGrellis, S., & Sharpe, S. (2002). Critical moments: Choice, chance and opportunity in young people's narratives of transition. *Sociology*, *36*(2), 335–354.

Tittenbrun, J. (2014). The death of class? *Przegląd Socjologiczny*, *63*(2), 35–53.

Tolson, A. (1977). *The Limits of Masculinity*. Tavistock.

Tomlinson, M. (2013). *Education, work and identity: Themes and perspectives*. A&C Black.

Tomsen, S., & Gadd, D. (2019). Beyond honour and achieved hegemony: Violence and the everyday masculinities of young men. *International Journal for Crime, Justice and Social Democracy*, *8*(2), 17–30.

Twenge, J. M. (2017). *iGen: Why today's super-connected kids are growing up less rebellious, more tolerant, less happy–and completely unprepared for adulthood–and what that means for the rest of us*. Atria.

Tyler, I. (2020). *Stigma: The machinery of inequality*. Bloomsbury Publishing.

Unluer, S. (2012). Being an insider researcher while conducting case study research. *Qualitative Report*, *17*(29), 1–14.

Veness, T. (1962). *School leavers. Their aspirations and expectations*. Methuen.

Vogt, K. C. (2018). The concept of the work situation in class analysis. *Current Sociology*, *66*(6), 849–866.

Waling, A. (2019). Rethinking masculinity studies: Feminism, masculinity, and poststructural accounts of agency and emotional reflexivity. *The Journal of Men's Studies*, *27*(1), 89–107.

Walker, G. (2006). Disciplining protest masculinity. *Men and Masculinities*, *9*(1), 5–22.

Walker, J. (1985). Rebels with our applause? A critique of resistance theory in Paul Willis's ethnography of schooling. *Journal of Education*, *167*(2), 63–83.

Walker, C., & Roberts, S. (2018). Masculinity, labour and neoliberalism: Reviewing the field. In C. Walker & S. Roberts (Eds.), *Masculinity, labour, and neoliberalism working-class men in international perspective* (pp. 1–28). Springer.

Walkerdine, V. (1993). Sex, power and pedagogy. In M. Alvarado, E. Buscombe & R. Collins (Eds.), *The screen education reader*. Macmillan Press.

Walkerdine, V. (2003). Reclassifying upward mobility: Femininity and the neo-liberal subject. *Gender and Education*, *15*(3), 237–248.

Walkerdine, V. (2016). Affective history, working-class communities and selfdetermination. *The Sociological Review*, *64*(4), 699–714.

Walkerdine, V., & Jiménez, L. (2012). *Gender, work and community after deindustrialisation*. Palgrave Macmillan.

Walkerdine, V., Lucey, H., & Melody, J. (2001). *Growing up girl: Psychosocial explorations of gender and class*. Palgrave Macmillan.

Wallace-Stephens, F., & Morgante, E. (2021). *Good work in the manufacturing and construction sectors in Europe*. Royal Society for Arts.

Wang, Y., Marosi, C., Edgin, M., & Horn, S. S. (2021). Adolescents' judgment of homophobic name-calling: The role of peer/friend context and emotional response. *Journal of Youth and Adolescence*, *50*(10), 1939–1951.

Ward, M. (2013). *The performance of young working-class masculinities in the South Wales Valleys*. [PhD Thesis, Cardiff University].

Ward, M. (2015). *From labouring to learning: Working-class masculinities, education and de-industrialization*. Palgrave Macmillan.

Warhurst, C., & Nickson, D. (2020). *Aesthetic labour*. Sage.

Watson, T. (2017). *Sociology, work and organisation* (7th ed.) Routledge.

Weber, M. (1948). Class status party. In H. Gerth & C. Mills (Eds.), *From Max Weber: Essays in sociology*. Routledge.

Weis, L. (1990). *Working class without work: High school students in a deindustrializing economy*. Routledge.

Welsh Government. (2018). *Employability plan*. Welsh Government.

Welsh Government. (2019a). *Wales 4.0: Delivering economic transformation for a better future of work*. Welsh Government.

Welsh Government. (2019b). *Welsh index of multiple deprivation*. Retrieved September 10, 2021, from https://wimd.gov.wales/explore?lang=en#&domain=overall&z=12&lat =51.5990&lng=-3.2734

Welsh Government. (2021). *Well-being of future generations (Wales) Act 2015: The essentials*. Welsh Government.

Wheelahan, L., Moodie, G., & Doughney, J. (2022). Challenging the skills fetish. *British Journal of Sociology of Education, 43*(3), 475–494.

Whitehead, S. (2019). *Toxic masculinity: Curing the Virus: making men smarter, healthier, safer*. Andrews UK Limited.

Wilkinson, R., & Pickett, K. (2010). *The spirit level: Why equality is better for everyone* (New ed.). Penguin.

Williams, S. (2008). What is Fatherhood? Searching for the Reflexive father. *Sociology, 42*(3), 487–502.

Williamson, H., & Williamson, P. (1981). *Five years*. National Youth Bureau.

Willis, P. (1977). *Learning to Labour*. Saxon House.

Wolfman, G., Hearn, J., & Yeadon-Lee, T. (2021). Hollow femininities: The emerging faces of neoliberal masculinities. *Norma, 16*(4), 217–234.

World Economic Forum. (2020). *The future of jobs report 2020*. World Economic Forum.

World Economic Forum. (2021). *Upskilling for shared prosperity*. World Economic Forum.

Yin, R. (2012). *Applications of case study research*. Sage Publications.

Yin, R. K. (2015). *Qualitative research from start to finish* (2nd ed.). Guilford Publications.

Index